ALBERT CAMUS
AND THE HUMAN CRISIS

ALBERT CAMUS
AND THE
HUMAN CRISIS

ROBERT EMMET MEAGHER

PEGASUS BOOKS
NEW YORK LONDON

ALBERT CAMUS AND THE HUMAN CRISIS

Pegasus Books, Ltd.
148 W 37th Street, 13th Floor
New York, NY 10018

First Pegasus Books cloth edition November 2021

Interior design by Maria Fernandez

Library of Congress Cataloging-in-Publication Data is available.

ISBN: 978-1-64313-821-3

10 9 8 7 6 5 4 3 2 1

Printed in the United States of America
Distributed by Simon & Schuster
www.pegasusbooks.com

In Memory of Germaine Brée

and

to my students

CONTENTS

Catherine Camus and her father in Sorel–Moussel, 1957

A Note from
Catherine Camus

T his is not a preface. It is simply a hand extended, across the oceans, to Monsieur Meagher, to his students, and to all those in the world who love my father.

I say "love" because in the forty years that I have been managing his writings, my greatest challenge has been to try not to disappoint the spontaneous impulse of fraternity, friendship, and warmth that has emanated from his readers. It is true that my father "touches not only the mind but the soul and the heart" of those who read him. This, I believe, is because he speaks to our humanity, clearly and with empathy.

So, when I read Monsieur Meagher's prologue, I was especially happy to find that his words were so like the very words that would come to me to write about my father. In saying this, I reach out my hand to him and to you for help.

I believe with my father that:

> Each generation doubtless feels called upon to remake the world. Mine knows, though, that it will not remake it, but its task is perhaps even greater. It consists in preventing the world from destroying itself. (Stockholm Nobel Speech, December 10, 1957).

For my part, every day I feel that I am watching the fall of the Roman Empire. By this I mean the West, where money and power have become the ultimate goals in life. Everything moves faster and faster, as billionaires prefer to launch themselves into space rather than help those who are only an "arm's reach" away. It seems that we humans today have become the "spontaneous generation" with no history and no past. The walls go up, and everyone sees noon at their own door, as the saying goes. But alone we are nothing.

When Monsieur Meagher writes "Far from affirming our common humanity, we dehumanize, demonize, dismiss, cancel, and degrade each other as a prelude to conflict, prejudice, and predation," I thank him. Optimistically perhaps, I am sure that there are many of us who think like him, but that does not interest the media. It is indeed true that "slogans replace dialogue."

I have met women and men from all over the world, from Chile to Malaysia, from Africa to Sweden. I have received hundreds of letters from Greece, Italy, the Americas, Australia. Believe me, we are not alone.

My father is not a "haughty, self-righteous Nobel Prize winner." He is human like the rest of us, searching, reaching out his hand and trying to find his way. He really listened to us and wanted us to live our lives. He still does. He is still doing good in the world today.

Thank you, Monsieur Meagher.

Catherine Camus

⁓

Ceci n'est pas une préface. C'est juste une main tendue, par-delà les océans, à Monsieur Meagher, à ses étudiants, et à tous ceux qui, dans le monde, aiment mon père.

Je dis « aiment » parce que depuis 40 ans que je gère son œuvre, la plus grosse difficulté a été de tenter de ne pas décevoir l'élan de fraternité, d'amitié, de chaleur qui émanait de ses lecteurs. C'est vrai que mon père

« touche non seulement l'esprit mais l'âme et le coeur » de ceux qui le lisent. Je crois parce qu'il parle à hauteur d'homme, empathique et cohérent.

Alors, en lisant le prologue de Monsieur Meagher, j'ai été tellement heureuse de trouver si exactement les mots qui me viendraient pour parler de mon père, que me voilà en train de lui et de vous tendre la main ! Help !

Je crois en effet que « chaque génération, sans doute, se croit vouée à refaire le monde. La mienne sait pourtant qu'elle ne le refera pas. Mais sa tâche est peut-être plus grande. Elle consiste à empêcher que le monde ne se défasse. » (Discours de Stockholm, 10 décembre 1957). Et j'ai l'impression, tous les jours, de voir la chute de l'Empire romain. Je parle de l'Occident où l'argent et le pouvoir sont devenus des buts ultimes. Tout va de plus en plus vite, les milliardaires préfèrent se lancer dans l'espace plutôt que d'aider celles et ceux qui sont « à leur portée ». Il semble que les humains soient devenus une « génération spontanée » sans histoire et sans passé. Les murs montent, chacun voit midi à sa porte. Mais seuls nous ne sommes rien. Lorsque Monsieur Meagher écrit « Far from affirming our common humanity, we deshumanize, demonize, dismiss, cancel, and degrade each other as a prelude to conflict, prejudice, and predation, » je lui dis merci. Et, optimiste peut-être, je suis sûre que nous sommes très nombreux à penser comme lui mais cela n'intéresse pas les médias. C'est vrai que le « slogan placé le dialogue ».

J'ai rencontré des femmes et des hommes du monde entier, du Chili à la Malaisie, de l'Afrique à la Suède, j'ai reçu des centaines de lettres de Grèce, d'Italie, des Amériques, d'Australie. Croyez-moi, nous ne sommes pas seuls.

Mon père n'est pas « un Prix Nobel hautain et moralisateur ». C'est un homme parmi les hommes, qui cherche et qui tâtonne, comme nous. Il écoutait vraiment et il nous laissait vivre. Aujourd'hui encore il fait du bien.

Merci, Monsieur Meagher

Catherine Camus

ALBERT CAMUS
AND THE HUMAN CRISIS

PROLOGUE

L ike countless others in my generation, I first read Camus in
the early 1960s, beginning with *The Stranger* and moving on to
The Myth of Sisyphus. I stopped there, and for the next six years carried the
"existentialist" Camus with me during my own political awakening and
early engagement in the peace movement. For me, who until then had
studied mostly ancient literature and philosophy, as well as early Christian
theology, reading Camus was a rite of passage into the unknown. It was
both threatening and exciting. The truth, however, was that I had barely
discovered Camus, much less understood him. The Camus section on
my library shelf and in my mind was a mere inch wide, comprising two
very early and very thin volumes. That suddenly changed in the winter of
1970, when, as a rookie recruit in the Notre Dame faculty of Theology,
I was summarily assigned to present a paper at an upcoming Memorial
Conference sponsored by the university to mark the tenth anniversary of
Camus's death. A handful of towering figures had been invited to speak,
and then far below, at pavement level, there was I, who for the next month
read my way through Camus's major works, well beyond *The Stranger* and
The Myth of Sisyphus, in the hope of being able to make a contribution that
would neither humiliate me nor do an injustice to the man I already revered,
but about whom I still knew precious little.

What began as a burden soon became a boon. My free dive into the
writings of Camus brought one wonder and challenge after another. I have

no recollection or copy of what I wrote to deliver at the conference, no doubt because it was far from memorable. Not so the electrifying lecture given by the conference's keynote speaker, Professor Germaine Brée, who had been a friend of Camus's and Francine Faure's, his second wife, for decades. She wove into her lecture a number of personal anecdotes about Camus that revealed just how extraordinary a man he was in life and not just in print. After waves of applause and well into the question period that followed, one student asked Brée (whose name the university daily, the *Observer*, misspelled as Bray) to tell more stories, and she generously obliged. Every time she tried to bring the session to a close, however, she was met with polite but insistent pleas from the audience for more stories. For the next forty-five minutes, the slight-of-stature and great-in-mind Professor Brée graciously gave way to more curtain calls than Johnny Cash had received months earlier. The following day, after a wrap-up panel discussion, Professor Brée walked over to me to say that she had appreciated my earlier remarks, and that she was surprised they had come from an under-graduate student. When I thanked her and explained that I was actually on the Notre Dame faculty, her immediate embarrassment and our ensuing laughter proved to be the beginning of a close friendship that lasted thirty-one years, until her death at the age of ninety-three in 2001.

After I moved to Massachusetts to join the founding faculty of Hampshire College, I invited Germaine to speak and meet with my students on multiple occasions, each time a highly memorable event. She found those long discussions with my students so rewarding that she told me that she would, from then on, gladly come for free. She knew, as did I, that their enthusiasm was not all about her but rather about Camus. Reading him and sharing our ideas, as if communing over a convivial meal, ignited our minds and kept them simmering long afterwards. It was that way for me across fifty-two years in the classroom, until I retired in the summer of 2020. During that long span, no other class I taught was as consistently rewarding, and sometimes life-altering, as my class entitled quite simply Camus. Most classes at Hampshire draw in the neighborhood of fifteen to twenty students, but on occasion the Camus class numbered close to a hundred. Camus spoke not only to the minds but also to the hearts and souls of my students, as no one else seemed to, no matter which state or nation they came from. And over the years, many of those same students have written to me to say that he continues to challenge, embolden, and support them in their struggles to keep going and to make a difference in the world.

This book on Camus, like the one that preceded it forty-two years ago,[1] took root in the classroom, working with students. While they might have imagined themselves sitting at my feet, learning from me, I sat equally at theirs, learning from them. Education is not like a blood transfusion, after all, with donors on one end and recipients on the other. When it works, it's a partnership. I am hopeful that the experience of reading this book will feel a bit like sitting in on a class. As in a class, the expectation is that you have done the basic reading, or will go back and complete it soon. No lecture in a class or chapter in a book can substitute for primary sources—in this case the fiction, drama, philosophy, journalism, notebooks, speeches, and correspondence of Camus. This book will draw from all of these to uncover and echo his voice. Think of this book, then, as a master class on Albert Camus by a humanist scholar who has taught the life and writings of Camus for a half century. As it draws all but exclusively from primary texts and original sources, the reader is brought straight to the core of Camus's enduring contribution to today's challenges and crises.

The emphasis here, as in all my classes, is on Camus's work, rather than on the critical contributions of Camus scholarship, however valuable and thought-provoking they are. In academia today, the balance between primary sources and critical commentary is often radically tipped in the latter's favor. In the conversations between critics it is sometimes hard, it seems, for Camus to get a word in. Few world authors have been more widely read, personally loved, and yet thoroughly misunderstood than Camus. The aims of this book are to try to correct the record when necessary, to increase even further the number of his readers, and to deepen their appreciation of his life and works in our time. My strategy in this effort is simple: to let Camus speak for himself. Perhaps the most egregious example of critics and commentators not listening to Camus is their pervasive insistence, from the 1940s to the 2020s, on labeling him an existentialist and an atheist, despite the fact that he never ceased explicitly denying both claims. Surely Camus's voice and vote should decide the matter here; so, in these and other debated matters, I have endeavored to let him speak for himself and to help him be heard. Essential to this endeavor is to point out and highlight, throughout this book, the depth of his lifelong dialogue and engagement with ancient Greek philosophy and literature, the Bible, and the early Church fathers, particularly Augustine. Their collective influence played a large part in making him an often solitary and prophetic voice then and now.

Why, anyone might ask, would I, after more than fifty years in the classroom, want to return there now, in career retirement and COVID-19 quarantine, to offer a final class on Camus? The answer to this is simple: our world, and our nation in particular, are in crisis, and we need the moral clarity and prophetic wisdom of Camus as never before. As I sat at my desk and began this book, with Camus's 1946 New York speech, "The Human Crisis," in one hand and the day's news in the other, these fierce words of the playwright Euripides came to mind:

> The truth is our country has gone mad.
> Its schemes are wild.
> And it is sick with dissent and division.
> It's come apart.
> Otherwise how would you ever have come to power?[2]

In Euripides's drama *Herakles Gone Mad*, the Chorus of citizens threw these barbed words at the tyrant Lykos. I had someone else in mind in summoning them. Unfortunately, there is no end to their relevance.

In *The Descent of Man*, Charles Darwin concluded that of all the things distinguishing human beings from lower animals, it is the moral instinct or conscience that is the most decisive. Looking today at the world around us, we may well wonder just how close our moral instinct is to extinction. No small concern, as without conscience there is no human being left. Many today already claim that we live in a post-human world. The very idea of a common humanity, in which we have a solemn stake, is widely dismissed as "essentialist" and naively anachronistic. Far from affirming our common humanity, we dehumanize, demonize, dismiss, cancel, and degrade each other as a prelude to conflict, prejudice, and predation. Our daily denial of the human "we," the human community, and the common good in the name of radical personal freedom and atavistic tribalism wears away at whatever bonds us to each other and makes possible mutual recognition and goodwill. Cooperation and compassion—the human signature since the first emergence of our species—daily decompose into mutual indifference and contempt. At best, we are an endangered species.

Camus's voice speaks like few others to the core of the cancer that infects our country and our world, a world divided against itself, consumed in a war of all against all. His generation called him the Conscience of Europe. That same voice speaks to us and our world today with a moral integrity and eloquence so sorely lacking in the public arena. In Camus's writings we often find the words we need to speak to one another in what he called the language of our common humanity. It begins with dialogue. "There is no life without dialogue," wrote Camus in 1949. "And in the major part of the world, dialogue has been replaced today by polemics. . . .

> But what is the mechanism of polemics? It consists in considering the opponent as an enemy, consequently in simplifying him and refusing to see him. We have no idea of what the man we are insulting looks like, or whether he ever smiles, or how. Having become three-quarters blind by the grace of polemics, we no longer live among men but in a world of silhouettes. There is no life without persuasion. And today's history knows only intimidation. Men live and can only live on the basis of the idea that they have something in common on which they can always get together. [3]

Dialogue, friendship, and community begin with stories. It has been said that an enemy is a person whose story we have not yet heard. Stories help keep the human flame alive, a flame we kindle every time we form a circle and tell our stories to each other. In the human circle the storyteller is always welcome. According to Homer, there are actually three types of strangers whom we are always glad to see at our door: the physician, the carpenter, and the storyteller. We are glad to see them because they can fix what is broken and there's always something broken, something that needs fixing, whether in our bodies, our houses, or our souls. Albert Camus was many things: journalist, novelist, playwright, actor and director, philosopher, political activist, editor, moralist, humanist, husband, father, lover, and friend. Through all this, from his youth to his last breath, he was an artist, a storyteller. As he went to his death, he carried in his briefcase and his imagination what was to be his consummate story, a story he never finished telling us.

Our Paleolithic ancestors—hundreds of thousands of years ago if it was a day—carried their fire kits with them everywhere they went, because survival depended on never being without fire or the capacity to kindle it. Fire brought light, safety, warmth, and the fellowship of the human circle. Today, our human survival depends on carrying our stories, whether in a backpack, a Kindle, a smartphone, or in our memory. Stories keep the most endangered parts of us alive. The human fire is always in danger of going out and not coming back. We can all say with Albert Camus that "the years we have lived through have killed something in us. And that something is simply the old confidence that humanity had in itself, which led us to believe that we could always elicit human reactions from each other if we spoke in the language of a common humanity."[4] That language, I would suggest, is the one preserved in great world literature and in the diversified works of Albert Camus. That language, I am confident, is not a dead language. It is the human voice, the human imagination, and its stories that first create community. Listening to each other across all our differences and divisions fosters the recognition and acceptance that bring healing and hope.

On the first day of class, I would go around the room and ask everyone to tell us something about themselves, what brought them here, and what expectations they have from the experience. It need not be any different with you, the readers of this book. I invite you to tell me something about yourself, about your interest in Camus, and where this book takes you, hopefully somewhere worth your time and effort.

Lastly, I want to acknowledge with gratitude my closest companions in this book, two friends who have read and discussed with me each chapter as it has taken shape, offering both criticism and suggestions, and always encouragement to keep going: my beloved friend, wife, and fellow teacher Betsy; and my former student and teaching assistant, Jean Dupenloup, himself a gifted author. I hold in my heart, too, my former students, countless at this point, but never nameless or faceless. They reminded me, one year and semester at a time, why I became a teacher and why it was so important for all of us to spend time together with Camus. I am still searching for words adequate to express my debt and my thanks to Catherine Camus. The gift of her kind words to this text and of her warm welcome to its readers is incalculable. She has, throughout her life, been an ark for her father's words and works, assuring that with the passage of time they are not lost, forgotten, or misunderstood. For that, we are all in her debt. Thank you, Madame Camus.

Robert Emmet Meagher

CHAPTER ONE
The Human Crisis

NEW YORK 1946

On Monday, March 25, 1946, Albert Camus, aboard the freighter *Oregon*, sailed into New York Harbor. The first sight he took in and noted in his journal was Coney Island. It reminded him of the Porte d'Orléans, and he found it depressing. The sky was a grim grey, and the air raw. The distant, mist-laden skyscrapers of Manhattan left him cold and unmoved. Then again, he arrived in America with the flu and a fever and a mission. He was thirty-two years old (though A. J. Liebling later remarked that he looked barely twenty) and already a legend in the making, the Conscience of Europe.

A fierce conscience that was, like his flu, contagious.

The first to greet Camus were the immigration inspectors, who interrogated him at length, detaining him until the French Cultural Services intervened. Well before his arrival, Camus (alias P. F. Corus) had been under surveillance by the FBI for his former membership in the Communist Party, his service in the French Resistance, and the fact that he was both French and a philosopher, two categories J. Edgar Hoover considered suspect.* Hoover was, as it happened, onto something. The radical message that Camus (whose name Hoover misspelled as Canus) would deliver three days later called for revolt and resistance. Camus brought word of a plague that everyone knew had devastated Europe but few recognized as having already infected America. Camus had been invited as a cultural ambassador from a broken France to a victorious United States. Heralded as the boldest young writer of his generation, the expectation was that he would share with New Yorkers his own engaged, insider's précis of current French philosophy, literature, and theater. This was not what they got. They didn't know the man they had invited. Those who had read *The Stranger* found themselves confronted with a stranger. Camus later explained that what he most admired about Meursault was that he refused to lie. The same was true of Meursault's creator. New York had invited an existentialist and found themselves confronted by a moralist. Instead of a French Hemingway, they got an Algerian Jeremiah.

On Thursday evening, March 28, every seat and open space in Columbia University's McMillin Theater was taken. Those who still stood in line and hoped for entry were out of luck. The scene was without precedent. No lecture delivered in French at Columbia had ever drawn more than two or three hundred listeners, and yet four or five times that many had come to hear Albert Camus read his prepared remarks entitled "La Crise de l'Homme" ("The Human Crisis"). What they heard was not the cultural excursion they had come for. Instead, it was arguably the most prophetic and unsettling speech Camus ever gave. On that night, in less than thirty minutes, he somehow managed to distill and convey his deepest fears and steepest challenges in words that have lost none of their urgency or relevance in the seventy-five years since he spoke them. Before we move on to what he had to say that evening, the chosen title of his brief talk calls for careful scrutiny. We know from his published *Carnets*, or *Notebooks*, in which Camus chronicled his memories and musings from 1935 to 1959, that

---

* The fact that Camus had since 1943 served as editor-in-chief of *Combat*, whose masthead read "From Resistance to Revolution," must have contributed to Hoover's suspicions.

he took titles seriously, laboring over them, trying them on until he got the right fit. "The Human Crisis" was likely no exception. "Crisis" could have pointed to any one of many possible or current emergencies—economic, political, medical, climatic, etc.—and "Human" suggested that this emergency was global rather than regional or national. If this was what Camus meant, however, then he had chosen his title rather carelessly, because it just didn't fit what followed. As is so often the case with Camus, we have to dig deeper, well beyond the obvious, to get his meaning.

What every close reader of Camus knows is that he was steeped in myth, both Greek and Christian. His writings are, as it were, marinated in the classics and in the Bible. At the time when Camus wrote "The Human Crisis," the myth that preoccupied him was Hesiod's Prometheus, whose multiple incarnate avatars people the pages of such works as *The Misunderstanding, The Plague, The Just*, and *The Rebel*. In Hesiod, the character of Prometheus is defined by an episode described as not merely *a* crisis but *the* crisis that defines humanity and sets it on its own unique, irreversible course. It is the Greek counterpart to the story of Adamah (הָאָדָם), the mortal earthling, in the Garden of Eden. It is a crucial moment of decision from which there is no going back. A moment of "crisis"* in this sense is one in which a line has been drawn, what we might today call a "red line" or a "line in the sand." A moment of crisis is, put simply, a critical turning point, a time of reckoning. The question then is: What did Camus see as the line that humanity was about to cross or had already crossed; and what was at stake in doing so?

As for what was at stake, the answer was clear: humanity, the common bond that defines us as a species and, less abstractly, as a community beyond borders. The "Good War," as it came to be called, was over and had been won. But the "crisis" had not passed. What Camus called "the struggle for life and for humanity" was immediate and ongoing. The "Good War" had released a pestilence, and the world remained in a state of plague. Camus

---

* French *crise* and English *crisis* are etymologically derived from the Greek word κρίνειν (*krínein*), which means "to define or separate," "to decide or contend," "to judge or bring to a reckoning."

made the point that Europeans knew this, while most Americans as yet did not.

> The French people sense that mankind is still under threat. And they also sense that to continue living they must rescue a certain idea of mankind from the crisis that grips the whole world.[1]

Camus's task that night in McMillin Theater was to convince an enthusiastic, overflow Francophile crowd, come to see a cultural celebrity, that "Yes. There is a human crisis." *Is*, not *was*. To accomplish this, Camus summoned his superpower. He told stories, in this case four terse stories, in an attempt to bridge the awareness gap between the people he was there to represent and the people he was there to instruct. For Camus and his French compatriots, these stories were all too familiar: "about a time the world is beginning to forget, but which still burns in our hearts."[2] Narrative fragments of everyday life in occupied Europe, embedded memories, that like shrapnel defied extraction. Camus's audience, on the other hand, were mostly American students, callow and hopeful. They could not forget what they had never known, nor were they haunted by it. These were the stories, best described as parables, that Camus shared with them that evening:

1. In an apartment building occupied by the Gestapo in a European capital, two accused men, still bleeding, find themselves tied up after a night of investigation. The concierge of the building begins her careful household chores in good spirit, since she probably just finished breakfast. Reproached by one of the tortured men, she replies indignantly, "I never interfere with my tenants' business."

2. In Leon, one of my comrades is dragged from his cell for a third round of questioning. Since his ears have been badly torn during a previous session, he is wearing a bandage around his head. The German officer who interrogates him is the same man who

conducted the previous sessions. And yet he asks him, with an air of affectionate concern, "How are your ears doing?"

3. In Greece, after an underground resistance operation, a German officer prepares the executions of three brothers he has taken as hostages. Their old mother throws herself at his feet and he agrees to save one of them. But only at the condition that she designate which one. She chooses the oldest because he has a family, but her choice condemns the two others. Just as the German officer intended.

4. A group of deported women, including one of our comrades, is repatriated to France by way of Switzerland. As soon as they enter Swiss territory, they notice a funeral taking place. And the mere sight of this spectacle sets off their hysterical laughter. "That's how the dead are treated here!" they say.[3]

In prefacing the body of his talk with these four parables, Camus must have known that if they failed to convince his audience of the human crisis—the moral bacillus that infected them and their world—then there would be no point in his going on to say anything more. He and they might just as well exit the auditorium, in silent despair.

In each related episode, something formerly alive lay dead on the floor, like the proverbial canary in the tunnel. Upon inspection, what lay dead, or missing, was humanity. If anyone then or now were to comment that these were war stories, aberrant accounts from a dark time long gone, they would miss the point, Camus's point. Camus knew that what was nowhere to be found in these stories was still missing, and quite possibly gone forever. He made this very point clearly several months later when he wrote, "The years we have gone through have killed something in us. And that something is simply the old confidence man had in himself, which led him to believe that he could always elicit human reactions from another man if he spoke to him in the language of a common humanity."[4] We may describe, explain, or make excuses for the death or demise of humanity in otherwise seemingly intact, healthy, successful people in any number of ways; but the fact remains that "in today's world we can contemplate the death or the torture of a human being with a feeling of indifference, friendly concern, scientific interest, or simple passivity."[5] "Yes," Camus continues:

> There is a human crisis. Since putting a person to death can be regarded with something other than the horror and scandal it ought to provoke. Since human suffering is accepted as a some-what boring obligation, on a par with getting supply or having to stand in line for an ounce of butter.[6]

Camus warned against the common postwar complacency that took false comfort in the fact that Hitler was dead and the Third Reich had fallen. Yes, the serpentine beast was dead, but "we know perfectly well," he argued, "that the venom is not gone, that each of us carries it in our own hearts."[7] All around him in the postwar world, Camus saw disheartening evidence of global community transmission of a murderous indifference many imagined to be contained and controlled. "Look around you," urged Camus,

> and see if it isn't still the case. Violence has a stranglehold on us. Inside every nation, and the world at large, mistrust, resentment, greed, and the race for power are manufacturing a dark, desperate universe in which each man is condemned to live within the limit of the present. . . . Perhaps you who dwell in this still happy America do not see this or cannot see it clearly. But the men I am talking about had been seeing it for years, and had felt this evil in their flesh, read it on the faces of those they love, and deep in their ailing hearts. . . .[8]

It may be that Camus was too polite a guest to have referenced the act that, more than any other, disrobed the human crisis and demonstrated how perilously near humanity was to moral extinction. "We can sum it all up in a sentence," wrote Camus on August 8, 1945, two days after the thermonuclear holocaust of Hiroshima: "The civilization of the machine has just achieved its ultimate degree of savagery."[9] He went on to note the spontaneous, indecent celebration of the event in which much of the world had indulged and thus "shown itself incapable of exerting any control while remaining indifferent to injustice or even mere human happiness."[10] Camus expressed how hard it was to breathe in this world, and he was not referring to his collapsed lung. He was living with moral, not just tubercular, pain. He put it simply: "Mankind has probably been given its last chance."[11]

Camus's suffering, spiritual and physical, only deepened in the fourteen years between his New York visit and his sudden untimely death sixty miles southeast of Paris. Whether that lethal car crash was an accident or a Soviet assassination, as some recent evidence suggests, Camus had written his last words and spoken for the last time. Or so it seemed on January 4, 1960. Since then, however, previously private manuscripts have found their way into print, and his voice has, if anything, grown ever more forceful and compelling. Three years after his death, in a review entitled "The Ideal Husband," Susan Sontag commented that "Kafka arouses pity and terror, Joyce admiration, Proust and Gide respect, but no modern writer that I can think of, except Camus, has aroused love. His death in 1960 was felt as a personal loss by the whole literate world."[12] Never silenced and still loved, Camus is far from forgotten. His books are devoured by the young and go on to companion them through their years. Inspiring people he never knew, addressing events, conflicts, and crises he cannot have witnessed, Camus's voice has somehow lost none of its urgency and relevance.

This very point was made several years ago by Madeleine Dobie of Columbia University when, seventy years after Camus's first and last visit to New York, she published an article in the *National Book Review* entitled "We Are in a 'Camus Moment.'" To support her claim, she cataloged the remarkable number of recent Camus anniversary celebrations, autobiographies, critical studies, novels, narrative and documentary films, translations, and newspaper columns focused on or spawned by Camus and his works.

In case we might imagine that this energy was confined to Western intellectual circles, Dobie assured her readers that

> Camus's broad appeal can also be attributed to his elevation of ethics over politics, and individual decision-making over collective ideologies. By searching for meaning in the face of life's absurdity, his essays and novels provide a moral framework that can be applied to everyday situations. This relevance to everyday life is at the heart of French director Joël Calmette's *Living with Camus*, in which ordinary people from around the world share their experience of turning to Camus for solace and moral guidance. The most moving sequence features the *"Camus émus"* (literally those who are "moved by Camus") a youth group in Douala, Cameroon, run by a resourceful literature student who introduces adolescents, who might otherwise be roaming the city's streets, to the works of Camus. "If I don't have bread to fill the belly [*la panse*]," she says, at least "I have Albert Camus's work to nourish the mind [*la pensée*]."[13]

"Until quite recently," Dobie continues, "Camus's image was that of the emblematic French public intellectual," whereas "the new Camus, by contrast, is a writer whose life and work are deeply marked by his Algerian origins. . . .

> The current incarnation of Camus as a figure torn between France and Algeria in an age of growing conflict has made him available for a new kind of moral and political reasoning. Camus has often been declared to be "relevant" to moral and political debates on issues such as suicide or the death penalty (of which he was a leading opponent), but today he's emerging as a privileged commentator on global politics, and in particular on relations between Western societies and Muslims living within and beyond their borders.[14]

As evidence of Camus's visionary relevance to current world issues, Dobie reminded her readers that seven decades earlier, in his New York address ("The Human Crisis"), "he identified the global rise of 'terror' as the leading problem of the age, tying it to the dehumanizing impact of bureaucracy and the hegemony of politics."[15]

Regrettably, Camus's words in "The Human Crisis" were largely lost on the postwar generation, for whom, as a rule, *The Stranger* was either the only work of Camus they bothered to read or else the prism through which all of Camus's other works were filtered. The memory of Camus endured, but that memory was mistaken. He was so often paired with Jean-Paul Sartre that their names were practically hyphenated. In 1945, when Camus and Sartre still shared a friendship, Camus had nevertheless found it necessary to make this much perfectly clear:

> Sartre and I are always astonished to see our names associated. We are even thinking of publishing a little advertisement in which the undersigned affirm that they have nothing in common and refuse to answer for the debts of the other.[16]

But he might as well have been talking to a brick wall. The point was lost. Camus was virtually tattooed with the label "existentialist," an identity Camus categorically denied. In fact, he was an outspoken anti-existentialist. When, on his New York visit, a student asked him outright if he was an existentialist, Camus only sighed and answered, "No."[17] He repeated this denial until his death, but for some reason his contemporary readers seldom took him at his word on this matter. Since his death, Camus's daughter Catherine has strenuously endeavored to set the record straight and to sever once and for all the unwarranted tether tying Camus to a school of thought he diametrically opposed. Her efforts to clarify her father's life and legacy and to ensure the posthumous publication and translation of previously inaccessible Camus manuscripts have notably expanded both the Camus library and the circle of his readers. That circle now includes not only Western scholars and students but also generations of extracurricular

searchers in Asia, Africa, the Middle East, and Latin America who find
in Camus the guide and companion they have been looking for and often
failed to find in the spiritual wastelands of contemporary greed, violence,
indifference, jargon-heavy ideology, and cold cynicism. The time is right
to revisit "The Human Crisis."

NEW YORK 2016

That was precisely the conclusion reached several years ago when, under
the umbrella title "Camus: A Stranger in the City," New York hosted a
monthlong festival of performances, readings, films, concerts, and other
celebrations to recall and evoke the first and last visit of Albert Camus to
America's shores. The centerpiece of this "Camus Moment" was a grand
commemoration of the pivotal address Camus delivered on March 28,
1946. This took the form of a "reenactment" of sorts. Seventy years to the
day after the original event, in the same McMillin Theater where it had
first taken place, a sold-out audience once again listened to "The Human
Crisis," in an English translation by Yale French professor Alice Kaplan
and others. Standing in for Camus and delivering his words that evening
was the Danish-American actor, author, and artist Viggo Mortensen, most
widely recognized as Aragorn or Strider in the epic film version of *The
Lord of the Rings*. Of lesser notoriety but of greater relevance here, he had
recently costarred as Daru, a war-weary schoolteacher, in the 2014 film
Loin des hommes (*Far from Men*), closely based on "L'Hôte" ("The Guest"),
a Camus short story included in the volume *Exile and the Kingdom*.

The New York and the America to which Camus "returned" in 2016,
and the audience that he vicariously addressed, were far different from
their 1946 counterparts. So, too, was this a very different Camus. He was
no longer such a stranger, and they were less starstruck. Instead, many of
them were "*Camus émus*," seeking not autographs but nourishment, while
others were paying tribute to a friend and mentor who, without their ever
having met him, had sustained them through dark times. Why, we might

ask, would they or should we revisit after seventy years this short speech that had left such a faint footprint? One suitable reason was offered by Camus's friend Nicola Chiaromonte, who, in the summer of 1960, thought back to "The Human Crisis" and reflected:

> It seems to me today that in this speech, which was a sort of autobiography, there were all the themes of Camus's later work, from *La Peste* to *Les Justes* to *L'Homme Révolté*. But in it there remained, discreetly in shadow, the other Camus, the one that I can call neither truer nor artistically superior, for he is simply "the other," jealously hidden in his secret being—the anguished, dark, misanthropic Camus whose yearning for human communication was perhaps even greater than that of the author of *La Peste*; the man who, in questioning the world, questioned himself, and by this testified to his own vocation. This is the Camus of the last pages of *L'Étranger*, and especially the Camus of *La Chute* in which we hear his deepest being, the self-tormenting tormentor, speak, resisting all forms of complacency and moral self-satisfaction. [18]

As a recent refugee, Chiaromonte, an Italian activist and writer, first met Camus in Algiers in April 1941, where they formed an instant friendship. They shared a visceral hatred of fascism together with a leftist rejection of Stalinist Communism. Camus deeply admired (and likely envied) Chiaromonte's service in the Spanish Civil War, flying in André Malraux's squadron in the Spanish Loyalist Air Force. For a while, before departing North Africa for America, Chiaromonte lived with Camus, delighting in his company and that of his many friends. Along with a shared "ecstatic admiration of the sea," Chiaromonte later remembered how they had both been "totally obsessed by a single thought: we had arrived at humanity's zero hour and history was senseless; the only thing that made sense was that part of man which remained outside of history, alien and impervious to the whirlwind of events." [19]

Five years later, Chiaromonte welcomed Camus to New York, and they rekindled their friendship. Chiaromonte, whom Camus called "my dear comrade," may be seen to have been a soul mate of Camus, one of many, actually. They were on the same page, as it were, from the day they first met. In a word, they "got" each other, which is why Chiaromonte's penetrating assessment of "The Human Crisis" is to be taken so seriously. Chiaromonte "got" Camus's point that evening, perhaps like few others in the audience, and years later came to realize that Camus had distilled in twenty-two minutes his life and work. With the pure simplicity of a Tibetan Buddhist singing bowl, the note struck and summoned that evening released the full range of overtones resonant in Camus's writings.

HUMANITY'S ZERO HOUR

When Aragorn, as appointed avatar, re-spoke Camus's words, his audience had long since lost the sanguine innocence of their 1946 predecessors. Camus's words no longer had to convince them there was a human crisis. That was why they were there. The Cold War, Vietnam, racial division, income inequality, "forever war" in the Middle East, global swarms of killer drones, routine school shootings, the remapping of the homeland into a clashing patchwork of red and blue tectonic plates, resurgent nationalism, born-again fascism, and an approaching election that every day looked more like a cliff . . . the American field had been plowed this time, the soil overturned to receive Camus's words. The "moral experience" of Camus's generation was no longer so removed from the moral experience of the American generation assembled in McMillan Theater. "As for our society's traditional morality, it seemed to us that it hadn't stopped being what it had always been: a monstrous hypocrisy."[20] Amen to that. Camus was now speaking to the choir.

America had finally reached, with the rest of the world, the "zero hour" when humanity might be lost, "left behind" in a godless rapture of its own making. Camus listed what he saw as "the most obvious symptoms of the crisis": the rise of terror; the impossibility of persuasion; the replacing of real men with political men for whom there is neither right nor wrong, only either winning or losing; and the decriminalization of murder. We might well wonder whether Camus somehow knew that what he said in 1946 would finally be heard and understood seventy years later in the same room. Truth, to borrow a phrase from Hannah Arendt, has a way of "coming home to roost."[21]

Camus, to the end—the end of his speech and the end of his life— "combined a pessimistic view of the world with a profound optimism for humankind."[22] His speech was a call, not to tears but to action. First comes communication: clear, simple words spoken in good faith, never lies, never more than one knows. "People can only really live if they believe they have something in common, something that brings them together. If they address someone humanely they expect a human response."[23] Next comes compassion, the bond that friends share, the recognition that what concerns you concerns me, and what happens to you happens to me.

> Yes, that was the great lesson of those disastrous years. That an insult aimed at a student in Prague affected a worker in the Paris suburbs. That blood spilled somewhere in the banks of an Eastern European river could lead a Texas farmer to spill his own on the ground of the Ardennes that he just got to know.[24]

That is the lesson of our own more recent disastrous years as well, the lesson of "I am Charlie Hebdo," of Black Lives Matter, and of "please somebody . . . please man . . . I can't breathe . . . I can't breathe," the lesson that we are in this together, as victim or as executioner. And in such a world, as Camus points out, there are finally only victims. Instead of further igniting political divides and burning down our common house, Camus called for putting politics in its place, behind morality, and "creating a universalism in which all people of goodwill can come together."

> In the end what does it all mean? It means that we must be modest in our thoughts and our actions, stand our ground and

do our best work. It means that we must create communities
and think outside parties and governments in order to foster
dialogue across national borders. The members of these communities will affirm, by their lives and their words, that this
world must cease to be the world of police, soldiers and money,
and become the world of men and women, of fruitful work and
thoughtful leisure.[25]

For Camus, this meant working for "a worldwide abolition of capital
punishment."[26] While Camus never expected to live in a world where
there would be no killing, he argued that killing can never, must never, be
justified. As he saw it, all killing is murder, and he found legal, efficient,
institutionalized murder the most abhorrent.

Camus's is a voice we need to hear and heed. Yes, there is a human crisis.
He has visited our shores to tell us this, and in "The Human Crisis" we
possess a guide to follow, a key to unlock the enduring truth of what he
had to teach.

One of the notable New Yorkers who came to know Camus during his
1946 visit was the philosopher William Barrett, who saw in Camus "the
advocate of what he (Camus) came to call 'ordinary values'—those elemen-
tary feelings of common decency without which the human race would not
survive."[27] Camus never saw himself as a philosopher. He was certainly
no academic. He came from poverty, from "ordinary" people, and it was
to them he was most concerned to speak. He became, on the other hand,
among many things, an intellectual, but with a difference. "There was a
quality about Camus that made him something different as an intellectual,
a quality indeed that most intellectuals lack: he was a man of the people
who remained in touch with our common humanity."[28]

It is that Camus, and his passion for asserting and preserving our
common humanity, that this book will seek to reveal and appreciate.

CHAPTER TWO

Mortality

T he weight that bore down on Camus in 1946, as we have seen, was what he called "the human crisis." While America was still basking in victory, Camus envisaged humanity on the brink. The war he had known and narrowly survived had been fought on many fronts but only won on some. In the luminous mushroom clouds over Hiroshima and Nagasaki, Camus had seen, as had Robert Oppenheimer, the face of "Death, the destroyer of worlds." The vengeful postwar purges and executions in France, the Stalinist death camps, the drawing of the Iron Curtain and the bristling of nuclear arsenals—all this and much more belied the euphoric postwar resilience of spirit and economic resurgence in the United States. America didn't know what Europe knew—that the world, humanity, was still at risk of defeat. The future of humanity was more in doubt and peril than at any time in the war. A line had been crossed without having been consciously drawn. Violence, indeed, had a stranglehold on us. Killing was the way we had learned to make peace, and so we had made our peace with killing. Without cracking a book, we had sided with Hobbes over Plato. Fear, not friendship, lay at the core of human community. We belong to history, and for the moment history seemed on our side in the inevitable war of all against all.

Camus's newfound American fandom was largely lost on him in 1946. His New York readers lay with Meursault and Marie on the sun-scorched beach of Algiers, while Camus labored with Rieux and Tarrou in plague-ridden Oran. He was expected to embody *The Stranger* while he was writing and still living *The Plague*. The truth, as we will soon see, is that he was never Meursault, never indifferent to an Arab's murder or a mother's death, and would never have wished for howls of hatred at anyone's execution, much less his own. Camus the writer, not Meursault the character, Camus the humanist, not the existentialist, was preoccupied with our common humanity, our shared human nature, our essence rather than our existence. In this obsession he had long since parted company with Meursault and Sisyphus; and, had he pursued these thoughts further in New York, he would have left most of his current literary entourage behind as well. These were not current thoughts. They were, in fact, quite ancient.

What few at the time suspected was that Camus, despite his youthful charm, had an old soul. It was not only that he had nearly died of tuberculosis at the age of seventeen* but also that in his youth he had spent so much time in silence, studying ancient philosophy, and returning each day to a silent home, convincing him to his core that life's most profound truths lay beyond the reach of words. This was one of the gulfs dividing him from Sartre, who revealingly entitled his autobiography *Les Mots* (*The Words*). Sartre's coming of age, his mind's birth, took place in his grandfather's library, where he learned to read, consume, and configure words. Camus, in contrast, grew up in an impoverished, illiterate household, along with his cancerous grandmother, hearing-impaired mother, marginally educated older brother, and partially paralyzed uncle. Their congested two-room flat was without running water, much less a library. A world not only without books but also largely without words. Camus's most intimate relationship was with his mother, an unschooled house cleaner who rarely spoke from the moment she learned of her husband's death in the First Battle of the Marne. Whether from shock or choice, or both, she and Camus communicated and shared their lives with few words. Whereas

---

* Camus's right lung was infected in 1930, and the other in 1935, leaving him in chronic pain and in need of recurrent intervention for the remainder of his life.

for Sartre something was real and understood only when put into words, for Camus the more real or profound the truth, the less it could or need be spoken. This was nowhere more evident than when Camus spoke or wrote of the "humanity" or "human nature" in which he believed but was all but at a loss to explain. Like the soul, our humanity is both innate and elusive. Its existence is a truism, eluding positive proof. We may only witness it in its absence. We may only experience it when we feel it slipping away. So it was for Camus in "The Human Crisis," when he shared four stark parables to convey the absence of humanity, the mortal threat to our souls, the unseen bacillus whose presence we nonetheless sense.

In his earliest writings we see Camus wondering and worrying about human nature, our humanity, its light side and its dark side. "To correct a natural indifference," he once explained, "I was placed halfway between poverty and the sun. Poverty kept me from thinking all was well under the sun and in history; the sun taught me that history was not everything."[1] Justice, he knew from his study of Greek philosophy, was a matter of giving to each thing its due. The sun, the earth, a mother's love, poverty, injustice, death. In the conclusion to his first book, *L'envers et l'endroit* (*The Wrong Side and the Right Side*), Camus wrote that "what counts is to be human and simple. No, what counts is to be true, and then everything fits in, humanity and simplicity."[2] It was of this modest inaugural text, published at age twenty-two and dedicated to his revered mentor, Jean Grenier, that Camus later wrote, "Every artist keeps within himself a single source which nourishes during his lifetime what he is and what he says. When that spring runs dry, little by little one sees his work shrivel and crack. . . . As for myself, I know that my source is in *The Wrong Side and the Right Side*, in the world of poverty and sunlight I lived in for so long."[3] In 1946, drained by the war and its aftermath, spring was running dry and Camus was struggling to write *The Plague*, trying to convince himself and others that there was still more good in humanity than there was evil. In that effort he drew once again from his sources: the sea, the sun, a mother's silence, and the deep roots of learning his teacher had once urged him to nourish.

As Camus was a *pupille de la nation*, the son of a fallen soldier, the State assured his basic education, but he owed his more privileged education in the Grand Lycée and then the University of Algiers to two mentors who perceived and fostered his promise and passion: his primary school teacher, Louis Germain, who shepherded him into secondary school, and Jean Grenier, who guided Camus through his studies in philosophy and literature and directed his thesis, entitled "Métaphysique chrétienne et Néoplatonisme" ("Christian Metaphysics and Neoplatonism"). At this point Camus would have embarked on a career in university teaching had not his tuberculosis permanently closed that path to him. The same impairment would exclude him from military service, as well as cancel his early aspirations to play professional soccer. The young Camus, like his mentor, would instead, and to the benefit of many, become a writer. "It was Grenier who introduced him to the first two books that strengthened his conviction that he, too, had something to say: a little-known novel, *La Douleur* (*The Sorrow*), and Grenier's own book of essays, *Les Iles* (*The Islands*)."[4] Camus, at eighteen, who had flourished in poverty and survived a collapsed lung, was nothing if not kindling, and Grenier lit the match. "Grenier," Camus once remarked in an interview, "gave me a taste for philosophical meditation."[5] A taste that led to hunger. In the ensuing years, under Grenier's tutelage, Camus consumed mounds of philosophy and literature, whatever Grenier piled on his plate and whatever he found on his own. "To Camus he (Grenier) transmitted his love of Greek literature, of the great tragic poets as well as the philosophers. It was through Plato and Plotinus that Camus first considered those problems of essence and existence . . . Camus's line of thought, unlike Sartre's, can be traced through St. Augustine, Pascal, Kierkegaard, and Chestov, with Plato and the Neoplatonists as a constant check and reference."[6]

The Greeks—the more ancient the better—infected the young Camus, deep and early; and the Greek landscape, drenched in a light like no other, addicted him. His soul, he discovered, was not only old but Greek. Passports aside, "Camus's true spiritual motherland was classical Greece."[7] Mystical, if not magical, thinking, yes; but there was in Camus a touch of the mystic, a "bug" he might have first caught from his pedagogue, Grenier, a Breton Christian who was himself "something of a mystic . . . and a passionate devotee of Greece."[8] It was Grenier who helped steer him through the turbulent waters of late antiquity to ponder "the passage from Hellenism to Christianity" in which Camus recognized "the true and only turning point in history."[9] This "turning point" had a name, Aurelius Augustinus, also known as Saint Augustine, whom Camus referred to as "the other Algerian." The kinship between Camus and Augustine began with the fact that they were born a mere forty-three miles from each other in northeastern Algeria, Camus in Dréan and Augustine in Souk Ahras. From the poverty that each of them knew as children there was but one escape—education—and for this they needed native brilliance, inner fire, and a hand up. They both had all three. The gap of nearly sixteen centuries that separated their birthdates lost much of its meaning as Camus dove into the writings of Augustine and found in them a well from which he drew for the remainder of his life.

This circumstantial kinship between Camus and "the other Algerian" turned into an enduring fellowship when Camus, in his late teens, was researching and writing his thesis on Christian metaphysics and Neoplatonism under the direction of Grenier. Regrettably little attention has been paid by Camus scholars and still less by his readers to this work and, more broadly, to the profoundly formative influence of Greek antiquity and early Christianity on the development of Camus's thought and writings. The intensity of Camus's active engagement in the issues and struggles of his day might mislead us. He was, yes, a man of his times, *engagé*, but not only *his* times; for his words resonate today, over sixty years since his death, with the same, if not greater, force. To relegate him to history is to dismiss him as a guide, to lose him as a companion on the human journey. Camus knew better in making the acquaintance of the ancients. He made his intellectual friends and foes where he found them, even and especially in the past. Though belonging to different centuries and millennia, he and they nevertheless shared a common world and a common humanity.

History represented for Camus, as for Heidegger, the human spectrum, the repetition of the humanly possible. He engaged the past as he engaged

the present: passionately. "The world moves toward paganism," wrote
Camus, "and it still rejects pagan values. They must be restored, to paganize
belief, Graecize Christ and restore balance."[10] There was much in "pagan"
Greece that Camus admired and embraced, but there was also much that it
failed to comprehend or offer. In Camus's eyes, Christianity comprehended
the reality of evil as Greek wisdom never had, and offered a conversion
of soul inconceivable to the Greeks. All this he found in Augustine, the
father of Western Christian philosophy, at the time of whose death "Christianity was formed into a philosophy. It is now sufficiently armed to resist
the tempest in which all will founder. During the long years, it remains the
only common hope and the only effective shield against the calamity of
the Western world. Christianity had conquered through its universality."[11]
From these words we might easily imagine that Camus, like his mentor
Augustine, had undergone conversion and embraced Christianity, but in
this we would be mistaken. "Greek in his need for coherence, Christian in the anxieties of his sensitivity, for a long time he remained on the
periphery of Christianity."[12] This was how Camus described the young
Augustine; in doing so, he might as well have been describing himself.
On balance, he seemed more comfortable with Hellenic values than with
Christian ones, explaining that "I feel closer to the values of the ancient
world than I do to the Christian ones. Unfortunately, I cannot go to Delphi
to become initiated."[13] Neither was he willing at this point to revisit or
confirm his ritualized baptism as an infant.

Camus never saw himself as a philosopher, much less a Christian. In
1946, on the day after his arrival in New York, he was asked at a press
conference about his philosophical position, to which he responded that
"his philosophy consisted of doubts and uncertainties."[14] Although, like his
mentor Grenier, Camus had a taste, even a hunger, for philosophical meditation, he never created a system. Indeed, Camus might have been looking
into a mirror when he wrote of his other mentor, Augustine, "There is this
curiosity about the author of the *Confessions*, namely, that his experience
remains the perpetual reference for his intellectual pursuits."[15] Books and
his own sentient being—these were the richest sources of Camus's early

philosophical meditations. The French public school curriculum and the reading list for his thesis offer rich clues to the shape of the book-world that Camus inhabited and explored as a student, while his early essays and the posthumous *First Man* paint a vivid picture of his experiences as a growing boy "placed halfway between poverty and the sun." The sea, the sun, the bond of friendship, the excitement of first love, the awakening of mind, the leap of imagination, the sculpting of language—these were among the experiences that seeded the young Camus's philosophical reflections. So, too, there was the experience of pervasive poverty, with all the daily hardships and humiliations it entailed, and the experience of death, the death of a father he never knew, and a taste of his own death when barely seventeen, a death that he would carry with him for the duration. As we will soon see, these experiences led him to common ground with the Greeks and Augustine, and decisively shaped his future work.

Camus, like Socrates and like Augustine, began, as it were, standing before a looking glass, with a singular focus on the human and the self. Lying in bed alone and awake at night in the year 386, Augustine carried on a series of extensive conversations with himself and then recorded them in an early text entitled *The Soliloquies*, which he introduced with these words:

> For long I had been turning over in my mind many various thoughts. For many days I had been earnestly seeking to know myself and my chief good and what evil was to be shunned. Suddenly someone spoke to me, whether it was myself or someone else from without or from within I know not. Indeed, to know that is my main endeavor. [16]

Augustine decided to call this inner voice Reason (*ratio*). He was talking to himself, and one of their initial exchanges went like this:

> *Reason.*—What then do you wish to know? . . . Briefly summarize it. *Augustine.*—I desire to know God and the soul. *R.*—Nothing more? *A.*—Nothing whatever. [17]

Years later, in his *Confessions*, Augustine pursued the same line of self-interrogation, putting it this way:

> I directed myself to myself and to myself I said, "You, who are
> you?" And I responded, "A human being."[18]

This response, however, hardly settled the matter for Augustine, because it simply begged the question, rendering Augustine, as he put it, a question to himself: "What am I then . . . What nature am I?"[19] This line of inquiry had also been the point of departure for Socrates, who saw no sense in asking other questions or pursuing other directions until he had an answer to this one.

> I can't as yet "know myself," as the inscription at Delphi enjoins,
> and so long as that ignorance remains it seems to me ridiculous
> to inquire into extraneous matters. Consequently I don't bother
> about such things . . . and direct my inquiries, as I have just said,
> rather to myself, to discover whether I really am a more complex
> creature and more puffed up with pride than a Typhon,* or a
> simpler, gentler being whom heaven has blessed with a quiet,
> un-Typhonlike nature.[20]

With this conviction Camus, too, was in full accord, affirming that "like the Greeks I believe in nature,"[21] by which he meant human nature. "Human condition. Human nature." reads another fragmentary entry in his *Notebooks*, "But if there is a human nature, where does it come from? Obvious that I ought to give up all creative activity so long as I don't know."[22] We can easily imagine Camus nodding his head in appreciation of these sentiments expressed by another of his major influences:

---

* In Greek mythology, Typhon was the son of Gaia (the goddess Earth) and Tartarus (the netherworld). Typhon was a deadly, hundred-headed serpentine monster who, with his mate Echidna (half woman-half snake), sired a host of monstrous offspring.

> If one can sometimes remember with a certain sense of relief that
> Caesar burned the entire Alexandrian library, one could also in
> all good will wish that our superfluity of knowledge could be
> taken away, in order that we might again learn what it means
> to live as a human being.*

This point by now is clear. Camus was committed to unearthing and understanding a concept that the modern world and most of his peers had long discarded and buried as naive and obsolete, not to say inconvenient. It was not idle, esoteric curiosity that drove Camus to inquire into human nature but rather an intuitive realization that if he, as a human being, had a nature, he would do well to live in accord with it, as would everyone else. It made simple, common sense that to violate your own nature would be folly and would carry a heavy price.** This inquiry into the nature of human being—so fundamental to ancient Greek and early Christian philosophy—formed the core of Camus's most enduring and consequential writings, from *The Stranger* to *The Fall*. Consequently, we will follow that same inquiry here, letting it focus and guide our discussion of those writings.

So what, we might ask, would Camus have learned first and taken with him from the Greeks regarding the nature of human being? From his study of Homer and Hesiod, who arguably shaped the classical Greek mind, Camus could not have missed the truth that human beings are defined by mortality. "O suffering mankind," chants Aristophanes's Chorus of birds, "lives of twilight, race feeble, and fleeting."[23] In the ancient Greek triad of beings that comprise the hierarchy of sentient life, "humanity, in reality, is poised midway between gods and beasts."[24] While there are myriad differences that might be noted between divine,

---

* Søren Kierkegaard, *Concluding Unscientific Postscript*, p. 229. A further indication of Camus's esteem for Kierkegaard may be that he named his dog "Kirk" after him.

** A drowning chicken I once rescued was enough to convince me of this. It thought it was a duck.

bestial, and human beings, the Greeks focused on two: rational conscious-ness and mortality, which fuse to create the consciousness of death or conscious death. In this scheme, beasts obviously die, which is to say they are finite, bounded. They live and then they die. They don't live with their death. Gods, on the other hand, live and never die, or only rarely in myth. Gods live forever, or at least for "aeons," which from a human perspective amounts to the same thing. Humans—halfway between the two—are as finite as beasts and as rational or conscious as gods, and in this they are unique. The gods, in Greek literature, are "deathless" (ἀθάνατοι); animals are "perishable" (φθαρτοί). Humans, on the other hand, are uniquely "deathful" (θνητοί). As Heidegger put it, human being is "Being-towards-death" (*Sein-zum-Tode*). In addition to being alive, we are, in every moment of life, also in the process of dying; and we know it, however far off the actual moment of our death might be. Knowing this, however, is not the same as daily living with it.

There are countless truisms (Time flies, Money doesn't grow on trees, No one is young forever); but we rarely break our stride to take them seriously. "I know another truism: it tells me that man is mortal," wrote Camus. "One can nevertheless count the minds that have deduced the extreme conclusions from it."[25] As Camus pointed out, most people live in denial of death, in particular their own death, as long as they are able to run or distract themselves from it. Life offers countless escapes from the consciousness of death, but none from death itself. If the experience of death were required to become conscious of mortality, no one would ever achieve it, since death marks the cessation of consciousness. No one has to be a Buddhist, however, to come to the first of the Four Noble Truths, the truth of suffering, of inevitable diminishment, the universal reality of sickness, old age, and death. We need only to use our imaginations to see ourselves in others—in the sick, the aged, and the dying—to realize that we will one day be them.

Why, we might ask, would we want to live with the consciousness of death, our death? The simple Greek answer to this is that our humanity depends on it. Ready or not, we *are* mortals, and when we pretend and act as if we are not, we all too often adopt the postures and presumptions of gods. Our imagined ascent into divinity, however, is in truth a never-ending descent. Euripides, another of the young Camus's ancient mentors, made this point relentlessly in his tragedies: the gods are not to be admired, much less imitated. They are selfish, callow, cruel, and capricious. Unable to die or truly suffer, and unaccustomed to labor, they don't know the price of anything; accordingly, they act blindly. Human would-be gods, too, are blind and monstrous. To illustrate this truth and drive it home to his fellow Athenians, Euripides staged the story of a young prince so fabulously wealthy, privileged, and spoiled rotten that, when death knocked on his door, he expected his father and convinced his wife to die in his place. His name—Admetus—literally means "untamed," and he wore it like a placard. It took the besotted yet clear-sighted Herakles, Admetus's only real friend, to break the truth to him, set him straight, with these lashing words:

> You there, c'mere.
> I'm gonna make you a wiser man.
> Do you know what's what?
> I mean do you know what it means to be human?
> I don't think you do.
> Anyway, you listen to me.
> We all gotta die.
> There ain't one of us alive today
> That knows whether he'll be around tomorrow. . . .
> So there, that's it.
> You heard what I got to teach. . . .
> When you're mortal, you gotta think mortal thoughts.[26]

Camus came to the same truth when, in his brother Lucien's words, he vomited "buckets of blood" and was carried off to a public ward in Algiers's Mustapha Hospital. Speaking of himself in the third person, Camus later recalled those days in these words:

At the worst of his illness, the doctor showed no hope for
him. He had had no doubts about it. Besides, the fear of death
troubled him considerably.[27]

For the seventeen-year-old Camus, mortality was no casual truism. If not
before, from that time on he "thought mortal thoughts." He had learned
an essential truth, a "noble truth," and would live it. He carried his death
around with him and felt its presence with every breath. Philosophy, Camus
once commented, used to teach us how to die, but now it only teaches us how
to think. Modern philosophy, all too often, is an effete, low-stakes parlor
game for members only. Not so for Camus, who felt uncomfortable in the
presence of French intellectuals. "Uncomfortable! That's hardly the word
for it," commented Camus's close friend Germaine Brée. "Camus came to
feel almost physically distressed in their presence."[28]

When, with one collapsed lung, Camus resumed his studies and
received his baccalaureate degree, he found the course of his life permanently altered. He would never teach, serve in the military, or tend
his soccer team's goal. Instead, for the remainder of his life, he would
mostly sit at a desk, read, and write, in relative solitude. What he
loved most was his work in theater, where he drew strength and found
joy in the experience of close community and collaboration. For the
next several years Camus continued his university studies, receiving
certificates in sociology and ethics, psychology, classical literature,
and logic and general philosophy, culminating in his thesis, "Christian
Metaphysics and Neoplatonism," for which he was awarded the *diplôme
d'études superieures*. At the same time, he honed his writing skills and
published his first two volumes of essays, entitled *L'envers et l'endroit*
(*The Wrong Side and the Right Side*) and *Nuptials*, in humble print runs
of 350 copies each. Neither book made an appreciable ripple, much less
a splash. What they did do was launch a life.

The journals or *Notebooks* (*Carnets*) that Camus began writing during
this period, at the age of twenty-two, provide an early window into his
churning imagination and ranging agenda. One of the first entries in

volume one reads: "People can think only in images. If you want to be a philosopher, write novels."[29] Advice he took to heart. In fact, Camus would soon be writing philosophy in multiple genres—fiction, nonfiction, and plays. Indeed, in the journal entries that followed, he revealed that he was already mapping out the first cycle of his work that would include *The Stranger, The Myth of Sisyphus, Caligula,* and *The Misunderstanding* (a novel, a philosophical essay, and two plays). Each cycle would have its own distinct patron or paradigm drawn from Greek myth and its own focal idea or concept. For the first cycle, in which Camus would address the "absurd," he chose Sisyphus as his patron. Before we turn in detail to the Sisyphus Cycle, however, we would do well to consider what Camus saw in Sisyphus, that drew him, indeed how he might have seen himself, and for that matter all of us, in this minor, arguably insignificant, figure, neither a god nor a hero.

In his own retelling of the myth, Camus highlights three qualities of Sisyphus's character that recommend him to our attention as an absurd hero: "His scorn of the gods, his hatred of death, and his passion for life."[30] Absurd heroes aside, what we cannot help but notice first is how vividly these qualities define the young Camus. His passionate love of life leaps from his earliest writings. "I am happy in this world," he announces in the first pages of his *Notebooks*, "for my kingdom is of this world."[31] Amid the Roman ruins at Tipasa, he virtually sings out, "I love this life with abandon . . . it makes me proud of my human condition."[32] Then, years later, at the age of forty-five, Camus looks back at his youth and recalls how "the lovely warmth that reigned over my childhood freed me from all resentment . . . I lived on almost nothing, but also in a kind of rapture.[33] This appetite for the feast that life affords, even in poverty, was made only more voracious as he faced his own imminent death at an absurdly young age, a death that he both feared and hated. From his immersion in Greek philosophy, Camus would have understood that human life, human becoming, represents a volatile fusion of being and nothingness. We are, as a result, defined by *eros*, an insatiable desire on a collision course with death.

As for his scorn of the gods, we might consider an episode related by Camus's boyhood friend Max-Pol Fouchet, who was on a walk with Camus from the hilltop village of Bouzaréah, when they witnessed an accident.

> A Moslem child had been hit by a bus and seemed to be in a coma. They watched the huddled crowd, listened to a wailed Arabic lament as long as they could stand it. Walking away, Camus turned toward the landscape of blue sea and sky. Raising a finger toward the heavens he said: "You see, He says nothing."[34]

This episode speaks for itself about a boy's scorn for a world without answers to suffering, injustice, and death, a world where "in the normal order of things, no one is ever recognized."[35] Camus's brother Lucien once recalled a moment when his deathly ill younger brother, too weak even to read, looked up and moaned, "What will I do if I don't get better?"[36] If he'd had the strength, he might well have raised his finger to the heavens and decried the absence of a response. Already, in this boy of seventeen, we hear the voices of Sisyphus and Meursault, Marie and Caligula, keenly aware that "men die; and they are not happy"[37] and struggling to summon a human response.

CHAPTER THREE
Happiness

T wo idyllic villas, separated by seven hundred miles and over fifteen hundred years. What of significance could they possibly hold in common? One is an affluent sub-Alpine farm in Cassiciacum, near Lake Como, belonging to a Milanese professor by the name of Verecundius, a friend of Augustine's. The other is a more ordinary dwelling with an extraordinary view, perched on a hilltop, high above the Bay of Algiers. More accurately, the space in question is only the second floor of this villa, rented by Camus and three friends, and nicknamed by them "the House Above the World." In these two rural retreats—Cassiciacum in 386 and the House Above the World in 1936—Augustine and Camus, in moments of uncanny synchronicity, may be seen to have briefly lived parallel lives. Both men, recently converted to philosophy as a way of life, were writing their first books, books on the same subject—happiness.

Augustine's brief sojourn in Cassiciacum was no generic getaway. What he was getting away from in this case was his former life. He had recently converted to both philosophy and Christian faith, dismissed his lover of fourteen years, retired from his professorship, abandoned his political ambitions, and embraced celibacy. He was weary, fragile, distraught, quick to tears, and spiritually hungry. He was a single father awaiting baptism and imagining a new life. Meanwhile, he was celebrating his thirty-second birthday with a small cohort comprising, in historian Peter Brown's description, "a pious old woman, two uneducated cousins, and two private pupils, aged about sixteen."[1] The pious old woman was Monica, his ever-hovering mother, who had followed him from North Africa to Milan, then the capital of the Western Roman Empire. They were all there for a taste of cultured leisure, *otium liberale*: country air, farm-to-table food, literary discussion, and philosophical dialogue, convened and led by Augustine, who urged the participants to put down their books, leave time for leisurely meditation, and give themselves over to shared engagement in the pursuit of wisdom. Their curriculum was guided by the writings of Virgil, Cicero, and Plotinus, who had once envisioned a city of philosophers to be called Platonopolis, a grandiose plan to which Augustine's philosophical house party could only modestly aspire.

The House Above the World, needless to say, was no Platonopolis, though not for lack of aspiration. It was closer to a commune or ashram, housing its four charter residents (Camus, Jeanne-Paule Sicard, Marguerite Dobrenn, and Christiane Galindo), and serving as a meeting place and cultural center for a wider circle of young intellectuals and artists, a circle that recognized Camus as its center. The House was an experiment in community, a family of like-minded friends and comrades, and a pop-up salon when the right people showed up. For Camus, personally, who often had it to himself, the House Above the World was a refuge, his "secret garden" or bolt-hole, a haven of recovery, a place to read and write. As it happened, he was reading Augustine and Plotinus, writing his thesis on their historic intersection, and mapping his first venture into philosophical fiction. In its first incarnation it was called *A Happy Death*, only to be reborn as *The Stranger*. Both were about happiness and both were infused with Augustine's reflections on *The Happy Life*, the title of Augustine's first major philosophical work, composed at Cassiciacum.

So, we see that both Augustine and Camus began their philosophical journeys focused on the question and meaning of human happiness. It is also the case that they retained this focus throughout their philosophical lives and works. "If there is one constant running through all of Augustine's thinking," Robert J. O'Connell assures us, "not only in this early period but throughout his career, it is his preoccupation with the question of happiness. From the *De Beata Vita* to the *De Civitate Dei*, this is always the focal question."[2] This is no less true of Camus and the arc of his writings. "When I do happen to look for what is most fundamental in me," explained Camus, "what I find is a taste for happiness."[3]

Augustine and Camus began their lives in philosophy, sharing not only a focal question—the desire for happiness—but also sharing an ancient understanding of what it means to be a philosopher. Both men pursued philosophy not as an academic profession but as a way of life. They *were* philosophers. They *did* philosophy, an activity increasingly rare today and, in some circles, illegitimate, a fact lamented by Camus:

> The ancient philosophers (quite understandably) meditated more than they read. That is why they clung so closely to the concrete. Printing changed all that. We read more than we meditate. We have no philosophies but merely commentaries. . . . considering that the age of philosophers concerned with philosophy was followed by the age of professors of philosophy concerned with philosophers. Such an attitude shows both modesty and impotence. And a thinker who began his book with these words: "Let us take things from the beginning," would evoke smiles. It has come to the point where a book of philosophy appearing today without basing itself on any authority, quotation, or commentary would not be taken seriously.[4]

For the young Camus, Plotinus, Plato, Aristotle, and Augustine were living mentors. He was their protégé. "I was nourished by Greek philosophy," Camus announced to a welcoming audience in 1955 Athens, "I am the son of Greek philosophy."[5] To any legitimate son or daughter of Greek philosophy, to anyone actually *doing* philosophy, there is no such thing as a dead philosophy or philosopher, not so long as their words and ideas survive and provoke reflection. Conversations across centuries and millennia can be and often are as illuminating, lively, and inspiring as those between contemporaries. Augustine, in *The Happy Life*, begins his dialogue, as Camus says real thinkers do, taking things from the beginning, which is what we will do here in considering that work and the ways in which it contributed to *A Happy Death* and eventually *The Stranger*.

The Happy Life is a real-time dialogue in which Augustine engages his interlocutors, challenging them to think, express their opinions, and raise questions. I say "real-time" because the text that has come down to us is an actual edited transcript of the proceedings recorded by on-the-scene short-hand scribes enlisted by Augustine and paid for by his mother. We know from this transcript that all those present concurred in the assertion of two fundamental, self-evident truths: that we are composed of soul and body, and that we all desire to be happy. Camus was in accord with these assertions in writing *A Happy Death*. "What matters—all that matters, really—is the will to happiness, a kind of enormous, ever-present consciousness."[6] Not just happiness, but conscious happiness, happiness of soul and body, happiness in the face of death. Consciousness—Death—Happiness. These realities shaped all the early writings of Camus comprising what he called the cycle of the absurd, in which "men die and they are not happy."[7]

In Augustine's intimate circle of more or less like-minded family and friends, it was agreed that to be happy "means nothing else than . . . to be wise."[8] And to be wise is to know God and thus to possess him. The consensus reached at Cassiciacum—that "whoever possesses God is happy"[9]—brought no closure or consolation, however, to Camus in the House Above the World. Camus was no atheist, but neither was he a believer. With neither religious faith nor metaphysical sight at his command, both God and wisdom were beyond Camus's reach, which in no way lessened his longing for them, his "appetite for the absolute."[10] The desire for happiness is one thing; the impossibility of its attainment another. With this realization "the absurd" experience is born.

As eavesdroppers on the distant dialogue between Camus and Augustine regarding happiness, we may well wonder what they both meant by "happiness" and how it might relate to "human nature." For a relevant response to both these queries we would do well to turn to classical Greek philosophy and more specifically to Aristotle. For a start, we need to realize that what Augustine and Camus understood by "happiness" is far from what we commonly mean by the term today or what the Declaration of Independence had in mind by our inalienable right to "life, liberty, and the pursuit of happiness." Our modern notion of happiness, and the etymology of the word itself, have a lot to do with luck, things working out, life going well, as each of us would define that for ourselves. Your happiness might be my misery. Your anguish my bliss. To each his own. *Vive la différence.*

In the ancient Greek philosophical tradition, from which both Augustine and Camus drank deeply, happiness is not only a different word—*eudaimonia* (εὐαιμόνια) in Greek, *beatitudo* in Latin; more critically, it is a very different reality from what we ordinarily reckon it to be. The idea of human happiness and the idea of human nature are so intertwined in Greek philosophy as to be inseparable. Put simply, happiness is the full realization of human nature. Happiness is human *being*, the end or *telos* (τέλος), of human *becoming*. Happiness lies in reaching that goal, crossing the human finish line, as it were. But who is it that draws that line? If we are to understand human nature as the Greeks understood it, we must consider their word for nature, *physis* (φύσις), which describes the full wondrous arc of a thing's coming-to-be, from seed to flower and from flower to fruit, from first breath to last gasp. Aristotle, on multiple occasions, cites the example of the acorn and the oak tree as an illustration of the coming-to-be of what potentially already is. The acorn, after all, is from the start somehow an oak tree. It is "on its way," "a work in progress," we might say. The poet Mary Oliver makes the same point when she writes, "Is it not incredible, that in the acorn something has hidden an entire oak tree?"[11] Plant an acorn and all you will ever get is an oak tree. Not a much larger acorn and certainly not an elephant or an owl. Quite evidently, it is the nature, or in the nature, of an acorn to become and be an oak tree. In *Physics*, Aristotle contrasts this with the planting of an artifact, such as a bed. A bed, planted in the ground, will eventually rot and revert to its prior state as wood. Never will it sprout another bed. We speak of a living thing's nature, then, as what it is in its full fruition, "for a thing is more properly said to be what it is when it has attained to fulfilment than when it exists potentially."[12] A bed has a form but not a nature. This is because, in Aristotle's terms, there is no "being-at-work" in it, no *energeia* (ἐνέργεια), from which we get the word *energy*.

Aristotle explains further how, in a world of becoming, a world like ours of motion and change, every natural thing possesses its own *energeia*, its own inner being-at-work, its own direction and momentum. Fire, he says, rises when ignited, whereas a stone, when released from a hand that holds it, falls. Flames don't fall any more than stones fly. So, too, acorns become oak trees, never rabbits. All very obvious, all common sense, until we turn to human beings, to us. Plant a human being and you never quite know what you will get, a saint or a scoundrel, or as Plato once put it, a gentleman or a monster. It's clear we are not acorns. We have a more fluid, unpredictable energy at our core. No particular genius is required to notice this. The song "Plant a Radish" from the musical *The Fantasticks* lays it all out plain and simple:

> Plant a radish.
> Get a radish.
> Never any doubt.
> That's why I love vegetables;
> You know what you're about!
>
> While with children,
> It's bewilderin'.
> You don't know until the seed is nearly grown
> Just what you've sown.[13]

What distinguishes human beings from oak trees, apart from the leaves, is free will, freedom of choice. Although Camus and Augustine were at radical odds with each other over the scope and degree of that freedom, they agreed that it is the human will that makes all the difference between one life course and another. Here, too, we turn to Aristotle for illumination. Gravity might well explain why stones fall and flames rise, but not why one person chooses a life of crime and another a life of service. In the case of a human being, Aristotle suggests, we need to picture an archer. He notches the arrow, draws the bow, aims, and releases the shaft to take its course. It's all in the drawing of the bow, and of course the aim. They determine the arrow's arc, its direction, and its reach. The arrow's *energeia*, or "energy," is the archer's doing. It is the archer who chooses the arrow's target, just as human beings choose their life's goal. What, we may ask, are the options to choose from?

On the one hand, turning to Camus and Augustine for a response, we see that there is really only one goal in life, desired and pursued by all of us: happiness. On the other hand, we are far from any consensus on what that means. "Verbally there is very general agreement," writes Aristotle, "for both the general run of men and people of superior refinement say that it is happiness, and identify living well and doing well with being happy; but with regard to what happiness is they differ, and the many do not give the same account as the wise." [14] Each of us lives in accord with our highest expectations. Our worlds have different horizons. We can aim no further than we can see. In general terms our goal is to pursue pleasure and avoid pain; but there are different kinds or spheres of pleasure and of pain. Aristotle offers three: physical, moral, and intellectual. These correspond, in general terms, to three "ethics," three modes of life: the life of enjoyment (ὁ βίος ἀπολαυστιχός), the life of politics* (ὁ βίος πολιτικός), and the life of contemplation (ὁ βίος φιλόσοφος). "It is clear," explains Aristotle in *Eudemian Ethics*, "that everyone relates happiness to one or other of three lives: the political life, the philosophical life, and the hedonistic life." [15]

Aristotle speaks of three distinctly different lives here because all too often individual human beings decide to situate themselves within one ethos or one way of life and stay there. In laying out the same options, the Danish philosopher Søren Kierkegaard—a mentee of Aristotle and a mentor to Camus—spoke of these three "ethics" as "stages on life's way"

---

* The "political life" meant something very different for Aristotle than it means for us, particularly at this time in the United States. It meant life in the public realm, a life of civic virtue, a life of service to the common good, even at the expense of our private interests.

(the title of one of his books). For Aristotle they were stages on the way
to happiness, stages on the way to full human being. There is a level of
pleasure or satisfaction proper to each stage, but true human happiness,
true human realization, requires all three:

> There are three items reckoned as elements of a happy life—the
> three mentioned earlier as the greatest of human goods, namely,
> virtue and wisdom and pleasure—so too we see three lives that
> all who have the opportunity for choice choose to live, namely
> the political life, the philosophical life, and the hedonistic
> life. The philosopher aims to devote his life to wisdom and the
> contemplation of truth, the politician to noble deeds (conduct
> that manifests virtue), and the hedonist to the pleasures of
> the body.[16]

The takeaway from all this is clear: humanity, being fully human, is
optional, not inevitable. Happiness is a matter of relentless striving, not
resting on our laurels as a species and hoping for a bit of luck. Human
nature is not like the nature of anything else. It doesn't account for the
way people act or for the lives they live. Remember the archer and his
freedom. Human nature doesn't determine *what* we do, it only determines
what we *ought* to do. It describes what is right for us, the being-at-work
in us, our true and full happiness. Human nature sets a goal we are free
to fail, draws moral boundaries we are free to trespass, but at a high cost.
The consequence of falling short of our goal, of violating our nature and
its ethical limits, is unhappiness—physical, moral, intellectual—whose
myriad symptoms include malaise, guilt, shame, despair, arrogance, cynicism, and delusion. The young would-be "hero" Neoptolemos, son of the
great Achilles, put it this way: "All is disgust when one leaves his own
nature and does things that misfit it."[17] As soon as we become aware of
ourselves, our world, and our possibilities, we discover that we are able to
do more, less, or other than what we ought to do. The essential "limits" we
encounter are not the design or doing of any civic or social law, laid down

by states or sovereigns. They are inscribed within, at our core, and often learned only when we violate them, as Neoptolemos did.

The pursuit of happiness is none other than the pursuit of full humanity. It is, in the end, a matter of all or nothing, an all-consuming passion, not some halfhearted sideline. It is a quest most people give up on partway and never finish.

> The backward pupil in a school is usually known by his habit of coming forward with his paper scarcely ten minutes after the task has been set, announcing that he has finished it—which must be extremely tiresome for the teacher. So also do all the mediocrities in life come running at once with the announcement that they are through, and the greater the task the more quickly they finish it.[18]

Patrice Mersault, looking back at his unfinished life, came to precisely that realization in *A Happy Death*:

> All his life he had pursued single mindedly a happiness which in his heart he believed was impossible. In this he was no different from everyone else. He had played at wanting to be happy. Never had he sought happiness with a conscious and deliberate desire. . . . Innocent, overwhelmed by joy, he understood at last that he was made for happiness.[19]

What, we may wonder, does it mean to no longer "play at wanting to be happy"? To be "made for happiness" means that it is implanted in us, defining our nature, human nature. Our soul or mind demands happiness with all the intensity with which our body demands water, our conscience demands justice, and our mind demands meaning. "The mind's deepest desire," Camus writes in *The Myth of Sisyphus*, "even in its most elaborate operations, parallels man's unconscious feeling in the face of his universe: it is an insistence upon familiarity, an appetite for clarity."[20] In this assertion

Camus is only echoing Aristotle, who in the first line of *Metaphysics* states, "All men by nature desire to know." Every word here is crucial. *All*—not just some—desire to know, and that uniquely human *desire* is ignited and driven by human *nature*. A closer look at the word conveying "desire" (*orégo*, ὀρέγω) reveals the desperate urgency here. The word Aristotle employs doesn't just mean "to want" but rather to "reach out or strain for," to "yearn." The human desire to know, when recognized and affirmed, is a hunger, a thirst, a longing, not a passing fancy.

Camus's desire to know was unrelenting. He never quit. At no point in his life do we see him, like Kierkegaard's "backward pupil," bringing forth his work "announcing that he has finished it." Instead, as we have seen, he confessed that his philosophy consisted of "doubts and uncertainties." He was at one with Aristotle, Augustine, and Kierkegaard in the desire to know, the desire for transcendent truth. His mind—the human mind—was made for it; but the world, it seemed to him, was not made for his mind. His cry for meaning was met only with silence. "If I were a tree among trees, a cat among animals," he writes, "this life would have a meaning, or rather this problem would not arise, for I should belong to this world."[21] Sensory sight is one thing and intellectual sight another. "Nothing you ever understand will be sweeter," writes Mary Oliver, "or more binding, than this deepest affinity between your eyes and the world."[22] Camus knew this well and reveled in the beauty of the sea, the sky, the earth, the human body—the splendorous, sensual cyclorama of the Mediterranean world. He knew this happiness, as did Meursault in the first half of *The Stranger*. But this was a fragile happiness, a partial truth, "stage scenery masked by habit."[23] Even in this "kingdom" of his, which he so loved, he found himself a stranger in a foreign land, like the young, lost hero in Kierkegaard's *Repetition*, who, sticking his finger into the world to smell where he is, smells only nothingness. "Where am I," he complains, ". . . how did I get into the world? Why was I not asked about it, why was I not informed of the rules and regulations?"[24]

The reality of this radical mismatch between the inquiring mind and the mute universe is the experience of the absurd, the cornerstone of existentialism, which Camus claimed "has its origins in Saint Augustine."[25] In saying this, Camus was acknowledging that the insatiable human hunger for truth and happiness is ultimately the desire for God, for the experience of transcendence, for the soul's unity with the One. Camus identified with this yearning, expressed in the most famous words ever written by Augustine, words spoken in prayer: "Our heart is restless until it rests in you."[26] Camus shared this much with the saint—a "restless heart" (*cor inquietum*). What he didn't share was Augustine's embrace of Greek metaphysics or Christian faith. These, for him, represented unwarranted "leaps" driven by desperation and nurtured by blind hope. Camus saw these as forms of "philosophical suicide," in which the mind turns to ventriloquism to answer its own questions. Camus never ridiculed the "One" of the Platonists or the "Word made flesh," as did and do so many others, for he knew that ridicule never amounts to refutation. Neither did he silence his restless heart in its cry for the transcendent. Instead, he insisted on it, rebelliously, to the end. In doing so, he ultimately chose the companionship of Augustine over that of Sartre, with whom he had far less in common. While Camus would only cite or invoke Augustine by name a handful of times in his writings, the footprint of "the other Algerian" on his work is pervasive and unmistakable. After their close encounter in Camus's youth, Augustine held his place among the inner circle of his muses.

As it happened, after completing his thesis on Augustine, Camus soon shelved his first major work of fiction, *A Happy Death*, and launched into another, *The Stranger*, which might be seen as *A Happy Death 2.0*. *The Stranger*, though, amounted to far more than a recycling of that earlier effort. It represented, instead, a fresh revisioning of the whole and the adoption of a writing style refreshingly spare and controlled after the often effusive excesses of its predecessor. Augustine, too, years later in his *Retractions*, would record his dissatisfaction with his earliest work, *The Happy Life*, to which he never returned. Both men moved on to more ambitious and mature work. Camus did so with Augustine and Aristotle as guides.

With the benefit of retrospect we are able to survey the several cycles of Camus's creative and philosophical writings that he envisioned in the

ensuing years. As early as June 1947, in his *Notebooks*, we see that he has a
preliminary plan for five series or stages:[27]

> Myth of Sisyphus—Absurd—*Stranger, M of Sisyphus*, Caligula,
> Misunderstanding
> Myth of Prometheus—Revolt—*Plague, Rebel*, Kaliayev
> Myth of Nemesis—Judgement—The First Man
> Love Sundered
> Creation

Two years later, in this brief entry, he focused on the philosophical essays
in his scheme:[28]

> The Myth of Sisyphus (absurd)—II. The Myth of Prometheus
> (revolt)—III. The Myth of Nemesis.

While no one can miss the imprint of Greek mythology on the names
given to each of the first three cycles—Sisyphus, Prometheus, and
Nemesis—the deeper and more significant influence of Greek philosophy
on the progression from one cycle to the next is less evident and rarely
noted. Across his life and career as a thinker and writer Camus never
discarded or discounted his focal concern with human happiness and
human nature. In fact, the stages of human becoming and the distinct
modes of life proper to each, as understood by Aristotle and adopted by
Augustine and Camus, may be discerned in the curricular progression
from the Absurd to Revolt to Judgement to Love. What is commonly
overlooked in Camus's literary/philosophical scheme is its dialectical character. Each stage is an experiment in truth, a test, just as each mode of life
set forth by Aristotle—the life of physical enjoyment, the life of ethical
engagement, and the life of philosophical contemplation—represents an
attempt at happiness. When hedonism, for instance, fails to deliver happiness, and when the active pursuit of justice runs aground in disillusionment
and despair, we discover that what we thought was the truth is no more

than a half or partial truth. One road dead-ends where another begins, while the horizon recedes with every step taken. So it was with the dialectical progression of Camus's cycles, wherein we see that the foundations laid in his youthful studies of Greek and Christian antiquity under the guidance of Jean Grenier erected the infrastructure for all that was to follow. Simply stating this, however, is surely not convincing. It must be shown and seen to be believed.

We begin here where Augustine and Camus began, with happiness. Camus, we know, made two first attempts at this topic: *A Happy Death* and *The Stranger*. For each, he chose a two-part structure. In *A Happy Death*, he gave titles to the parts: Part One / Natural Death and Part Two / Conscious Death. In *The Stranger* he numbered the parts but gave them no titles. Nevertheless, these two titles strongly suggest themselves and would be a good fit: Part One / Natural Happiness and Part Two / Conscious Happiness. The permeating centrality of happiness and death to both books is obvious to any reader and will be explored in the next chapter. What is less obvious and more interesting is the line drawn in each book between the "natural" and the "conscious" and the movement from the one to the other. The emergence of consciousness, it appears, is transformative and irreversible.

For Augustine, this movement represented a conversion. He relates in his *Confessions* how, as a student still in his teens and a passionate materialist, he struggled to accept the reality of incorporeal substances. Nothing to him was real beyond what could be grasped by the senses. Happiness was to be pursued, tasted, and enjoyed physically as long as he had breath. Even words were raw material—like marble to be sculpted or musical notes to be arranged—and Augustine savored them. He was at this point a would-be wordsmith, not a thinker. This changed, he tells us, when he stumbled one day on a text by Cicero as yet unknown to him (and long lost to us), a dialog between the author and a rival politician named Quintus Hortensius Hortalus, in which Cicero exhorts his interlocutor, and thereby his readers, to take up philosophy as a way of life. It excited Augustine, and changed him.

The book changed my feelings. . . . It gave me different values
and priorities. . . . For I did not read the book for a sharpening
of my style, which was what I was buying with my mother's
financial support. . . . I was impressed not by the book's refining
effect on my style and literary expression but by the content. . . .
"Love of wisdom" is the meaning of the Greek word *philosophia*.
This book kindled my love for it.[29]

Put simply, Augustine realized for the first time that words could
not only be well crafted; they could also be true. This first taste of truth
changed the course of Augustine's life. It was the first of his conversions,
the conversion to philosophy. While Camus never recorded so sudden and
dramatic a moment of conversion in his youth, his philosophical studies
under Grenier and the writing of his thesis on Augustine and Neoplatonism
clearly changed him. From his lyrical celebration of sensual happiness, his
untimely face-off with death, his immersion in ancient philosophy, and
his bonding encounter with Augustine, Camus emerged committed to the
pursuit of truth, to philosophy as a way of life, not a way to make a living.
He was a "philosopher"—a "lover of truth"—who wrote novels to incite
and sustain in others the same love.

CHAPTER FOUR

The Zero Point

O n a sleepless spring night in 1940, an exhausted Camus attached his signature to the manuscript he had just completed and shared the news in a letter to his fiancée, Francine Faure: "I'm writing you in the middle of the night. I've just finished my novel. . ."[1] The corresponding entry in his journal reads simply, "*The Stranger* is finished."[2] To Francine, however, he admitted that it probably wasn't finished. He was unsure of what he had written—one minute proud, the next dismissive. He would put it aside for two weeks and then go back to it. He was only twenty-six years old and was far from knowing that the book on his desk would launch him.

At the moment, he felt anything but launched. Trapped was closer to the truth. He was a stranger in Paris, where he had gone for work six weeks earlier, to take up a position offered to him by his former boss and friend, Pascal Pia. Camus's outspoken critiques of French colonial abuse had made him all but unemployable in Algeria, and he had just about worn out his welcome staying in the Oran home of Francine's family. In addition to a reliable paycheck, his less-than-challenging new work as a layout editor at *Paris-Soir* offered Camus the creative time and freedom to focus on *The Stranger* and finish it with journalistic dispatch. He had traveled light when he'd sailed from Oran on March 15, 1940, but he had carried what there was of *The Stranger* at that time, a narrative jigsaw slowly revealing itself in bits and pieces. One of these early fragments survived intact to become the opening lines of the novel:

> Maman died today. Or yesterday maybe, I don't know. I got a telegram from the home: "Mother deceased. Funeral tomorrow. Faithfully yours." That doesn't mean anything. Maybe it was yesterday.[3]

Camus had entered those iconic lines into his journal on an unspecified date in the fall of 1938,[4] after he had shelved *A Happy Death* and while he was envisioning several projects: *Caligula*, *The Myth of Sisyphus*, and *The Stranger*, the first to make it to the finish line.

The metamorphosis of *A Happy Death* into *The Stranger* is as dramatic as that of a sluggish caterpillar into a soaring butterfly.[*] In both cases the chrysalis conceals the mystery. Camus carried *The Stranger* within him during this stage, silently, except for the occasional revealing entry in his journal. What emerged in 1940 was a masterwork, brilliant in design and compelling in its eloquent simplicity. In it he demonstrated how a true work of art can be one that conveys the most by saying the least.[5] *A Happy Death* was meandering and wordy. *The Stranger* was neither. From the wreckage of *A Happy Death* Camus salvaged a handful of passages and scrapped the rest. He also retained the two-part structure—the focus on happiness and the murder, or rather *a* (very different) murder, in Part One. Mersault, the calculating murderer in *A Happy Death*, bought his happiness with his crime. Meursault, his predecessor's reincarnation in *The Stranger*, forfeits his happiness when he pointlessly murders an anonymous Arab. What a difference one letter *u* makes!

The narrative movement in *A Happy Death* from unhappiness to happiness is reversed in *The Stranger*, wherein Meursault moves from the sun-soaked beach where he is happy to the barren cell where he awaits death.

---

[*] Alice Kaplan has brilliantly traced the evolution of the manuscript in her book *Looking for "The Stranger."*

In both cases, murder marks the turning point and makes all the differ-ence. *The Stranger*, like *A Happy Death*, is all about happiness and death, physical and conscious, body and soul. The structure of the tale is tight and transparent. Part One begins with the death of Meursault's mother and ends with the death of the Arab. Part Two proceeds on a different plane toward the death of Meursault. From Meursault's first moment in prison, he mirrors his mother in the last months of her life. His prison, like her old folks' home, is for people awaiting death. As we shall see, however, in these "dying places" Meursault and Maman rediscover life. In their final days and moments, like Sisyphus they descend in full conscious happiness to shoulder the rock and begin again. They and their will to happiness are unbroken.

There's no denying that *The Stranger*, from one generation to the next, has cast a spell over its readers. A surprising number of those readers will always be able to recall, if asked, where and when they read it for the first time. It is for many a coming-of-age text, a "moment," not just a book. They're all there, the preoccupying concerns of youth—sensuality, self-absorption, sex, mortality, and the simple, spontaneous honesty that the world out there and the life ahead will never accept. *The Stranger*, once read, is rarely forgotten, yet many readers never move on from there to what Camus had to say next. They don't realize that the final sentence of *The Stranger* leaves us hanging, like the final episode of the first season of an ongoing dramatic series. *The Stranger* is so absorbing and compelling by itself that most readers fail to see that it is only the first act, not the final word. This helps explain why Camus is frequently and falsely identified with the character of Meursault, whom he once described as his photo-graphic negative, his opposite, and why to this day Camus is still widely labeled an existentialist.

In plotting the narrative of *The Stranger*, Camus was also laying out the first steps in a philosophical argument, formulating a thesis to which he already anticipated the antithesis and an eventual synthesis. In simpler terms, he was making one point in order to make a further point, telling a half-truth in order to pursue the fuller truth. In other words, according to plan, he was thinking as a philosopher and writing a novel. That he was writing a novel is lost on no one. That he was unfolding a philosophical argument is less self-evident. Camus himself acknowledged the pivotal influence of the American crime writer James M. Cain, and more specifically Cain's hit thriller *The Postman Always Rings Twice*, on the story line and style of *The Stranger*. What is less evident and more rarely acknowledged is the comparably formative influence of Augustine and ancient philosophy on the shape of the story and the truths it reveals.

Camus didn't suspend his philosophical inquiry into human nature when he turned to writing fiction. On the contrary, he sustained it. We recall here, from our discussion of Augustine's *The Happy Life*, that the first and foundational consensus reached by those gathered at Cassiciacum to reflect on happiness was that we, all humans, are made of body and mind or soul. This much was a given, the point of departure for any further reflection on human realization, human becoming, and human being. This same foundational footprint is evident in the two-part structure of *A Happy Death*, in the movement from natural or physical death to conscious death. Less explicit but no less evident is the movement from Part One to Part Two in *The Stranger*, a movement from body to mind, from sense to thought, from the half-light of pre-consciousness to incandescent lucidity, from sentience to selfhood.

Part One of *The Stranger* begins on an odd note, with several of the most famous entry lines in 20th-century literature:

> Maman died today. Or yesterday maybe. I don't know. I got a telegram from the home. "Mother deceased. Funeral tomorrow. Faithfully yours." That doesn't mean anything. Maybe it was yesterday.[6]

Meursault's confusion over the exact day of his mother's death is understandable. He may have already missed her funeral. What's odd here is his fixation on the timing of his mother's passing, rather than the fact. The telegram has provoked puzzlement but no grief. He's in his head at a moment when we would expect him to be in his heart. Whatever his mother might have been to him—loving, devoted, negligent, abandoning, abusive—we would expect some ripple of response to her death. Even if his mother were nothing to him, her death would be news. He might be curious to know how she died, and not just when. On our side, as readers, this passage should suffice to disabuse us of any notion that the character of Meursault represents a self-portrait of the author, whose love for his mother was profound. We can only imagine Camus's bottomless grief had he outlived her.*

Meursault, here and throughout Part One, is somehow both "off" and "on," "with it" one moment and "out of it" the next. His oddity or strangeness is many different things, depending on the moment: puzzling, appealing, humorous, disconcerting, admirable, shocking. But he's no simple "loser" or "outsider."** Meursault has a job as a shipping clerk, and he's good at it, good enough for his boss to offer him a promotion and transfer to Paris. He has a pretty, young girlfriend who loves him enough to want to marry him. He has friends who enjoy his company. Strangers talk to him, taking him into their confidence. He takes an interest in people he observes or meets. Most everyone seems to like him. At least before he murders a man. In this light, we can see how Camus once considered entitling the book *A Man Like Any Other* or *An Ordinary Man* (*Un homme comme les autres*). But is he ordinary, like anyone else? As readers, we are privy to Meursault's personal thoughts, his inner voice, and so we hear and not just see how often he misreads situations, misses social cues, and crosses moral lines as if they weren't there. The world often bewilders him, as he bewilders the world. In today's world, we might be inclined to place him somewhere on the autism spectrum, Asperger's syndrome, perhaps. He has by various critics been called a freak, a psychopath, a maverick, a misfit, a

---

* Catherine Hélène Camus (SINTES) died nine months after her son Albert, on September 20, 1960.

** *The Outsider* was the title given, without consultation, to the British edition of *L'Étranger*.

free spirit, a racist, a misogynist, a messiah, and by Camus, paradoxically, "the only Christ we deserve."[7]

Another provisional book title Camus tried on for size was *A Happy Man* (*Un homme heureux*). And there's no disputing that Meursault was just that—happy, at least until he found himself behind bars. Even then, however, a condemned man, he found his way back in the end to happiness. Like Sisyphus and Meursault's mother, we must imagine him happy. In Part One, Meursault's happiness lies in his attunement with the natural world, the physical world. He is a man at home in his skin, at one with his body. This is something he later, in prison, came to realize about himself. Looking back, he explained that "my physical needs often got in the way of my feelings."[8] That is to say that his body silenced his mind, his senses drowned out his thoughts. The blazing sun, the hum of insects, a cool breeze, two buzzing hornets, a coffee, the sucking sound of toothless gums, a woman's choking sobs, a smoke, a doze, silence, an old man's sagging red ears, the smell of hot leather and horse dung. These and countless other discrete moments were, for Meursault, the sensuous sum of his mother's funeral. Soon, almost seamlessly, they gave way to cooling waters, soft breasts, laughter, brief tumultuous pleasure, and sweet sleep.

In *A Happy Death*, Patrice Mersault imagined happiness to be like a stone, warmed in the sun and cooled in the rain, wide open to each moment, without resistance, without regret. And so, in his final passing, "stone among the stones, he returned in the joy of his heart to the truth of the motionless worlds."[9] Meursault the Stranger, however, will not die so natural a death, in bed with his lover near. Instead, he will lose his head to a guillotine amid cries of hate from a mob eager to watch. For now, however, in life, in Part One, the sensual accord between Meursault and his tactile world is near perfect. Swimming in tandem with Marie, matching his movement with hers, tangling with her in love, and then letting the night air cool their bodies, running and leaping into a moving truck with his pal and laughing, letting Sundays drift by under his balcony, he is happy in this world so well suited to him. "What is happiness," Camus explains, "except the simple harmony between a man and the life he leads."[10]

The most revealing label given to Meursault and *The Stranger* comes, not surprisingly, from Camus, in his journal, where he explains,

> My work will count as many forms as it has stages on the way to an unrewarded perfection. *The Stranger* is the zero point. Likewise *The Myth of Sisyphus*. *The Plague* is a progress, not from zero toward the infinite, but toward a deeper complexity that remains to be defined. The last point will be the saint . . .[11]

What this brief note makes clear is that *The Stranger* represents the beginning, not the end, of a development, a striving. It marks the starting line, not the finish line. *The Stranger* is a requisite first stage, nothing more. Readers of *The Stranger*, and of its companion philosophical essay, are cautioned not to embrace or emulate Meursault or Sisyphus or the absurd as embodiments or expressions of any full or final truth. The way ahead leads to deeper complexity, and the goal is the infinite, and the perfection of a godless saint, as yet beyond our understanding, much less our reach. The progression and stages that Camus alludes to here, in these notes to himself, are those he learned from Augustine and Greek philosophy. The road mapped out by Camus is the arduous ascent to happiness and full human being, from physical pleasure, to moral commitment, to truth and wordless well-being, *eudaimonia*, happiness.

Meursault, like Sisyphus, is an absurd hero, yes, but this makes him suitable for only very selective emulation. Camus made very clear what he affirmed in Meursault, what he found most admirable in him:

> . . . he refuses to lie. To lie is not only to say what isn't true. It is also and above all, to say more than is true, and, as far as the human heart is concerned, to express more than one feels.[12]

It angered Camus when careless, literal-minded critics utterly missed the point of *The Stranger*, blurring any line between author and protagonist,

and reading the text as Camus' last word on life and death. To one such
critic he responded sharply in a letter he wrote but never sent:

> You have gratuitously attributed to me a ridiculous philosophy.
> Nothing in the book, in fact, can allow you to assert that I
> believe in the natural man, that I identify a human being with
> a vegetable, that human nature is foreign to morality, etc., etc.[13]

The Stranger is an experiment in thought, not an exercise in realism.
Meursault is meant to provoke thought, not inspire a following. In Part
One of the text, he is in the earliest stages of human becoming, *en route*,
not *arrivé*, as a human being. He is a sentient human being, with limited
consciousness, a full-grown infant, as it were. Think of him as a human
acorn, the whole tree *but not yet*, a human being at the zero point. This
is no place for a literal mind. No wonder Camus was distraught. "Three
years to make a book, five lines to ridicule it."[14] The nascent stage in
human becoming that Meursault embodies is indeed human and to be
affirmed as such. It's just that there is more to humanity than "brief
emotions, devoid of the long echo that memory gives. The sensitivity of
dogs is like that."[15]

Imagining Meursault as a dog is actually not an absurd conceit. In a
brief conversation I once had with James Watson, one of the team that
discovered the double helix structure of DNA, he remarked that most
everything anyone needs to know about life can be learned from dogs:
courage, companionship, cleverness, loyalty, honesty, and love. He spoke
with such enthusiasm and affection for *man's best friend* that I wondered
if, at that point in his life, shortly before a death he knew was coming,
he might have preferred canine to human companionship. Dogs are
everything Watson said of them, and Camus might have had similar
regard for his dog Kirk. Like Meursault, dogs make the most of every
moment. The moment is what they have, where they live. Dogs would
be confused if offered a promotion, asked about marriage, or expected
to behave at a funeral. They understand loyalty, but not morality. Once

they become your pal, your enemies are theirs. It's not a matter of racism or misogyny. Indeed, as strange as it may seem, Part One, or much of it, falls comfortably into place if we imagine Meursault with four legs. All that changes, however, on a sandy, sweltering beach, when four deafening shots shatter the illusion.

There is no episode or act in *The Stranger* that is as inexplicable as the murder of the nameless Arab. In the moment, it just happens. Before that moment, however, we can see it coming. Tempers have flared, fists have flown, blood has been shed, grudges have simmered, and racial resentment has turned up the heat. It seems only natural that someone was going to lose control and make a mistake. What defies reason is *how* it happened. If we take Meursault at his word—and the one thing he doesn't do is lie—he didn't consciously pull the trigger. It just happened, an act of nature, an unconscious autonomic response.

> It seemed to me as if the sky split open from one end to the other to rain down fire. My whole being tensed and I squeezed my hand around the revolver. The trigger gave; I felt the smooth underside of the butt; and there in that noise, sharp and deafening at the same time, is where it all started.[16]

As Meursault later recalls and relates this episode, he insists that it was not an act. It was something he experienced, not something he did. He felt it happening to him. This is not so outrageous a claim for someone who displays little or no sign of executive functioning; what *is* outrageous, however, is the apparent absence of such functioning in an adult with a gun in his hand. Meursault, to the end, will declare his innocence, his purity, as it were. Indeed, it could be argued that he was never so pure as he was in the moment he murdered the Arab, provided we agree that

> to be pure means to rediscover that country of the soul where one's kinship with the world can be felt, where the throbbing

of one's blood mingles with the violent pulsations of the after
noon sun. [17]

Mystical language, however, does not have a long shelf life in courts of
law. Camus knew this all too well from his experience as a criminal court
reporter in Algiers, where he covered a number of murder trials for the *Alger
républicain*. No wonder the prosecutor and eventually the jury couldn't see
past the four additional shots fired into the Arab after the first shot had
brought him down. If they weren't deliberate, what was?

Meursault's detachment from the murder is nearly as shocking as the shots
fired. In his first-person account of the moment, the inert body in the sand is
irrelevant. The gunshots are somehow not about the Arab and the fact that
his life has abruptly ended on that beach. For Meursault what stood out was
how "in that noise . . . it all started."[18] The Arab's murder was just noise to
Meursault. To focus on the dead Arab is to miss the point. He explains very
clearly what really happened on that beach, what really matters:

> I knew that I had shattered the harmony of the day, the excep-
> tional silence of a beach where I'd been happy (*heureux*). Then
> I fired four more times at the motionless body where the bullets
> lodged without leaving a trace. And it was like knocking four
> quick times on the door of unhappiness (*malheur*). [19]

What stands out and defines this moment for Meursault is his passing
from happiness to unhappiness, not the Arab's passage from life to death.
Meursault, the Arab, the sun, the shots—this scene has a primordial feel
to it, closer to myth than fact. It is the scene of Meursault's fall from innocence and expulsion from his Eden. It is at the same time the fratricidal
sin of Cain. Meursault is no innocent. From now on, whether he notices
it or not, he bears the mark of Cain on his brow. Murder is not an act that
Camus overlooks or lets pass.

In Part Two, the door of Meursault's unhappiness opens slowly at first.
He doesn't lose his accustomed happiness as suddenly as the Arab lost his

life. The world of judicial procedures and barred cages intrigues Meursault at first. It's all very new to him. He's the focus of a lot of attention, admittedly not all pleasant. There is much that confuses and agitates him, but he does his best to get along with the people he meets. He's uncomfortable with having to talk a lot, especially about himself. "It's just that I don't have much to say," he explains to the examining magistrate. "So I keep quiet."[20] The truth is that he doesn't have the answers to what the magistrate most wants to know: why he behaved as he did at his mother's funeral; and why, after firing once, he then fired four more times. After days of interrogation, Meursault grows "tired of repeating the same story over and over. It seems," he explains, "as if I had never talked so much in my life."[21] It is the screaming, crucifix-waving magistrate, however, who shows more signs of distress and exhaustion than does Meursault. These heated interactions eventually become more cordial once the magistrate makes up his mind about Meursault and loses interest in him. Time passes and Meursault finds his new world quite inhabitable, even congenial.

> I started to breathe more freely. No one, in any of these meetings, was rough with me. Everything was so natural, so well handled, and so calmly acted out that I had the ridiculous impression of being "one of the family." And I can say that at the end of the eleven months that this investigation lasted, I was almost surprised that I had ever enjoyed anything other than those rare moments when the judge would lead me to the door of his office, slap me on the shoulder, and say to me cordially, "That's all for today, Monsieur Antichrist."[22]

But there is a darker, more disturbing side to Meursault's confinement, one that he does his best to avoid thinking about, much less talking about. So long as he is caught up in the novel experiences prison life offers, he can avoid facing what he has lost. "In fact, I wasn't really in prison those first few days."[23] Things were happening, time was passing and carrying him in its flow from one moment to the next as it always had.

I was sort of waiting for something to happen. It was only after
Marie's first and last visit that it all started. From the day I got
her letter (she told me she would no longer be allowed to come,
because she wasn't my wife), from that day on I felt that I was
at home in my cell and that my life was coming to a standstill
there.[24]

Being now "at home" in his cell meant that Meursault was no longer
touring or visiting the prison world. He was not a guest. It was his world
from now on, his only world, his last home, a dead end. This was where
he lived now and where he would die. He would not go back to the world
in which he had been happy, and that world would not come back to him.
Marie "meant the world" to Meursault. She was his link to the world he
lost, his way back. Now she was out of his life and the way back was gone.

So what was it that "all started" for Meursault after Marie's first and
last visit? In *The Myth of Sisyphus*, Camus explains that "during every day
of an unillustrious life, time carries us. But a moment always comes when
we have to carry it."[25] Marie's exit was just such a moment for Meursault,
one that "inaugurates the impulse of consciousness. It awakens consciousness and provokes what follows."[26] Camus once explained how his purpose
in *The Stranger* was "to describe a man with no apparent awareness of his
existence."[27] True enough in Part One, but that all changes when Meursault
finds himself alone in a bare cell, with a single high window open only to
the sky, no longer thinking the thoughts of a free man but rather those of
a prisoner tormented by the desire for a woman, any woman. His solitary
prison cell amounted to a sensory deprivation chamber in which nothing
ever happened. In this blinding, blank silence, Meursault found himself
having to "carry time" instead of its carrying him. Until now, he had always
relied on his body to interest and entertain him, to keep him occupied
moment by moment. What was a body for without a world to engage it,
enliven it? The only consciousness he had ever known was sentience, and
what good was that now—sentience without sensations? What other kind
of consciousness was there? What other kind of world was there for him to

inhabit? In his deepening *malheur*,* Meursault was about to make a great discovery.

In *The Sickness Unto Death*, Søren Kiekegaard describes men like Meursault, who imagined themselves happy but in truth were not. Such a man, writes Kierkegaard,

> is generally very far from wishing to be torn away from that delusion . . . the sensuous nature and the psychosensuous completely dominate him . . . he is too sensuous to have the courage to venture to be spirit or to endure it . . . (such people) have no conception of being spirit.[28]

Indeed, until now Meursault had "no conception of being spirit" or of having an inner self. Kierkegaard understands this vacant oblivion as a form of despair, a soul-sickness. He also sees it as commonplace, an ignored epidemic. In this regard Meursault is, in fact, "a man like any other." Picture this, suggests Kierkegaard:

> In case one were to think of a house, consisting of a cellar, ground floor and *premier étage*, so tenanted, or rather so arranged, that it was planned for a distinction of rank between the dwellers on the several floors; and in case one were to make a comparison between such a house and what it is to be a man—then unfortunately this is the sorry and ludicrous condition of the majority of men, that in their own house they prefer to live in the cellar. The soulish-bodily synthesis in every man is planned with a view to being spirit, such is the building; but the man prefers to dwell in the cellar, that is, in the determinants of sensuousness.[29]

---

* *Malheur* (simply translated as "unhappiness") has a range of meanings, including misery, destitution, grief, distress, squalor, sorrow, and misfortune. All of these reveal different dimensions or shades of Meursault's condition in prison.

As much as Meursault had preferred and enjoyed his life in the "cellar" and imagined himself perfectly happy there, that life was no longer an option for him. The cellar had become uninhabitable. Less dramatically, to be sure, than Adam, driven from paradise by an angel with a flaming sword, Meursault found himself exiled from the world he knew. There was only one thing left to do, and that was to take the steps he had ignored to the ground floor and from there to the *premier étage*. He had nothing left to lose and his overlooked humanity to gain. He was starting late the task of becoming human, having imagined it finished. And now he was running out of time.

CHAPTER FIVE

Prison

Nature, as the saying goes, abhors a vacuum. Human nature is no exception. Solitary and starved for stimulation, Meursault did the only thing he could do. He escaped. He fled the "cellar" and began the ascent to spirit. "A human being is spirit," writes Kierkegaard. "But what is spirit? Spirit is the self."[1] This pursuit of spirit took Meursault not out but in. "Out" was not an option. The walls were too thick, the bars too strong. What he found was a new, inner world. The material, sensuous world he knew so well and had enjoyed so mindlessly—the world his body craved and clung to—opened into a vast other world he had never known was there, so near and until now so peripheral and superfluous. Each step he took startled him and revealed a marvel.

Meursault's inward explorations and discoveries occurred, not surprisingly, during two periods of extended isolation. The first of these spanned the time between Marie's visit and the trial; the second period stretched from the conclusion of the trial to the brink of his execution. These were sensuous dry spells, times when Meursault was at a loss. His days and nights were empty, and so was he. The early months of active interrogation had occupied, even fascinated, Meursault, as would the ritual drama of the trial proceedings. The cessation of each sent him back to a stagnant cell, without physical distraction, much less delight.

"The main problem," Meursault explains, "was with killing time."[2] Then
he discovered something, a trick that had somehow never occurred to him
before, a skill he had not needed. "Eventually," he relates, "once I learned
how to remember things, I wasn't bored."[3] Unable to glide through the
walls of his cell and return to his old apartment, he reconstructed it in his
memory, down to the last detail, every stick of furniture, every chip in the
paint. As his memory sharpened, the details multiplied and time flew, "so
that after a few weeks

> I could spend hours just enumerating the things that were in
> my room. And the more I thought about it, the more I dug out
> of my memory things I had overlooked or forgotten. I realized
> that a man who had lived only one day could easily live for a
> hundred years in prison.[4]

Meursault's disarming admission here strains credulity. At his age
could he really be discovering memory for the first time in his life? Of
course not. Camus is very clear that *The Stranger* is not about realism. It
is a thought experiment, a parable. "Camus was, like many of our writers
at the present mid-century," wrote French scholar Henri Peyre in 1958,
"seduced by parables."[5] In this parable, Meursault is *becoming* human,
discovering and embracing his nature. It is that simple and wondrous. In
time-lapse photography, we are given to witness processes, unfoldings,
rarely observable in real life: an acorn becoming an oak tree, the quickening
of consciousness as sensuality expands into spirit. We know they happen,
but we don't see them happening in what we call "real time." We can't slow
ourselves down sufficiently to match the rhythm of such events. Here, in
fiction, the pace is accelerated. Months are distilled into days and days are
condensed into paragraphs.

In less than three pages, months pass as Meursault discovers the boundless depths and expanses of his mind. Memory is only the beginning. Then
come sleep and dreams, another inner world in which time passes effort-
lessly. Once a poor sleeper, Meursault becomes a champion, sleeping sixteen

to eighteen hours at a crack, leaving him with less time on his hands. More exciting, however, than all the time slept away atop his mattress is what he finds under it one day—a scrap of torn yellowed newsprint reporting an unusual murder committed in a Czech village.* A case of mistaken identity. A man killed by his own mother and sister. The story captivates Meursault. He loses himself in it, loses track of time. He's stumbled into another wing of his house, another world to explore, the world of narrative. Stories—real-life stories or made-up ones—are portals. He can walk through them into other lives, other lands, other loves. Not only can he find stories; he can create them, inventing experiences he never had, and never would have. Whether he gives it a name or not, Meursault has discovered imagination, which is another way of saying he has found his mind, where time takes on a new meaning.

> Of course I had read that eventually you wind up losing track of time in prison. But it hadn't meant much to me when I'd read it. I hadn't understood how days could be both long and short at the same time; long to live through, maybe, but so drawn out that they ended up flowing into one another. They lost their names. Only the words "yesterday" and "tomorrow" still had meaning for me.[6]

These lines make it very clear that Camus was writing *The Stranger* with Augustine close at hand. Meursault's astonishing personal discoveries here in Part Two, chapter 2, trace and echo Augustine's own explorations in Books 10 and 11 of his *Confessions*, where he redefined the Western understanding of time.

The traditional, indeed canonical, conception of time, inherited from Aristotle's *Physics*, saw time as the measure of motion, the motion of bodies

---

* A news story of a similar episode appeared in the January 6, 1935 edition of *L'Echo d'Alger*. In that case the incident had occurred in Belgrade. The story that Camus inserted into *The Stranger* and that served as the plot for his play *The Misunderstanding* was likely inspired by the factual crime in 1935 and/or by a traditional Central European folktale with the same basic story line.

from place to place, an observable, measurable phenomenon. Augustine was concerned with inner time, psychological time, time as a dimension of mind, not matter. His reflections on time and memory in Books 10 and 11 of the *Confessions*, the first autobiography in Western literature, were revolutionary and remain foundational for the study of subjective time and autobiographical memory. Together with Augustine's fuller meditations on the inner life of the mind in his treatise *On the Trinity*, they stand among the most illuminating and influential writings in Western philosophy.[*]

The path traced by Augustine begins with a simple, fundamental question, a question he puts to himself: You, who are you?[7] He directs this question to himself because only he can answer it. The ancient Greeks maintained the opposite conviction, that only after death can someone be truly known and their story told, which renders autobiography futile. Any life can only be assessed and its story told from without, never from within; in retrospect, never in the midst. "One must look always at the end of everything—how it will come out finally."[8] A life, like a race, must be over before we can call it won or lost. It was a truism in the ancient world that no one should be called happy until he is dead. Augustine, however, was convinced otherwise and set out in Book 11 of the *Confessions* to demonstrate why.

In Book 11, Augustine conducts an experiment in thought. He realizes that to respond fully and truthfully to the question he has put to himself—Who am I?—he must expand the question and ask himself, Who was I in the past and who will I be in the future? After all, he is extended in time. The human self, like music or narrative, exists in time and so has a beginning and an end. As for the present, it is always being driven into the past by the incoming future. If we have any doubt that Camus was mentored by Augustine and joined him in these reflections, we may recall

---

[*] For an in-depth exploration of both texts, see Meagher, *Augustine on the Inner Life of the Mind*. In reflecting on Meursault's evolving interest in and understanding of time as a human experience, it is illuminating to compare his development with that of children as studied and discussed by Jean Piaget in *The Child's Conception of Time*.

Meursault's comment "Only the words 'yesterday' and 'tomorrow' still had meaning for me."

Returning to Augustine's thought experiment, he argues that the past does not exist because it is no longer and that the future does not exist because it is not yet. Neither can be said to "be," to have any objective or real existence. They *are not*, even though, respectively, the past once *was* and the future one day *will be*. This leaves Augustine solely with the present. At this point, by process of elimination, only the present can be said to exist. But, as he proceeds, he comes to realize that the present is no less problematic and threatened than the past or the future.

How so? What we call the present is, when we examine it, actually divisible into past and future. This year, 2020, is not the present because, as I write this on the last day of August, every day of 2020 and of August prior to today, the 31st, lies in the past and therefore no longer exists. Neither does tomorrow or any day, month, or year after today exist. At least not yet. Anyone can see where this is going. The only indivisible present moment would be one without extension, and such a moment cannot be said to exist, precisely because it is without extension. Such a moment in time is like an object that has no extension in space, no width, no height, no depth. In geometry, we call this a point. We mean by this not a visible point we make with chalk on a blackboard or with a pencil on paper. Such points have extension. Otherwise they would be invisible. A true geometric point exists only in the mind, in thought. It is a concept. Likewise, as we shall see, the self exists only in the mind.

To sum up. Augustine concludes that the past does not exist, the future does not exist, and the present does not exist. This means that time does not exist, and therefore that the self does not exist, because the self is essentially temporal. Augustine, we recall, began this inquiry by asking himself, Who am I? Now he has arrived at an impasse, a dead end, where he is forced by his own argument to admit that "I do not exist." But Augustine refuses to accept his own nonexistence. Anticipating Descartes by twelve centuries, he asserts that his past exists in the act of memory, his future exists in the act of expectation, and his present exists in an act he calls *contuitus*, "attention." He had only to turn inward (as we have watched Meursault do in Augustine's footsteps) to escape the constraints of his physical existence and to discover the reality of time as a *distentio* (extension) of his mind.

Like the divine Creator in the book of Genesis, staring out over the timeless void, Augustine summoned himself from the void of nonexistence by his own creative, imaginative activity. He imagined his past and his future in an extended present of his own making. This is what happens when we engage our past in memory and imagine our future in expectation. As Augustine understands it, *memoria*, "memory," is the presence of the past, and *expectatio*, "expectation," the presence of the future—presence to mind, in images. We form these images, create them, when we step out of physical time and step into mental time, when we cease doing and begin thinking. This is where Meursault found himself—deep in thought—when in his cell there was nothing at all for him to do and nothing at all being done to him or around him. This is when Meursault encountered himself, and made his most startling and transfixing discovery yet.

> One day when the guard told me that I had been in for five months, I believed it, but I didn't understand it. For me it was one and the same unending day that was unfolding in my cell and the same thing I was trying to do. That day, after the guard had left, I looked at myself in my tin plate. My reflection seemed to remain serious even though I was trying to smile at it. . . . I moved closer to the window, and in the last light of day I gazed at my reflection one more time. It was still serious—and what was surprising about that, since at that moment I was too? But at the same time, and for the first time in months, I distinctly heard the sound of my own voice. I recognized it as the same one that had been ringing in my ears for many long days, and I realized that all that time I had been talking to myself. [9]

Meursault was no longer simply alone, he was alone with himself. He was no longer merely conscious of what was happening to or around him, he was conscious of what was happening in him. He was, in a word, self-conscious. But conscious of what self? The serious self, the smiling self, the silent self, the talking self . . . ?

The discovery of inner time and imagination is no final solution to the problem of selfhood, no definitive answer to the question of identity. The problem now is not the existence of the past and the future and the self, but their multiplicity. Every act of memory and of expectation takes place within an extended "present" created by the act of *contuitus*, "attention." *For me it was one and the same unending day that was unfolding in my cell and the same thing I was trying to do.* When I step out, as it were, of the relentless flux and flow of my life to remember my past and anticipate my future, I have a fleeting, partial glimpse of myself, of who I am. The problem with this glimpse, however, is that it is a product of that moment. It is biased by that moment. If I look at my education, my career, my marriage, my finances, my health, or any other aspect of who I am in a moment of loss, betrayal, misunderstanding, injury, or failure, for example, then I am likely to see the past and the future as a series of losses, betrayals, misunderstandings, injuries, or failures, and so on. The moment of *contuitus* inevitably serves as a filter, a finite lens through which past and future are imagined; and in that autobiographical moment, all that exists, all that we have of our past and future, are the images we create. They represent, to a great extent, the present moment expanded, blown large. If I hold still my life and take a look at it in a moment of despair, I am all too prone to despair at what I see. In a godless moment we see a godless life, and in a moment of deep faith we see a life infused with the divine presence. The question Augustine put to himself—Who am I?—has, with this realization of chaotic multiplicity, become for him a nightmare: "I have flown apart into moments whose order I know not, and my thoughts, the deepest workings of my soul, are shredded by the havoc of change."[10]

The critical question now becomes, When? When should I step out of my life in order to see it? What is the privileged, the nonarbitrary moment? When is the moment of truth? For Augustine that proved to be the moment of his conversion, the moment when he heard the insistent voice of an unseen child singing the words *Tolle et lege*, "Take up and read."[11] And so Augustine lifted the scriptures, closed his eyes, pointed to a random page, opened his eyes, and read the words that changed the course of his life. Of what he experienced at that moment, the realization he came to, he wrote these words: *Caro mihi valent stillae temporum*, "Loving and loved, every grain of sand in the glass of time became precious to me."*

It is easy to lose ourselves in *The Stranger*, in the terse, relentless pace of the narrative; it is easy to overlook the fact that, like the *Confessions* of Augustine, *The Stranger* is a philosophical autobiography told in the first person. Just as Meursault suddenly realizes that he has been hearing his own voice, so we realize that it is Meursault's voice we have been hearing. His story is one of self-discovery. We watch him, hear him, discovering time, inner time, lifetime, narrative, and self. "If we wish to know about a man," writes clinical neurologist Oliver Sacks,

> We ask "what is his story—his real, inmost story?"—for each of us *is* a biography, a story. Each of us *is* a singular narrative. . . . Biologically, physiologically, we are not so different from each other; historically, as narratives—we are each of us unique. To be ourselves we must *have* ourselves—possess, if need be re-possess, our life-stories. We must "recollect" ourselves, recollect the inner drama, the narrative of ourselves. A man *needs* such a narrative, a continuous inner narrative, to maintain his identity, his self.[12]

But where is the voice we hear? Where is Meursault's voice in *The Stranger*? Where is it located? Where is he located? Not in space (we

---

* Augustine, *Confessions*, 11.2. The Latin *stillae temporum* literally refers to water drops, not grains of sand, because ancient Greeks and Romans used water clocks, not sand clocks. The Greek word for a water clock was kleyuvdra (*klepsydra*), "water thief" and thus "time thief."

know the answer to that—in his cell) but in time. It's the autobiographical moment, the moment of truth, as it were, that we are looking for. What is the moment in Meursault's life that corresponds to the moment of conversion and confession in Augustine's life?

Meursault's moment of truth must be after his trial. Otherwise, how could he describe the trial and the events that followed it? His detailed account of the trial proceedings is clearly memories of the past. Those memories offer plain if subtle evidence of how he has been transformed by his discovery of self and his evolving self-consciousness. For the very first time since the murder he realizes his guilt, rather than experiencing only annoyance. What occasions this awareness is a mere "stirring" in the courtroom as the caretaker from his mother's home relates again Meursault's oddly detached behavior at his mother's wake, the fact that he had declined to see his mother's body but had instead accepted a smoke and some coffee, and then dozed off.

It is the emergence of emotion that is perhaps most striking in Meursault's trial memories. Meursault remembers how the prosecutor, when asked if he had any further questions for one witness, had exclaimed,

> "Oh no, that is quite sufficient!" with such glee and with such a triumphant look in my direction that for the first time in years I had this stupid urge to cry, because I could feel how much all these people hated me. [13]

More striking and poignant than this was Meursault's response to the testimony of Céleste, who ran a restaurant Meursault had frequented. Céleste had dressed up for the occasion. He'd wanted to make a good impression and help his friend. Meursault later remembers how, when asked if Meursault was a customer of his, Céleste had replied,

> "Yes, but he was also a friend"; what he thought of me, and he answered that I was a man; what he meant by that, and he stated that everybody knew what that meant. . . [14]

The presence and testimony of Céleste truly moved Meursault, and even more than what Céleste said, it was what he found no words to say.

> And as if he had reached the end of both his knowledge and his goodwill, Céleste then turned toward me. It looked to me as if his eyes were glistening and his lips were trembling. He seemed to be asking me what else he could do. I said nothing. I made no gesture of any kind, but it was the first time I ever wanted to kiss a man.[15]

After the trial, Meursault entered the second and final period of isolation. It was also a period of waiting. Judged guilty and sentenced to the guillotine, he was awaiting death. Now, quite literally and inescapably, in Heideggerian terms, he embodied Being-towards-death (*Sein-zum-Tode*). Not that he didn't look for ways to escape. That was about all he did after the trial. "Looking" in this instance meant imagining. There was nothing any longer lacking in his imagination. It had become his strongest point. It was where he lived.

> All I care about right now is escaping the machinery of justice, seeing if there's any way out of the inevitable. They've put me in a different cell. From this one, when I'm stretched out on my bunk, I see the sky and that's all I see. . . . Lying here, I put my hands behind my head and wait. I can't count the times I've wondered if there have ever been any instances of condemned men escaping the relentless machinery.[16]

He regrets not having done research on the history of the death penalty and of executions. Surely there must have been accounts of escape. Just one would suffice for him to be able to hope. But there were none on record, not with the guillotine. It was different with hangings and firing squads. Ropes could snap and shooters could miss, but guillotines are flawless, foolproof. The certainty of death irked him, unsettled him, but eventually served as a metaphor for the mortality that everyone faces, not just men on death row.

He came to see himself as privileged. Everyone lives under a death sentence. No exceptions. What is exceptional is that some men, like him, get to stand before a judge passing the sentence publicly to a packed courtroom. He knew he was going to die. He could read it in the newspaper. And that had its advantages. The appeal he hoped for and never came would change nothing. Appeals and pardons don't cancel death. They only delay it.

In his new cell on death row, Meursault was fixated now not on the past but on the future. He was lost not in memory but in expectation. His days were spent in his imagination. He realized just how much he had changed. "I've never had much of an imagination. But still I would try to picture the exact moment when the beating of my heart would no longer be going on inside my head. But it was no use."[17] After having refused twice to see the never-give-up chaplain, he let him in. Night would come soon and *they always came at dawn*. In another story, this would be the perfect moment, the classic moment, for a gallows (or in this case a guillotine) conversion, for a turn to God in exchange for eternal life. That was precisely what the priest was there to offer. "Every man I have known in your position," pleaded the priest, "has turned to Him."

> I acknowledged that that was their right. It also meant that they must have had the time for it. As for me, I didn't want anybody's help, and I just didn't have the time to interest myself in what didn't interest me. [18]

The priest—annoyed and agitated—wondered, "Have you no hope at all? And do you really live with the thought that when you die, you die, and nothing remains?" To which Meursault responded with a simple "Yes."[*]

---

[*] Camus, *The Stranger*, p. 117. At a later point in the prison-priest's last-ditch effort to stir in Meursault's soul some tremor of hope in another life, he asked what kind of afterlife Meursault might imagine and desire. Meursault's answer—"One where I could remember this life!"—echoes Augustine's vision of the eternal happiness of the saved in *The City of God*. In Augustine's theology, this vision is linked to the resurrection of the body, the retention of selfhood, and the memory of one's earthly life. Camus would not have encountered this teaching anywhere in Plato, Aristotle, or Plotinus. Meursault's imagined afterlife in which he would remember this life represents one more debt to Camus's shadow-mentor Augustine.

As we will discuss in the next chapter, in Camus's eyes what the priest offered Meursault, and the reader for that matter, was not life but suicide, philosophical suicide, false hope. This life in exchange for a future life. In the view of another French philosopher, Blaise Pascal, Meursault had nothing to lose by embracing faith. If he was right that "nothing remains," faith cost him nothing; but if he was wrong and the priest was right, then he purchased "the pearl of great price" for practically nothing.[19] For Meursault, however, who never lies, the price was too high.

Admittedly, the chaplain's deathbed manner left much to be desired, but he had given it his all. What tipped Meursault over the edge was the priest's calling him "my son" and asking why Meursault kept calling him "monsieur" and not "father."

> Then, I don't know why, but something inside me snapped. I started yelling at the top of my lungs, and I insulted him and told him not to waste his prayers on me. I grabbed him by the collar of his cassock. I was pouring out on him everything that was in my heart, cries of anger and cries of joy.[20]

Meursault's conversion, his moment of truth, had arrived, triggered not by the voice of a child chanting "Take up and read" but by a pitying priest telling Meursault his heart was blind. The priest seemed so sure of himself and his beliefs, but it was Meursault who was certain of himself and of his life and his death. In this moment, the moment of confession, the extended autobiographical present, the entire narrative—from "Maman died today" to "they greet me with cries of hate"—takes form in consciousness, summoned, imagined, and spoken inwardly. Meursault, in the long, lucid, sleepless night before his execution, looks back in memory and forward in expectation, and tells his story to himself and so to us.

Augustine, in just such a moment of confession, looked back at his life and wrote, "Such was my life, but was that a life, my God?"[21] Looking back over his life, Augustine knew perfectly well what he had done and what he hadn't. All that, all those moments were *who* he was. When he had first put to himself the question, You, who are you? the answer that came back at once was "a human being." At that point he had become, by his own admission, a question to himself. Until he knew what it was to be a human being, until he understood his nature, human nature, he didn't know how to regard who he was. He had turned to himself to ask, Who are you? because *who* he was, his self, was his doing, his creation. He had made himself who he was. But he knew that he had not created *what* he was. He, as a human being, was a creature, not the Creator. So he turned elsewhere. "What am I then, my God? What nature am I?"[22] Augustine knew he had failed his Creator, violated his own nature, sinned. But that didn't tell him how to regard his messy, conflicted, flawed life. His question was more fundamental. He laid his life out before his Creator and wanted an opinion, a judgment. The answer came in the garden when *loved and being loved, every grain of sand in the glass of time became precious to him.* God is love and he, Augustine, was loved unconditionally, in every moment of his life. It was what it was, and it was all good.

Søren Kierkegaard, in *The Sickness Unto Death*, defines the moment of faith, when every trace of despair is uprooted from the self, in these words: "In relating itself to itself and in willing to be itself, the self rests transparently in the power that established it."[23] In other words, in the extended moment of self-consciousness, the moment of confession, when I not only see who I am but also will who I am, affirm who I am, I am grounded in the transcendent power, the reality, that created me. We are not mistaken in hearing these words echoed in Meursault's moment of confession, his moment of truth, when he sees his life, affirms his life, accepts his death, and embraces the indifferent power that established him and his world.

> I was sure about me, about everything . . . sure of my life and sure of the death that I had waiting for me. Yes, that was all I had. But at least I had as much of a hold on it as it had on me. I had been right. I was still right, I was always right. I had lived my life one way and I could just as well lived it another. I had done this and I hadn't done that. I hadn't done this thing but

I had done another. And so? It was as if I had waited all this
time for this moment and for the first light of this dawn to be
vindicated. Nothing, nothing mattered, and I knew why. . . . I
opened myself to the gentle indifference of the world. Finding
it so much like myself—so like a brother really—I felt that I
had been happy and that I was happy again.[24]

In this moment Meursault stands beneath an indifferent sky, before
an indifferent universe, and sees that he has been faithful to that indifference in every decision he made in life: he could see his mother's body
or not see it, he could marry Marie or not, take a promotion or not, kill
the Arab or not. It had never mattered what decision he made in these
moments or in the countless other moments of his life. Nothing had ever
been at stake. Nothing is ever at stake in a world where the outcome of
every life is the same, where every life is lived under a death sentence.
The universe, the nearest Meursault could come to a conception of the
divine, was an indifferent executioner, and Meursault had imitated
the universe in his life, and most dramatically on the beach where he had
been happy and had temporarily lost that happiness.

Now he is happy again. Happy in life, happy in death. He is at one
with, even brotherly with, the universe, the lethal indifferent universe. He
imagines all is well, but is it? There is a crowd of spectators gathering at
this moment, ready to greet him "with cries of hate." *The Stranger* has come
to an end, but we are not through with it.

CHAPTER SIX

Toothing-stones

*T*he *Stranger*[1] is neither realism nor fantasy," wrote Camus in 1954. "I see it rather as a myth in the form of a person, but deeply rooted in the physicality and intensity of everyday life. People have tried to see in it a new kind of anti-morality, which is utterly wrong."[2] Myths convey truths. These truths may be only partial truths, but they are not made up. They are found, not fabricated. Myths convey what is, not what may or may not have happened once. Meursault came to certain truths, found them, the night before he died. As he put it, "I was . . . sure of my life and sure of the death I had waiting for me. Yes, that was all I had." He claimed to have more, though, claimed that "nothing, nothing mattered," and he knew that he had lived as if that were true. But this is where his truths betrayed him, where his wisdom failed him. Meursault died convinced that it didn't matter and never would that he had killed the Arab. But are we meant by Camus to put down *The Stranger* and walk away sharing this conviction, this "new kind of anti-morality"? Camus made it clear that we would be "utterly wrong" to do so. Yes, he made it clear in 1954, fourteen years after he completed *The Stranger*. By that time a generation of readers had gotten it "utterly wrong," and innumerable readers (but not all) since then have followed in their mistaken path. What did they get wrong? How did they miss the point? Did Camus really only make it clear in 1954 that there was something wrong, something not to be admired or imitated, in Meursault's murderous amorality?

Before we address this question, we need to address another. If *The Stranger* is a myth, as Camus wrote to Hädrich, what myth does Camus have in mind? The answer to this is clear. *The Stranger* belongs, in Camus's creative scheme, to the Sisyphus Cycle, the cycle of the absurd, in which the philosophical companion work to *The Stranger* is *The Myth of Sisyphus*, written alongside *The Stranger* and published seven months after it in December 1942. Sisyphus, we know, is all about his signature rock, his eternal burden, and we will return to that rock in a moment after we have taken a closer look at this archetypal figure of whom Meursault was a literary avatar. In various ancient versions of his myth, Sisyphus was far from uniformly admirable. He was a rogue, a thief, a killer, a snitch, and a cheat, whose high-profile philandering reputedly led at one point to his surreptitious engendering of Odysseus. But these were not the primary qualities that recommended him to Camus. Camus admired and chose him for his cleverness, his rebellious cunning, "his scorn of the gods, his hatred of death, and his passion for life."[3]

Sisyphus's story is summed up in two of his ancient epithets—the Runaway and the Stone-roller—pointing on the one hand to his crime and on the other to his punishment. Sisyphus clung tenaciously to life, which pitted him against death, his own and others'. When Hades, the Lord of Death, came for him, Sisyphus turned the tables, trussing Hades and holding him captive. With Hades in bondage, no one could die, a situation that particularly irked Ares, the god of war, because it clearly put him out of business. Ares freed Hades, his enabler, and handed over Sisyphus. Not for long, however, did Sisyphus remain in Hades, tricking Death a second time, securing a temporary furlough from the netherworld to see to his own proper funeral rites, promising Persephone to return in three days. Those days turned into weeks and Sisyphus was once more dragged below and condemned to his rock as a way of keeping him in Hades forever.

The punishing task laid on Sisyphus, we know, was to shoulder a massive rock and shove it, one step at a time, upward to the crest of a steep netherworld hill. Presumably, he imagined at first, or at least hoped, that this would be a one-off feat. If he were somehow able to reach the summit, he and Hades would be even. This is what he must have told himself, as anyone in his place would. It was what kept him going, making the effort. Each footfall brought him closer to his goal.

> At the very end of his long effort measured by skyless space and time without depth, the purpose is achieved. Then Sisyphus watches the stone rush down in a few moments toward that lower world whence he will have to push it up again toward the summit. He goes back down to the plane. It is during that return, that pause, that Sisyphus interests me. [4]

Camus would have us imagine what went through the mind of Sisyphus in that moment when Sisyphus steps away from his rock, only to watch it tumble down the hill and come to a crashing stop where the brutal ascent had begun. In this moment that Camus called "the hour of consciousness," Sisyphus witnessed the total erasure of all his efforts, the undoing of all his labor.

For Meursault, the hour of consciousness came as he waited for the first light of dawn that would bring his executioners. It was precisely then that he realized and accepted that "nothing mattered." And he knew why:

> Throughout the whole absurd life I'd lived, a dark wind had been rising toward me from somewhere deep in my future, across years that were still to come, and as it passed, this wind leveled whatever was offered to me at the time, in years no more real than the ones I was living. [5]

With acceptance came peace: "The wondrous peace of that sleeping summer flowed through me like a tide." [6] The fading brilliance of the night sky, the cooling "smells of night, earth, and salt air," awakened his long-deprived, dormant senses, and he was happy again, as he had been on the beach. He was at one with the beauty and indifference of the universe, so like him, so well suited to him.

Sisyphus, too, accepting his fate, knows a "silent joy" in his descent to take up his rock again. "In the universe suddenly restored to its silence, the myriad wondering little voices of the earth rise up."[7] He, like Meursault, is happy. "His fate belongs to him. His rock is his thing."[8] Meursault is Sisyphus. Sisyphus is Meursault. The one's rock is the other's "dark wind." Each is an absurd hero, striking a balance "between the needs of his body and the demands of his mind."[9] Each is ready to start anew, Sisyphus to take up his rock, Meursault to "live it all again" as his mother did, when she took a "fiancé" on the brink of her own death. But neither of them do. We leave them on their descent, which is unfortunate, because both are on the cusp of a crucial discovery.

Sisyphus, incarnate in Meursault and in all those who live the absurd without appeal, is not without integrity despite his many failings. He follows the logic of the absurd and embodies its demanding ethic: always more life rather than less life. This is what Camus labels the quantitative ethic. Many lives are better than one single life, longer lives are better than shorter lives. Living consciously, demanding happiness, meaning, and reason in the face of their denial, and the denial of life itself, by the lethal, irrational, indifferent universe—this is the code of the absurd hero.[*] "The present and the succession of presents before a constantly conscious soul," explains Camus, "is the ideal of the absurd man."[10] Sensuality and consciousness, flesh and spirit, affirming their needs and demands and living life fully, devoid of transcendent consolation or hope—this describes Sisyphus and Meursault in their hour of consciousness, in their descent to shoulder their rock and begin again.

In *The Myth of Sisyphus* Camus cites several illustrative exemplars of absurd heroism and the quantitative ethic: the seducer, the actor, the traveler, the conqueror, and the creator. We can see how each of these figures

---

[*] Camus might just as well have assigned the label "existentialist" to this code, the quantitative ethic, and to the heroism of those who live by it. Others have certainly done so ever since, assigning the same label to Camus, who in the Absurd Cycle designedly gives voice to existentialism's fundamental tenets and ideals.

quests after quantity, above all, at whatever cost. For the seducer, Don Juan is Camus's gold standard. Every night a different woman. It's all in the pursuit and conquest. Repetition is pointless, a waste of time, an illusory diversion into quality when only quantity matters.

> Don Juan does not think of "collecting" women. He exhausts their number and with them his chances of life. "Collecting" amounts to being capable of living off one's past.[11]

Needless to say, for the seducer to collapse into commitment, much less marriage, is apostasy.

The actor's, too, is a career committed to quantity. The actor plays many parts, lives many lives, does whatever the script calls for. Villainous roles have the same attraction as those of a saint. Horns are as good as halos. For an actor, being cast forever to play the same character may be a sinecure, but it is also cause for despair.

> Sweeping over centuries and minds, by miming man as he can be and as he is, the actor has much in common with that other absurd individual, the traveler. Like him, he drains something and is constantly on the move. . . . If ever the ethics of quantity could find sustenance, it is indeed on that strange stage.[12]

Next, Camus offers the conqueror as an icon of absurd heroism. The conqueror's obsession with quantity is again obvious. After each conquest the conqueror moves on. The aim is not to settle or govern but, like cancer, to metastasize. The last, and by Camus's rating, the "most absurd character," is the creator. In the final chapter of *The Myth of Sisyphus* Camus reflects on what he calls "absurd creation." This chapter and its discussion of philosophy, fiction, and freedom point well beyond absurdism and will be resumed in *The Rebel*, where they arguably belong and can be pursued fully. The truth is that all of the works in Camus's absurd cycle point beyond themselves. This is by design, not default. After the final line and period

of each of these works of fiction, philosophy, and theater, we are meant
to continue reading, as if we had not come to the end. In the absurd, or
Sisyphus Cycle, each work is like a movement in a symphony. At the end
of the movement there is silence and, if we are not in the know, we might
mistakenly begin clapping. The same is true after reading *The Stranger* or
Caligula, for example. Camus, on the one hand, wants us, his readers, to
pause and take in what we have just read, to consider what it would mean
if this were the whole truth, the final word. On the other hand, he wants
us to feel uneasy and sense that this can't really be it, that there must be
more. To assure us that this is the case and to point us onward, Camus
leaves clues in the endings of each of his absurd works, clues indicating
that there is more to come, more to say, more to discover. We will call these
indicators "toothing-stones."

Constructing a drystone wall is rarely the work of a single day. Most
walls take a good deal of time, so they are built in stages. No one wants
those stages to be plainly visible in the finished wall. For the sake of
both aesthetics and stability, the wall must be continuous, seamless—or,
in a word, "one" and not many. To ensure the integrity of the wall, the
builder never ends a day's work with a clean, straight edge, top to bottom.
Instead, the builder leaves an intentionally uneven edge, with multiple
protruding stones, jutting out and pointing the way ahead. These are the
"toothing-stones."* Among their functions is to make clear that this wall
is a work in progress, not a done deal.

The last-minute toothing-stone in *The Stranger* literally clamors for our
attention. The very last words of the text—*cris de haine*, "cries of hate"—
come as a sudden shock. The fact that Meursault wishes for such a welcome
at his public execution site is even more unexpected and unsettling. We
expect a cadence, and we get dissonance. Any notions we may have enter-
tained of Meursault as an exemplary character, an icon of evolved humanity,
are surely shattered at this point. Meursault, at best, is a work in progress.

---

* The same construction principles clearly obtain whether the building blocks are stones,
bricks, or even (for junior builders) LEGOs.

Starting as he did from scratch, from the zero point, he has come a long way, but he still has a long way to go.

By the end of *The Stranger*, Meursault has made his peace with the world and with his fate.

> I opened myself to the gentle indifference of the world. Finding it so much like myself—so like a brother, really—I felt that I had been happy and that I was happy again. [13]

He's happy. We may be happy *for* him. But are we happy *with* him? A man is dead, at his hands. He expresses no regret, no repentance over his murder of another human being, also so much like himself. How, we may wonder, can he possibly call the world or the universe *tendre*, "tender," "gentle," "kind," in its lethal indifference to human life? And what of Meursault? So like that universe, are we meant to regard him, in his indifference to the life and death of the Arab, as similarly *tendre*? A gentle killer—an odd and disturbing note on which to put down *The Stranger*.

Meursault, in his cell, thought back to his trial and remembered the hatred that had filled the courtroom, the hatred toward him: "I could feel how much all these people hated me."[14] The disconnect, indeed the gulf, between Meursault's expressive kinship with the inhuman universe and his hostile estrangement from the human community should at least make us pause before heralding Meursault as a hero for our times. An absurd hero, yes, an existentialist paradigm, yes; but we have seen that absurd heroes live by a merely quantitative ethic: more life. More life, that is, for me. Meursault actually failed even in that egotistic ethic, because his murder of the Arab cut short not only his victim's life but also his own. The death of the Arab and Meursault's consequent incarceration annoyed him. He was in prison, alone. He would rather have been with Marie, on the beach or in bed. His regret was understandable. At the same time he felt no remorse. None. To feel remorse, he would have to acknowledge a qualitative ethic in which some lives and some actions are better than others. Some right and some wrong, some good and others evil. Meursault was not there yet, and he wouldn't get there. It was too late. If, like his mother, he could have started over, begun again, even briefly, he might have had a chance. Instead, he was out of time, and went to his death a stranger to others, as they were strangers to him.

Meursault was close to realizing his brotherliness, his kinship, with other humans, when he realized that everyone lives under a sentence of certain death. All are condemned to a common fate. He was not singled out, only included. What he failed to realize is the profound implication of this universal death sentence—that we are all in this together and that this makes us brothers and sisters. It never occurred to him that there is a natural, compelling solidarity among the condemned. This was simply lost on Meursault. After all, in his cell, where he took his first steps into human consciousness, Meursault was alone. It was during prolonged periods of radical isolation that his mind first opened. After his first and last meeting with Marie in the visiting room, we find in the text no evidence of other inmates. He never mentions a fellow prisoner, much less another condemned man facing execution.

Meursault's lack of remorse and his inability to see himself in others and others in himself were failures of imagination. He was yet to experience

> how,
> once in a while,
> you can creep out of your own life
> and become someone else—
> an explosion
> in that nest of wires
> we call the imagination.[15]

Without imagination there can be no compassion and no unselfish solidarity. It was not that Meursault was entirely without imagination in his cell. He made strides, discovering and exploring interior time, memory, expectation, and narrative. He surprised himself with his own emotions, his rush of affection for Céleste and his rage at the man who called himself "father." Before prison, his inchoate imagination leaned on immediacy and sensory experience to take a step, even to take a leap. Looking back, Meursault remembered how this had happened once in Masson's beach house, with Marie and Masson's wife. Masson was talking with Meursault and the women were in the kitchen together.

> He told me that he spent Saturdays and Sundays and all his days off there. "With my wife, of course," he added. Just then his wife was laughing with Marie. For the first time, maybe, I really thought I was going to get married.[16]

This moment gave Meursault a pleasant experience, a taste of being a couple with Marie, together with another couple—an explosion in that nest of wires we call the imagination. Perhaps not an "explosion" in this case. More like a pop. But it was enough for him. So this is what marriage feels like! It felt good. He might just go there, maybe. Vicarious experience, we know, is a mode of imagination. It helps break down barriers between one life and another. We can only imagine what effect it might have had on Meursault if he had talked with fellow prisoners on death row as they'd prepared for their deaths, shared feelings with them, and even witnessed their executions.

Another notorious absurd hero and avatar of Sisyphus was the young emperor Gaius Caesar Augustus Germanicus, as scripted by Camus in his most successful drama, *Caligula*. Camus, an age-mate but obviously no contemporary of Gaius, was twenty-five when he wrote *Caligula*, the same age as the historical Caligula when he became emperor. In what Camus admitted later was an "artless intention," he wrote the play for himself, intending to play the part of Caligula in its first planned production. The war intervened and doomed the play's opening in Algiers, postponing the debut of Caligula to 1945, when Gérard Philipe at age twenty took on the title role in Paris's Théâtre-Hébertot.*

---

* The first English-language production of *Caligula* was staged by the Royal Shakespeare Company. Michael Cacoyannis, best known as a film and stage director, played the role of Caligula. Michael, a dear friend of mine for many years, once related to me how displeased Camus (who attended the first performance) was with his portrayal of the title character. It was clear that Camus still "owned" the part, though he never had an opportunity to play it.

When the curtain rises, there is turmoil in the imperial palace. Caligula is missing and was last seen fleeing, with a strange look in his eyes. When he finally returns after three days, he is not himself. "His legs are caked with mud, his garments dirty; his hair is wet, his look distraught."[17] To all appearances he has gone mad, but he insists that he has never been more lucid. Drusilla, his sister and lover, is no more, torn forever from his arms. Her death has taught him "a childishly simple, obvious, almost silly truth, but one that's hard to come by and heavy to endure. . . . Men die and they are not happy. . . . this world of ours, the scheme of things as they call it, is quite intolerable."[18] What he describes here is the absurd, the standoff between the incessant human longing for life and meaning and the endless silence of the universe. This is the truth Caligula must live, the truth he will teach to his subjects. In Caligula, wisdom and power have finally converged. Plato's philosopher-king is now incarnate in Rome.

Caligula's truth is no different from that of Sisyphus or Meursault; but he, unlike them, enjoys a captive following. Sisyphus was chained to his rock, Meursault executed. Neither were "talkers," much less teachers. Caligula, like his absurd siblings, is a rebel, but his metaphysical rebellion is on a whole different scale. Meursault came to the nihilistic conviction that nothing matters, but he had no way of convincing others of his truth. Caligula is empowered. He combines clout with his convictions. "Thenceforth," comments Camus in 1957,

> obsessed with the impossible and poisoned with scorn and horror, he tries, through murder and the systematic perversion of all values, to practice a liberty that he will eventually discover not to be the right one. He challenges friendship and love, common human solidarity, good and evil.[19]

He shares Sisyphus's "scorn of the gods, his hatred of death, and his passion for life" and, like Meursault, is an indifferent executioner; but unlike them he comes to the realization that he was wrong, not wrong about the absurd but wrong in the conclusions he drew from it, wrong about what it means, or ought to mean, to live the absurd.

Caligula arrives at this realization—the error he made—too late, only moments before he is assassinated, too late to start over. Caligula has found a kind of happiness in the murderous path he has taken, as did Meursault. And, like Meursault, he is in the end confronted with hate before he is killed. Before that, however, he, too, is offered a last chance to reconsider what he has done and how he has lived. This time the appeal comes from a loving woman, not a desperate cleric. "Happiness is kind," Caesonia reminds him. "It doesn't thrive on bloodshed," to which Caligula responds, "Then there must be two kinds of happiness. And I've chosen the murderous kind."[20] A debate follows between Caligula and his lover, a debate that she wins. With his assassins in the wings, hungry for his blood, Caligula screams his recantation: "I have chosen a wrong path, a path that leads to nothing. My freedom isn't the right one."[21] Caligula once believed, as does Caesonia, that "the only mistake one makes in life is to cause others suffering."[22] But he lost his way. He made this mistake, over and over, and suffered for it at the murderous hands of others who once revered him.

Caligula's embrace of "absurd freedom" was absolute. After his "con-version" to the absurd, occasioned by Drusilla's tragic, untimely death, he lived by a purely quantitative ethic, refusing to accept his friend Cherea's view that "some actions are—shall I say?—more praiseworthy than others." Caligula was clear in his rejection: "And *I* believe that all are on an equal footing."[23] This was clearly not Camus's belief when he wrote *Caligula*. It never was and never would be. Like Socrates in his dialogues, Camus pursued assertions and arguments he knew were ultimately false, pressing and interrogating them until they broke down and came to a dead end of their own making. The works of the absurd or Sisyphus Cycle were, as we have called them, experiments in truth, experiments that ultimately fall short, not as works of art but as counsels to live by. They offer only half-truths, unable to bear the full weight of a life worth living. They represent the jagged edges of an unfinished, as yet unstable, wall.

The last toothing-stone to consider here is the one that Meursault discovered under his prison mattress—the ragged newspaper clipping, whose
"crime story" he says he must have read "a thousand times."

> A man had left a Czech village to seek his fortune. Twenty-five
> years later, and now rich, he had returned with a wife and child.
> His mother was running a hotel with his sister in the village
> where he'd been born. In order to surprise them, he had left his
> wife and child at another hotel and gone to see his mother, who
> didn't recognize him when he walked in. As a joke he'd had the
> idea of taking a room. He had shown off his money. During
> the night his mother and his sister had beaten him to death
> with a hammer in order to rob him and had thrown his body
> into the river. The next morning his wife had come to the hotel
> and, without knowing it, gave away the traveler's identity. The
> mother hanged herself. The sister threw herself down a well.[24]

With few alterations this became the core of Camus's 1944 tragedy of
errors, *Le Malentendu* (*The Misunderstanding*),[25] written during his 1942–43
sojourn near the occupied French village of Le Chambon-sur-Lignon,
where he was witness to the selfless rescue of over five thousand Jews from
under the murderous eyes of Vichy and Nazi forces. *The Misunderstanding*
was first performed in an embattled Paris at the Théâtre de Mathurins on
August 24, 1944, one day before the German garrison surrendered the city.

Jan, the returning son in *The Misunderstanding*, prefigures Prometheus,
while his mother and his sister, Martha, embody Sisyphus, who robs and
murders wayfarers. Like Patrice Mersault in *A Happy Death*, they are bent
on murdering their way to personal happiness. More life for them at the cost
of less life for their victim. Jan, on the other hand, has journeyed a long way
to return to the village of his birth with only the happiness of his mother
and sister in mind, explaining to his wife, "No one can be happy in exile
or estrangement. One can't remain a stranger all one's life."[26] Maria, Jan's
wife, approves of his purpose but not his plan. His scheme is to prolong

what would otherwise be a simple homecoming. He will go incognito, as a stranger in need of lodging, and wait to see when and how his long-lost family recognizes him. Maria argues against her husband's proposed game. Sheer folly, as she sees it. And dangerous.

> But why not let them know the truth at once? There are situations in which the normal way of acting is obviously the best. If one wants to be recognized, one starts by telling one's name; that's common sense. Otherwise, by pretending to be what one is not, one simply muddles everything. How could you expect not to be treated as a stranger in a house you entered under false colors? No, dear, there's something . . . something morbid about the way you're doing this. . . . No, there's only one way, and it's to do what any ordinary mortal would do—to say "It's I," and to let one's heart speak for itself.[27]

Meursault, we know, agreed with Maria. Every time he read the story of Jan's murder, he came to the same conclusion that, in his words, "the traveler pretty much deserved what he got and that you should never play games."[28] Camus, not surprisingly, saw eye to eye with Meursault on this matter.

> For after all, it amounts to saying that everything would have been different if the son had said: "It is I; here is my name." It amounts to saying that in an unjust or indifferent world man can save himself, and save others, by practicing the most basic sincerity and pronouncing the most appropriate word.[29]

Saving oneself and others in an unjust or indifferent world is precisely the mission of Prometheus, but Jan failed as a would-be Promethean avatar because he forgot the one lesson to be learned from Meursault, Meursault's most admirable quality—sincerity. Meursault never lied or played games.

That said, Jan was right to turn his back on Sisyphus, Meursault, Caligula, and their purely quantitative ethic of private happiness. He points the way ahead. He knows that there is more to life than his happiness and stands his ground against his wife's urging that they go back and live the life they have made for themselves.

> Maria: Let's go away, Jan; we shall not find happiness here.
> Jan: It's not happiness we've come for. We had happiness already.
> Maria: Then why not be satisfied with it?
> Jan: Happiness isn't everything; there is duty too.[30]

With this simple declaration—*Happiness isn't everything; there is duty too*—we have left one myth and entered another, left the Sisyphus Cycle and made our way into the Prometheus Cycle. This should come as no surprise. As Camus was writing *The Misunderstanding*, he was also writing *The Plague*, surrounded by plague-fighters, deferring their happiness and risking their lives for the sake of others. Simply doing their duty. Soon he would be one of them.

CHAPTER SEVEN
Plague

O n February 21, 1941, Camus inserted this entry into his *Notebooks*: "Finished Sisyphus. The three absurds are now complete. Beginnings of liberty."[1] The "three absurds" referred to here, as we know, were *The Stranger*, *Caligula*, and *The Myth of Sisyphus*. Perhaps to mark this accomplishment and to signal a new departure, Camus left the next two pages blank. Then again, these blank pages might have meant that really he had no idea what was coming. In retrospect, that was surely the case, for "Beginnings of liberty" failed to predict or describe what the years ahead would be like for Camus, Algeria, France, and the world. Six months later, with these words, Camus acknowledged that "liberty" was not the word for where he now found himself: "Everything is decided. It is simple and straightforward. But then human suffering intervenes, and alters all our plans."[2]

France was already enduring great suffering, in a humiliating defeat and a shameful armistice that left its people at bitter odds not only with the Germans but with each other. More personally, Camus began the new year (1942) spitting blood, as he had at age seventeen. In August, with tuberculosis ravaging both of his lungs, he and his wife, Francine, fled the oppressive heat and humidity of Oran, sailed to France, and sought out the clean, crisp mountain air of the Massif Central. Here, in the hamlet of Panelier, he would hope to recuperate, receiving regular pneumothorax injections in Saint-Étienne, and at the same time diving into the writing of *The Plague*, a work he had already conceived in Algeria and ruminated on in his writer's journal. His work was, as noted there, making its way in stages "to an unrewarded perfection."[3] *The Stranger* and *The Myth of Sisyphus* had been the zero point. "*The Plague* is a progress, not from zero toward the infinite, but toward a deeper complexity that remains to be defined."[4] Upon arrival in his mountain retreat, Camus could hardly have anticipated just how deep and complex his life and writing would come to be during his fifteen months in this remote enclave in what was euphemistically labeled the "Free Zone."

Two months later, in October 1942, Francine Camus left Panelier to return to Oran and resume her post as a mathematics teacher. Camus planned to follow her shortly, before winter set in. In fact he had his transit papers in hand when, on November 11, the Allied forces under Dwight Eisenhower's command suddenly launched Operation Torch, a three-prong invasion of Vichy French North Africa, with landings in Algiers, Oran, and Casablanca. This effectively severed travel and communication between mainland France and Algeria. In response, the German Wehrmacht promptly invaded and occupied the French Free Zone, until now under the direct administration of the collaborationist Pétain government centered in the resort town of Vichy. Condemned to the fate of Oran's citizenry in *The Plague*, Camus and his new neighbors in the Vivarais hill towns were trapped, "like rats." Camus was a stranger here, like Rambert, the Parisian journalist in *The Plague*, "on assignment" so to speak, and separated from the woman he loved and the life in which he had been happy. Camus had come to Panelier to write *The Plague*, and now he was living it. The plague chronicle that Camus wrote at his desk was, at the same time, the historic drama he witnessed, as it were, from his window. One of the models for his text was Daniel Defoe's 1722 *A Journal of the Plague Year*. Camus was indeed writing his own journal of the plague year he lived in Nazi-occupied south-central France. *The Plague* is an intensely personal book, on the one hand autobiographical and on the other a composite biography of the community in which he found himself, quite by accident, in 1942–43.

What was Camus doing, we might wonder; how was he spending his days and nights until he left for Paris in the fall of 1943 to work as reader for Gallimard publishers and as editor-in-chief of the clandestine Resistance newspaper *Combat*? We know he was writing his book and recovering his health; and, as always, he was observing, listening, forming friendships, and sharing ideas. In addition, we have a clue to his other activities in a coded message, dated September 17, 1943, that he was finally able to send to his wife via Morocco, in which he wrote that he had spent the summer (of 1943) "mostly with children, big groups of children."[5] Who were these children and how was Camus involved with them? In retrospect, knowing now of the extensive Resistance activities taking place all around Camus that summer, we may make a reasonable guess.

The granite boardinghouse in which Camus resided and wrote *The Plague* was an easy walk from the larger village of Le Chambon-sur-Lignon, with roughly five thousand inhabitants. In the surrounding plateau lay numerous other villages whose aggregate population at that time was closer to twenty-four thousand. Neither of these numbers include the many thousand fugitives, nearly all Jews and mostly children, who found refuge and rescue here from December 1940 to September 1944. In Le Chambon and nearby parishes it is estimated that five thousand people were taken in, cared for, issued forged papers and ration cards, and escorted to safety in Switzerland. This all took place with first Vichy and then Nazi forces as omnipresent as ticks. Jewish children were often hidden in plain sight, attending Christian church services and even singing in the choir. In one case, a house harboring numerous Jewish children stood next door to the headquarters of the local German garrison. In no case, across four years, was a single child lost. No one in Le Chambon broke ranks. These humble, unarmed warriors didn't need André Malraux to teach or remind them that "the only response to absolute evil is fraternity."[6] No one fleeing for their life was turned away. Everyone knew what everyone else was doing, and there were no informers. In this village of secrets, secrets were sacred, like the lives they protected. The legendary rescue network centered in this village is regarded as the most extensive and successful operation of its kind in all of Europe during the Second World War.* So when Camus wrote evasively to his wife that he had been spending his time in the summer of 1943 with "big groups of children," there is every reason for imagining that Camus was in on the secrets of Le Chambon and somehow involved in its life-saving seditions.

The full extent of Camus's engagement in the Resistance is not well documented until he moved to Paris, carried multiple identity papers, and lived at least two lives, one public and one hidden, one as Albert Camus, noted author in the employ of Gallimard, and the other as Albert Mathé, the voice of *Combat*, known to his Resistance comrades as Beauchard. Before that, however, he was no neutral bystander to Vichy and Nazi atrocities. While at Panelier, his frequent excursions to Lyon, a center of Resistance activities, were unlikely all to have been innocent interludes with friends and fellow writers. In addition to his close friend and colleague Pascal Pia (Resistance code name Pontault),[7] Camus spent time in Lyon and Saint-Étienne with the Catholic Resistance poet René Leynaud, the regional head of the "Combat" movement, arrested and executed in 1944. Camus expressed his deep respect and enduring fondness for Leynaud by dedicating to him the *Letters to a German Friend.*

Panelier, Camus's own residence and workplace, was also a place where he met with various figures knee-deep in the Resistance, whether armed or unarmed, such as René Fayol, a local Maquis leader, and André Chouraqui, an Algerian Jewish biblical scholar, who tutored Camus on the biblical significance of the plague and worked with the OSE (the Society for Rescuing Children) to shepherd Jewish children to the relative security of Le Chambon and the plateau. Undoubtedly the most colorful new friend that Camus made at this time was Raymond Bruckberger, O.P., a Dominican monk. Any glimpse into his life is like peering into a kaleidoscope: pious priest, intellectual, combat veteran, prisoner of war, filmmaker, chaplain of

---

* Le Chambon and the Chambonnaise are the only community to be honored collectively as "Righteous Among the Nations" by Israel's Yad Vashem.

Free France and later of the Foreign Legion, associate of Charles de Gaulle, spiritual adviser to Georges Pompidou, and close friend to Albert Camus. Years after the war, in 1958, Bruckberger accompanied Camus on a holiday in the Greek islands, costumed as a cowboy, sporting a checked shirt. Whatever else might be said of this monk, Bruckberger ensured that Camus's view of the Catholic priesthood was and would remain complicated.

Like the great masters of the Renaissance who populated their canvases with the familiar faces of their contemporaries, Camus filled the pages of his fictionalized plague chronicle with the lives and labors of the Chambon "sanitary squads" who risked themselves for strangers simply because it was the right thing to do. Some of those portrayed by Camus in *The Plague* were known to him personally, others perhaps not. He, too, may be partially glimpsed, more or less veiled, in several of his characters: in Rambert the journalist, Rieux the chronicler, Tarrou the pacifist, and even Paneloux the Augustine scholar. With all of them, he shared the commitment to resist the plague in all its murderous forms, most immediately the "brown plague" (*la peste brune*), as the Nazi pestilence was known. We surely hear Camus's voice in Rieux's as he asserts that "when you see the misery it [plague] brings. You'd need to be a madman, or a coward, or stone blind, to give in tamely to the plague."[8] Camus, we know, wasn't, and didn't.

In Le Chambon and the surrounding villages during the war years, resistance to the "brown plague" (and before it the "grey plague"*) took two basic forms: armed and unarmed, violent and nonviolent. As Camus made clear in his journal:

> All fight—and each in his way. . . . Rieux: In any fighting group one needs men who kill and men who cure, I have chosen to cure. But I know that I am fighting.[9]

The resistance that prevailed in Le Chambon and for which it is remembered and lauded was nonviolent, inspired and led by the Christian

---

* The Vichy regime was known as *la peste grise*, the "gray plague."

Huguenot pastor of the Reformed Church of France André Trocmé, his
wife, Magda, and his assistant pastor, Edouard Theis.* As early as 1934,
in the first sermon Pastor Trocmé delivered to his new congregation, he
made perfectly clear where he stood: "No government can force us to kill;
we have to find the means of resisting Nazism without killing people,"[10]
which is what he and the people of Le Chambon did for the next ten years.
They found spare support for their pacifist resistance, however, from the
French Protestant Church or the traditional Catholic hierarchy in France.
Trocmé decried the rampant antisemitism and the passive, even complicit,
submission to Vichy and Nazi terror that infected France; on August 16,
1942, he called upon the Christian church to fall to its knees and beg God's
forgiveness for its cowardice and failures. We hear an echo of Trocmé's
unarmed militancy in the second sermon of Father Paneloux, where he
entreats his congregation not to listen to those "who told us to sink to our
knees and give up the struggle."[11]

    In his journal, Camus envisioned *The Plague* as a chronicle, and that
is how it comes to us, as penned by Dr. Rieux, in whom we are not mistaken in seeing Camus and hearing his voice. While Rieux's namesake
in Le Chambon-sur-Lignon was the elderly Dr. Paul Riou, his character
bears the unmistakable stamp of another village physician, Dr. Roger Le
Forestier, who, like Prometheus, was a great lover of humanity. Still in his
twenties, he arrived in Le Chambon from Africa, where he had worked
with Albert Schweitzer in Cameroon. Le Forestier, a pacifist Christian
Résistant and exuberant community leader in Le Chambon, was above all
a healer,** who aided in the rescue and care of refugees, treated combatants
and peacemakers alike, and reached out to anyone in need. His calling was
to cure and to care and to first do no harm. For all this his reward was to
be falsely accused of plotting against the German army. At his tribunal he

---

* Trocmé and Theis were both arrested in February 1943, sent to an internment camp, and
  released after four weeks. From that point on they went underground and continued their
  rescue efforts from there.

** Dr. Le Forestier happened to be skilled in the pneumothorax therapy that Camus was
   receiving in Saint-Étienne.

professed his uncompromising commitment to Christian nonviolence in words later summarized by Trocmé:

> We in Le Chambon resist unjust laws, we hide Jews, and we disobey your orders, but we do this in the name of the Gospel of Jesus Christ.[12]

The tribunal's head, Commandant Major Schmähling, a devout Catholic, was moved and convinced by Le Forestier, and acquitted him of any capital offense; however, the prosecuting attorney, Major Metzger,[13] insisted that Le Forestier be punished. This led to Le Forestier's transfer to Fort Montluc prison in Lyons, run by Klaus Barbie, the "Butcher of Lyons," from where he was taken and savagely murdered along with 119 Résistants and Maquisards, including several priests and twelve women.

In an age of ideologues and executioners, Camus offered his readers the compassionate voice of a doctor, committed to saving from murder and indifference all who could be saved. Even Father Paneloux, whose eyes were inclined to look upward, to God, was able to recognize the kind of man that stood before him in Rieux: "Yes, yes, you too are working for man's salvation."[14] As Camus was witnessing daily the murderous hatred of a world soaked in savagery, it was surely the good doctor Le Forestier and the people of Le Chambon who emboldened him to assert and believe, even if barely, that "on the whole, men are more good than bad."[15]

Another key inspiration and paradigm for *The Plague* and its chronicler is *The Peloponnesian War* by the 5th-century general and historian Thucydides. A seminal concept in Thucydides's narrative is expressed in the elusive word κίνησις (*kinesis*, from which we get "kinetic"). It means a movement or disturbance, an unfolding upheaval or happening. It often suggests turbulence and so might refer to a revolt, an earthquake, a hurricane, or a colossal conflict. In Thucydides's case the *kinesis* in question was war, and not just *any* war, not just *another* war. In his view, this war—the nearly thirty-year conflict between Athens and Sparta and the alliances they led—was the archetype, the "mother of all wars." It represented the greatest *kinesis*, the most world-altering conflict Greece had ever known. Under scrutiny it would reveal the very essence of war, the common nature of all wars. Thucydides was further convinced that when the war finally ended, it would not ever be truly over, simply a thing of the past. It would lie low and return, somewhere, sometime. And the only recourse against it would be to see it coming, to recognize it in advance, and to marshal every force to ward it off or to diminish its duration and severity. War, in other words, if studied, can be understood and confronted, like plague. As it happened, Thucydides knew both of these *kineseis*—war and plague—firsthand and made them the subject of his history.

Thucydides, as an elected Athenian general, was a veteran as well as an observer of the Peloponnesian War. He was also a victim of the plague that struck Athens twice in the course of the war, devasted its population, and arguably made a major contribution to its defeat. Thucydides, who survived both war and plague, was struck by how the one mirrored and shed light on the other. Each *kinesis*, or "movement," revealed its nature to him. Thucydides was preoccupied, we might say, with the concept of nature (φύσις, *physis*), most especially human nature, to which Camus was no stranger, as we discussed in chapter 3. This concept had its most decisive origin in the early study and practice of medicine in the school of Hippocrates of Kos, the reputed father of Western medicine. Thucydides was a contemporary of Hippocrates, widely regarded as the author of the ancient treatise *On the Nature of Man*.

To know the nature of anything, including human being, is to know its beginning, its unfolding, and its end point. Understanding the nature of any physical *kinesis* or phenomenon, therefore, whether benign or pernicious, from pregnancy to malignancy, begins with recognizing its earliest manifestations or symptoms. If I witness a strange rash, a bump, a growth, a sudden loss of smell or hair or whatever else for the first time, I won't know what caused it, what it portends or promises, and I certainly won't know what to do, or not do, about it. Amputate or ignore, apply heat or cold, feed or starve?—the possibilities are endless. Someone who has seen this before, however, will know firstly how to do no harm and secondly how to do some good. We call such a person a physician, someone who knows about *physis*—specifically, the nature of the human body. In the natural world, beyond the borders of our skin, the name for such a person-in-the-know is "physicist." In the case of both medicine and natural science, however, no one can rely solely on their own limited life experience. They must learn from those before them. In the field of medicine, the awareness of this need and possibility was precisely what Hippocrates contributed to the development of medical understanding and practice, and what led him and his students to promote the writing, collecting, and distribution of case histories.

In the Hippocratic tradition, physicians observed bodies in all their mutations, illnesses, afflictions, and responses to a range of treatments, and then they documented and shared with students and colleagues, far and wide, what they saw and did and how it all turned out. In this way the Hippocratic school amassed a growing body of shared experience and expertise that became ever more specific and complex over time, taking into account variations in climate, race, gender, age, etc. Consequently, every generation of physicians and physicists stand on the shoulders of those who went before them. When any individual sees or experiences something for the first time, it rarely means that this is the first time that anyone has seen or experienced anything like it. To imagine otherwise is foolishness, and fools dance to a music no one else hears. The ancient word for someone who claims that they and their experiences are unique and that others' seemingly similar experiences are irrelevant is ἰδιότης, *idiotes*—put simply, "idiot." Such a person lives in a fantasy world all their own, in which they are convinced no one has ever felt what they feel, enjoyed what they enjoy, suffered what they suffer.

Contrariwise, Hippocrates and Thucydides, and for that matter Camus, held the commonsense view that we all have human bodies, human minds, and human souls, and live and act in the same world as each other. Consequently, we can and must learn about ourselves and our world from each other. In the words of the 2nd-century B.C.E. Roman African playwright Terence, *Homo sum, humani nihil a me alienum puto*, "I am a human being, and therefore I regard nothing human as foreign to me." [16] Herodotus, Thucydides, and Camus were all, in this sense, historians, all storytellers.* They may also appropriately be called philosophers, whether or not they feel comfortable with the title, by virtue of their common pursuit of human nature as manifest in our bodies, our epidemics, and our wars.

What this comes down to is that Thucydides was not chronicling the Peloponnesian War and the Athenian plague as a "best seller" for the avid consumption of his contemporaries. He was not a journalist, much less a blogger. He was concerned not so much to inform his readers of specific events but to discern recurring patterns in those events and to disclose the enduring truths revealed in them. For example, from his narration of the infamous revolt in Corcyra (the island of Corfu), he drew these reflections on the nature of war:

> In times of peace and prosperity cities and individuals alike follow higher standards, because they are not forced into a situation where they have to do what they do not want to do. But war is a stern teacher; in depriving them of the power of easily satisfying their daily wants, it brings most people's mind down to the level of their actual circumstances. [17]

Similarly, when reporting on the plague that first struck Athens in 430 B.C.E. Thucydides comments that

> I myself will merely describe what it was like, and set down the symptoms, knowledge of which will enable it to be recognized, if it should ever break out again. I had the disease myself and saw others suffering from it. [18]

In writing as he did about the past and his own present times, Thucydides was writing to the future. He was offering not entertainment

* Their kinship under this common title is displayed in the various meanings of the word *history* (from ιστορία, *historia*): inquiry, body of knowledge, narrative of inquiries, story or account.

but instruction, guidance, and wisdom. "It will be enough for me," he explained,

> if these words of mine are judged useful by those who want to understand clearly the events which happened in the past and which (human nature being what it is) will some time or other and in much the same ways, be repeated in the future. My work is not a piece of writing designed to meet the taste of an immediate public, but was done to last forever.[19]

The Plague, too, is a book designed to speak not only to Camus's generation but to future generations for whom the mid-20th century and the "brown plague" would be ancient history. It was, quite simply, "done to last forever," though Camus would never have been so bold as to utter such a boast. And he didn't have to. The book has spoken for itself. The fact that today it is a best seller, more than seventy-five years later, in a country which Camus only visited once and briefly, tells us all we need to know about how and why it was written. We find ourselves where Camus found himself. He knew we would, *human nature being what it is*. It is no accident that *The Plague* speaks directly to the current coronavirus plague, as well as to the murderous, hate- and ignorance-driven pestilences that infect the body politic. *The Plague* is, after all, about the "human crisis" he warned us of in his 1946 New York address. It was about what he had witnessed in Europe—*I had the disease myself and saw others suffering from it*—and what he saw was already on its way to our shores. He told us as much:

> He knew what those jubilant crowds [think Times Square on VE Day] did not know but could have learned from books: that the plague bacillus never dies; that it can lie dormant for years and years in furniture and linen-chests; that it bides its time in bedrooms, cellars, trunks, and bookshelves; and that perhaps the day would come when, for the bane and the enlightening

of men, it would rouse up in rats again and send them forth to
die in a happy city.[20]

The fact that Camus wrote about the years of Vichy perfidy and Nazi
terror in shrouded terms, under the guise of a physical plague, disappointed
and displeased some in Camus's close circle, such as Sartre and Simone
Beauvoir. He had in their eyes blurred the line between natural evil and
moral evil, between the inescapable and the culpable. Plagues are no one's
fault. Not so with Vichy and Nazi atrocities. *The Plague*, however, focused
on solidarity and quiet heroism, not betrayal and psychopathic sadism. For
some few that was not enough. It declined to point fingers and draw blood.
Camus hadn't held people accountable by name. Witless rats brought the
plague to Oran and, unlike Pétain and Hitler, they were the first to die of
it. *The Plague* is neither journalism nor history. It is literature—allegorical,
poetic, woven with metaphors—and philosophy. And Camus saw no con-
tradiction in this.

> A novel is never anything but a philosophy expressed in
> images. And in a good novel the philosophy has disappeared
> into the images. But the philosophy need only spill over into
> the characters and action for it to stick out like a sore thumb, the
> plot to lose its authenticity, and the novel its life. Nonetheless,
> a work that is to endure cannot do without profound ideas. And
> this secret fusion of experience and thought, of life and reflec-
> tion on the meaning of life is what makes the great novelist. . .[21]

Camus wrote these words to introduce the work[22] of another writer,
Jean-Paul Sartre, whom he had yet to meet; but they speak with equal if
not greater force and relevance to his own work. Camus's philosophy of
revolt, "expressed in images" in *The Plague*, was soon to be developed at
great length in *The Rebel*, the novel's companion work. *The Rebel* would be
to *The Plague* what *The Myth of Sisyphus* was to *The Stranger*. As we shall
see in the next chapter, *The Plague* was not lacking in "profound ideas,"

and in it the "fusion of experience and thought, of life and the reflection on the meaning of life," was no secret. In it, Camus had come of age as a writer. *The Plague* demonstrated to the world that Camus was indeed a "great novelist" and of all his work made the most persuasive case for his reception of the 1957 Nobel Prize in Literature, an honor he nevertheless protested should have gone to André Malraux.

The conflation, not confusion, of natural evil and moral evil in *The Plague* was integral to Camus's plan, not only for this one work but also for the unfolding of his philosophy from the absurd to what he later labeled the philosophy of limits, from point zero to sanctity without God. He signaled his intentions when he inserted this admittedly elusive quotation from Daniel Defoe opposite the title page of *The Plague*: "It is as reasonable to represent one kind of imprisonment by another, as it is to represent anything that really exists by that which exists not."[23] This allusion comes to life in *The Plague*, when the as yet anonymous chronicler compares the fate and experience of convicts in cells with the citizens of Oran quarantined in a plague city:

> Hostile to the past, impatient to the present, and cheated of the future, we were much like those whom men's justice, or hatred, forced to live behind prison bars.[24]

The Plague begins where *The Stranger* left us, with a man facing execution but ready to resume his life and start over. We see Sisyphus, too, at the foot of the hill ready to shoulder his rock again. The difference is that now they are not alone. Their fate is shared. The cell is a city. The rock is ours, not just his. This is no longer the zero point. There is progress. The story is the same, but further along in the telling, and the living. "*The Plague* has a social meaning *and* a metaphysical meaning," explains Camus. "It's exactly the same. Such ambiguity is in *The Stranger*, too."[25]

In the absurd, each of us is in a one-to-one face-off with a murderously indifferent universe: a universe whose bright side affirms and rewards our desires for a time, sometimes generously long and sometimes capriciously brief, long enough in either case for us to crave more; a universe whose dark side, however, sooner or later cancels us forever, apparently on a whim. Meursault concluded from this that he should accord no more meaning to any of his actions or reactions than does the metaphysical regime into which he was born. Indifference is the best response to indifference. "When in Rome . . ." The world of *The Plague*, however, is more complex. It is more populated with others—all facing the same fate but not responding in the same way. In society, there are victims; there are executioners; and there are those who resolve to be neither. There is a bright side, as well as a dark side, to everyone. There is good and there is evil. In chronicling the story of what France and humanity had lived through, done and suffered in the war years, some readers wanted Camus to focus on the darkness, the evil, the evildoers. Camus chose a different path, deciding "to state quite simply what we learn in a time of pestilence: that there are more things to admire in men than to despise."[26] This is what he learned and shared from the villagers of Le Chambon, his Resistance comrades, and the simple decent people who said no to hate and murder. Camus found his voice in Rieux and came to realize that even "the plague has its good side; it opens men's eyes and forces them to take thought. . . . What's true of all the evils in the world is true of plague as well. It helps men to rise above themselves."[27]

For Camus, the problem of evil was a lifelong preoccupation. The presence of evil, though, is no mystery. We see it around us, and in ourselves. What is harder to explain and more urgent to understand, especially in dark times, is the presence of good. How it is that some, in the darkest of times, rise above themselves. Our demons speak for themselves. It is to our better angels that Camus listened and gave voice in *The Plague*.

CHAPTER EIGHT

Rats

R ats brought the plague to Oran. They were the first sign of its arrival. Rats, of course, were not new to Oran, a busy Mediterranean port. Neither was the death of rats a novel occurrence. So, when "on the morning of April 16, Dr. Bernard Rieux felt something soft under his foot" and found it to be a dead rat on the landing outside his office, "he kicked it to one side . . . without giving it another thought."[1] One or two rats, dead or alive, were a matter of no particular concern, except for the building's concierge, M. Michel, who insisted, "There weren't no rats here."[2] A dead rat is unseemly but not threatening—a mess to be cleaned up.

When one dead rat turned into many, and many rats turned into a mounting multitude, concern grew. What began as an ugly spectacle soon became a logistical nightmare—how to remove and dispose of thousands of dead rats per day? Then the daily rat count suddenly plummeted. The rats were gone, for good. This brought relief to the city, and those who had always loathed rats and found them filthy must have felt a certain satisfaction. Good riddance. When people, instead of rats, began dropping in the streets, however, there was panic. It was in M. Michel that the fatal bacillus made its first leap from rodent to human. The rat that was the first victim of the deadly malaise proved to be its first carrier. Rats, as it turned out, were both victims and executioners.

The course of the disease soon traced the same alarming trajectory among humans as it had among rats. Death spread among the townspeople just as it had among its vermin. From the moment of infection, the sick became spreaders, victims became carriers, evoking not only sympathy but fear and aversion. Even as the death toll mounted, the civic authorities were more concerned with not alarming the public than with diagnosing and effectively attacking the disease. When Rieux managed to persuade the authorities to convene a health commission, the Prefect remained convinced the whole matter was a false alarm. Calm rather than cure was at first the official priority. Eventually, however, as corpses and lab results piled up, the Prefect succumbed to the weight of evidence and issued a telegram that read, "Proclaim a state of plague—stop—close the town."[3]

This scenario of rats and people, the infected and the infectors, victims and executioners, mortality and murder operates on many levels. *The Plague* is a story of both biological epidemic and moral contagion, a commentary on lethal indifference that is both metaphysical and historical. The cursed rock that Sisyphus shoulders to no avail, the remote, incommunicable universe that snuffs out any and every life on a whim, the callous indifference of takers, torturers, and killers who witness or inflict the suffering of others without sympathy or pity—all these are the plague from which we can never fully exempt or exonerate ourselves. Camus makes it clear that the plague bacillus is in each of us and in our world to stay. Immunity and innocence are not options. What lies in our power is "the never ending fight against terror . . . by all who, while unable to be saints but refusing to bow down to pestilences, strive their utmost to be healers."[4]

The Plague is, as we have seen, in the words of Thucydides, "not a piece of writing designed to meet the taste of an immediate public, but was done to last forever."[5] It is an allegory open to being read in many ways at different times, because understanding the plague means understanding that it is "the same thing over and over and over again."[6] Nevertheless, like *The History of the Peloponnesian War*, *The Plague* was written at a specific time and place to address what its author was immediately witnessing and recording. However resonant *The Plague* might be with Stalinist terror, the Hungarian Revolt, or the COVID-19 pandemic, Camus's immediate plague was "the brown plague" (in league with the collaborationist "grey plague") as he experienced and survived it in France, first in the Vivarais hill towns of the Massif Central and later in occupied Paris. From this perspective the early narrative of Oran's rats might well describe the fate of France's Jews after the 1940 collapse of the French Republic and the establishment of the Vichy regime in the French "Free Zone."

In the sordid vision of Nazi and Vichy antisemitism, Jews were vermin, fit for removal and extermination. Vichy and Nazi officials and forces made common cause in ridding France and the Third Reich of their pestilent Semite presence. Aryanization, the expulsion of Jews from commercial life, led to stripping French Jews of their citizenship, excluding Jews from civil service, the army, the press, the media, and most professions. Roundups, internment, and death camps completed the process of isolation and disposal. Borrowing Jean-Baptiste Clamence's vile comment in *The Fall*: "What a cleanup! . . . that's a real vacuum-cleaning."[7] Like the death of rats in Oran, the plight of the Jews (or for that matter Roma and Communists) caused no great alarm and, in certain circles, brought sick satisfaction. When the "brown plague" caused suffering and brought death to the "human population," as it were, it was a different story. Anyone who assisted Jews or resisted the authorities in any way risked suffering the same Jewish fate. The Jews, it seems, like rats, were socially and politically contagious. Nazis and collaborationist French, likewise, were infected, except that their disease was moral. They festered and died from the inside out.

The oft-cited poem composed by German Lutheran pastor Martin Niemöller[*] describes the downward moral spiral that many arguably decent but silent French, like their German counterparts, found themselves on.

---

[*] Niemöller, a former U-boat commander in WWI, initially supported Hitler's rise to power but later turned against him and led a group of clergy opposed to Hitler. After his arrest, he was sent to Sachsenhausen and later Dachau, where he survived and was eventually liberated. After the war, he called for penance and worked for reconciliation.

First they came for the socialists, and I did not speak out—
Because I was not a socialist.

Then they came for the Republicans, and I did not speak out—
Because I was not a trade unionist.

Then they came for the Jews, and I did not speak out—
Because I was not a Jew.

Then they came for me—and there was no one left to speak
for me. [8]

Others, like the villagers of Le Chambon-sur-Lignon and the
"sanitary groups" of Oran, spoke out from the start. For them it was a
matter not of heroism but of common decency. In the words of Dr. Rieux,
"That's an idea which will make some people smile, but the only means
of fighting a plague is—common decency," [9] or ordinary people doing
the right thing.

Why, we might ask, did the Chambonnaise, from the start and for
the duration, choose to harbor the hated and the hunted, even at the risk
and often the cost of their own lives? But was it a choice? Is common
decency a choice? When put this question, one after another of the villagers of Le Chambon said that for them it was not a choice. They felt
they had no choice but to do what they did. Betraying Jews and others
was out of the question, unthinkable. What's more, in their eyes, they
were not heroes. They saw no heroism in what they did, only duty, only
decency (the same thing, as they saw it). Many of these ardent Calvin-
ists looked upon the Jews who came to them as "chosen people" and saw
their escapes as reflections of the biblical Exodus and, for that matter,
of their own persecuted Huguenot ancestors' flights to freedom in the
16th century. In fact, the roughly 190-mile escape route to Switzerland
on which they escorted Jews retraced the route taken centuries earlier by
their fleeing forebearers.

In the fictional narrative of *The Plague*, it is perhaps the dutiful temporary municipal clerk Joseph Grand,* who "had all the attributes of insignificance,"[10] that most resembles the ordinary villagers of Le Chambon. Grand also reflects Camus, who, with plague all around him, sat writing at his desk day after day, laboring to create a "flawless" literary work. Rieux, and we his readers, first come upon Grand on the occasion of a man's suicide attempt. The man, named Cottard, now slumped on his bed and sobbing, is going to need someone to watch him in the night. Without a moment's hesitation, Grand offers: "I can very well stay with him. I can't say I really know him, but one's got to help a neighbor, hasn't one?"[11] It is as simple as that. "In a certain sense," Rieux later noted, "it might well be said that his was an exemplary life. He was one of those rare people . . . who have the courage of their good feelings."[12] Grand, who lived a little, solitary life and called no attention to himself, in the end receives the highest praise of all in *The Plague*:

> Grand was the true embodiment of the quiet courage that inspired the sanitary groups. He had said yes without a moment's hesitation and with the large-heartedness that was a second nature with him.[13]

For the Chambonnaise and for Joseph Grand, as for many members of the French Resistance and of Oran's sanitary groups, there was indeed not a moment's hesitation in listening to their hearts and doing the right thing. Still, for those who have never been put to such a test, or for those who have and failed, there remains the question, Why did they do it? "In searching for an explanation of the motivations of the Righteous Among the Nations," writes Moredecai Paldiel,**

---

* Grand was the surname of Camus's peasant friend who lived in Panelier.

** When he was three years old, Paldiel fled in 1940 with his family from Nazi-occupied Belgium via France to Switzerland.

are we not really saying: what was wrong with them? Are we not
in a deeper sense, implying that their behavior was something
other than normal? Is acting benevolently and altruistically such
an outlandish and unusual type of behavior, supposedly at odds
with man's inherent character, as to justify a meticulous search
for explanations? Or is it conceivable that such behavior is as
natural to our psychological constitution as the egoistic one we
accept so matter-of-factly?[14]

It may seem implausible that doing the right thing, acting with honor
and decency, is "natural" in the sense of "in our nature" as human beings,
when we consider the weight of evil in our world, in history, and in ourselves. Once again, Augustine both companioned and challenged Camus
as he pondered this question. While Camus found himself at fierce odds
with the "other Algerian's" doctrine of "original sin," he was far from naive
on the question of human corruption. With good reason, Camus took
Augustine seriously on the problem of evil, which is not to say that they
found a lot of common ground on the subject.

> The only great Christian mind that *faced* the problem of evil
> was St. Augustine. He drew from it the terrible *"nemo bonus."*
> Since then, Christianity has striven to give the problem tempo-
> rary solutions. The result is evident. . . . Men took their time,
> but today they are poisoned by an intoxication that has been
> going on for two thousand years. They are fed up with evil, or
> resigned, and this comes to the same thing. At least they can
> no longer accept lies on the subject.[15]

High on the list of lies that Camus categorically refused to accept was
Augustine's *nemo bonus*, the unequivocal assertion that "no one is good,"
from which it follows that there is no such thing as innate human decency.
The traditional Christian doctrine of universally inherited moral broken-
ness meant that no one can ever become whole and upright, much less

aspire to "saintliness" (as does Tarrou in *The Plague*), without the gift of unmerited divine grace, freely bestowed by God on those predestined for salvation. The most extreme extension of this doctrine that so outraged Camus throughout his life was the teaching that unbaptized children are denied redemption from the curse of original sin. It is no wonder that Camus—wrongfully labeled a "pessimist" by many—bristled at this label, particularly when it came from a Marxist or a Christian.

> By what right . . . could a Christian or a Marxist . . . accuse me of pessimism? I was not the one to invent the misery of the human being or the terrifying formulas of divine malediction. I was not the one to shout *Nemo Bonus* or the damnation of unbaptized children.[16] I was not the one who said that man was incapable of saving himself by his own means and that in the depths of his degradation his only hope was in the grace of God.[17]

The truth is that Camus, while he admired human decency, was never able to account for it, for right action rather than wrong action, for good deeds rather than misdeeds. He was not alone in this. Plato and Aristotle met with the same impasse. Why should anyone be just, or compassionate, rather than cruel and murderous? Reasons come readily to mind, as they have for thousands of years, but are they enough to be convincing?

What does it mean for common decency not to be common? This is the kind of question haunting truly moral people if they find themselves, for instance, in occupied France, the Warsaw ghetto, apartheid South Africa, the ruins of Homs, or most anywhere else, or if they read or watch the daily news. Without divine commands and sanctions, without "thou shalts" and "thou shalt nots," and without heaven and hell, why is anyone good? Or evil? Why should anyone be the one rather than the other? Aristotle wrote two books on the subject—*Nichomachean Ethics* and *Eudemian Ethics*—but these texts explain to good people why they are on the right track. They confirm decisions already made and lives already lived. They help people reflect on and understand themselves and each other. What they don't do is help people radically alter the course of their lives. Ethical philosophy in the ancient world was about enlightening people, not radically changing them. Ethics was not about "conversion" because conversion of wills was not thought possible, at least not on any significant scale. Anyone's moral character depended on how they were brought up and what decisions they made early on. Decency, put quite simply, was an acquired habit. It was about a person's "second nature" rather than a universal human nature. Telling the truth is "second nature" to someone who is in the habit of being truthful, just as lying is to a liar. Neither is "natural" as we ordinarily understand that term, which helps explain why common decency is anything but common.

The young Augustine, on the other hand, was all about conversion. He was lost. He knew how he had been living as a youth and then as a young adult, and he wanted to change—not just a little but a lot. He desperately desired to break the habits he had formed, to remake his life rather than simply understand it. He knew what he had to do, but he was unable to summon the will to do it. Fortunately for him, radical conversion lay at the center of Christianity, to which he now felt drawn. Augustine had discovered timeless truths in the Platonists, but for conversion he craved inspiring narratives, stories of lives reversed, remade. And he found them in the Christian scriptures and in the conversion narratives of early Christian saints: stories of the apostles, dropping their lives and all they were doing and following Jesus in response to a single word, "Come"; and the testimony of St. Paul, thrown from his horse and transformed from Christian scourge to Christian martyr. Augustine was particularly moved by the conversion story of Anthony the anchorite, who turned his back on everything and everyone he knew and walked off into the Egyptian desert to be with his God. Much closer to hand and heart for Augustine was the conversion story of his close and dear friend Alypius, with whom he identified in so many ways. It made him realize that "if Alypius did it, so can I."

Ancient moral philosophy offers reasons for living a certain way, and Christian theology warns what will happen if we don't. Personal testimonies, on the other hand, inspire and motivate positive life change. They show how it's done, step by step, which makes a change of path and character seem possible. Modern-day recovery programs—whether from alcoholism, drug or sex addiction, battle trauma, or uncontrolled anger—all make use of shared storytelling and reveal its power to foster the breaking of habits and the altering of lives. The *Confessions* of Augustine, which Camus knew well, is at its core a conversion narrative, the story of a life transformed. Augustine attributed his transformation to the call and grace of God, convinced that without them he would have remained lost. "I was altogether unwilling to entrust the care of my languishing soul," writes Augustine in the *Confessions*, "to the philosophers."[18] Only the God who created him could convert him. This was true, he believed, for all who converted: "He who made us also remade us."[19]

Camus, although he witnessed conversion in life and wrote about it in *The Plague*, did not believe that it was only possible with divine intervention or grace. He rejected Augustine's *nemo bonus* and asserted instead that "on the whole, men are more good than bad."[20] Wherever people start out in life, many, if not most, eventually find the will and the courage to do the right thing when confronted with true evil. Camus did not come to this conviction easily and questioned it frequently in his life; but in the end, without being able to construct an argument that was likely to convince others, he clung to it. The alternative was too unthinkable, too painful. Instead of writing a treatise on common decency, he told stories and wove them together in *The Plague*. All of the focal characters in *The Plague*, which is to say all of the core members of the sanitary groups, with the sole exception of Joseph Grand, owe their commitment to what might be called a conversion: Rieux, Tarrou, Rambert, and Paneloux. As we have seen, Grand undertakes his anti-plague efforts without hesitation and seemingly without giving it any thought. You don't have to ask a bird if it will fly. It's what it does. So for Grand. Doing the right thing, responding to a request for help, is what he does. It is who he is. Rieux and Tarrou, on the other hand, by their own accounts, had to discern their proper calling and then act on it. They could have followed a different course. Finally, for Rambert and Paneloux the decision to accept the moral challenges of living and working in a plague city and so to join the sanitary groups was more tortuous. They had to struggle with themselves to get there. Each of these figures and their stories represents a different face in the human community; Camus could recognize himself, with greater or lesser clarity, in all of them. Paraphrasing the words of the playwright Terence, *He was human and nothing human was foreign to him.*

The Stranger is about one man, Meursault, and it is only Meursault's inner voice that we hear in it. Meursault doesn't change his life because he sees no point or purpose in doing so. He makes decisions, because decisions are inescapable—to marry or not, to change jobs or not, to kill or not—but he sees nothing ultimately at stake in these or any decisions. This isn't to say that his life doesn't change, because the decisions he made had consequences for him. But to the end he remains indifferent, because he lives under an indifferent sky. The only radical change he undergoes is in consciousness. He becomes self-aware and consciously relates to himself, which enables him to relate to others in a way he never has before. He begins to emerge from solitude, but the guillotine cuts short any move into solidarity with others. In turning to *The Plague*, we are left to wonder where and in what incarnation we would find Meursault in the plague city of Oran. Would he still be an outlier, more of a stranger than he had ever been in Algiers? Would he remain consistent with his character, join the black market, and play the plague to his own benefit, perhaps in the end killing himself after killing others, still a murderer and now a suicide? Or would he, who had already come so far, come still further and embrace others in the common struggle to fight plague in all its forms? In moving from *The Stranger* to *The Plague*, from the Sisyphus Cycle to the Prometheus Cycle, I am convinced Camus wanted us to ponder such questions.

Just as *The Stranger* is a study in solitude, so *The Plague* is a celebration of solidarity. If *The Stranger* were music, it would be an a capella solo, whereas *The Plague* would be polyphony, a weaving of multiple simultaneous melodies or story lines into a single, harmonic whole. Reading *The Plague* closely in its full complexity involves following each story line start to finish and, at the same time, appreciating how they together form a community of purpose and commitment. Plague-ridden Oran, sealed off from the rest of the world, is like a prison, a city of cells. As Camus noted, "In practice, *there are nothing but solitary people in the novel.*"[21] More precisely, solitary men. Apart from Rieux's mother, there are no even semi-significant women within the walls; only men, and they are at least for now celibate, some by choice, others by circumstance. All of them, regardless of their years, are "veterans," a term derived from the Latin *vetus*: aged, old, literally old or just old before one's time, experienced beyond one's years, worn, worn out. "To grow old," Camus reflects in his *Notebooks*, "is to move from passion to compassion."[22] There is no sex in *The Plague*, only friendship. The only "couple" in the narrative is Rieux and Tarrou. Their brief but defining friendship takes the place of Meursault's abbreviated affair with Marie. This parallel is nowhere more transparent than in Part Four, when Rieux and Tarrou break their own quarantine rules and slip outside the city's walls to the sea to take a swim, for "friendship's sake."

> It's one of the harmless pleasures that even a saint-to-be can indulge in. . . . Really, it's too damn silly living only in and for the plague. Of course a man should fight for victims, but if he ceases caring for anything outside that, what's the use of his fighting?[23]

As with Meursault and Marie, swimming occasions their first moment of shared sensuousness. "For some minutes they swam side by side, with some zest, in the same rhythm, isolated from the world, and at last free of the town and of the plague."[24] In *The Stranger*, Meursault and Marie's swim was a prelude to their union as lovers. Here, Rieux and Tarrou's moonlit swim marks the culmination of their bond as friends. Either way it is a matter of communion.

Each of the central melodies in *The Plague* follows a similar pattern, from consciousness to activism. We hear or see, in real time or memory, how each of the plague fighters, again with the exception of Grand, came to plague consciousness and moved from there to taking action. Rieux and Tarrou each explains that he recognized the plague and resolved to resist it well before pestilence came to Oran and closed the city. Rieux was already a physician, under oath to do no harm and to attend to others' wounds and afflictions. This much is to be expected of a doctor. What Tarrou wondered at was the intense fervor with which Rieux gave himself to his calling. "Why," he asked Rieux, "do you yourself show such devotion, considering you don't believe in God?"* This is of urgent interest to Tarrou, who aspires beyond all else to be a "saint without God."[25] The point here for Rieux was that "if he believed in an all-powerful God, he would cease curing the sick and leave that to Him."[26] He was "outraged by the whole scheme of things" and was "fighting against creation as he found it."[27] What taught Rieux this was watching people suffer and die in an indifferent universe. The truth was just that simple and obdurate: "Men die and they are not happy,"[28] and Rieux's labors to resist its weight meant, like those of Sisyphus, "a never-ending defeat."[29]

Tarrou, too, as a young man *outraged by the scheme of things*, came to see that his world is "shaped by death." Not just by mortality, but even more outrageously by murder. This is the death that human beings—driven by hatred, greed, ambition, prejudice, ideology, and ignorance—inflict on each other, counting on a numberless supporting cast of indifferent bystanders. For Tarrou, the founder of the sanitary groups, "the most incorrigible vice" is "that of an ignorance that fancies it knows everything and therefore claims for itself the right to kill."[30] To his great horror, it was that same murderous ignorance that Tarrou, in his youth, found seething in his father, who "to all appearances was a kindly, good-natured man . . . a very decent man as men go."[31] Tarrou's father, an esteemed prosecuting attorney, apart from mastering the French criminal code, obsessively studied train schedules and committed them to memory. Not that he was a frequent traveler, any more than he was a criminal. He dwelt happily in a world of abstractions, and in the satisfaction that trains ran on time and that the wheels of justice turned smoothly.

The day Jean Tarrou lost his "innocence," as well as his reverence for his father, was when his father invited seventeen-year-old Jean to see him at work

---

* Camus, *The Plague*, p. 116. Though directed to Rieux, Tarrou's question seems aimed at Augustine, who maintained that no one can be good (*"nemo bonus"*) without the grace of God.

and hear him address the court in a front-page murder trial. In the courtroom, the sight of the defendant—a young man obviously horrified by what he had done and by what would likely be done to him—suddenly shattered Tarrou's comfortably abstract notions of justice at work. He saw only a "living human being" and men in robes bent on killing him. Then Tarrou's father rose to speak. This was the moment his father had wanted him to witness.

> In his red gown he was another man, no longer genial or good-natured; his mouth spewed out long, turgid phrases like an endless stream of snakes. I realized he was clamoring for the prisoner's death, telling the jury that they owed it to society to find him guilty; he went so far as to demand that the man should have his head cut off.[32]

From that day on, Tarrou viewed his father's railway directories with disgust and took "a horrified interest in legal proceedings, death sentences, [and] executions."* Fixated on the death penalty and the social order organized around it, Tarrou set out on a life of engagement aimed at opposing any law, idea, belief, or institution that advocated or justified murder. His plague was the human death machine, and he knew that he was complicit in its workings. He, like everyone else, was infected with it.

> I came to understand that I . . . had had plague . . . I had had an indirect hand in the deaths of thousands of people; that I'd even brought about their deaths by approving of acts and principles which could only end that way.[33]

With that haunting realization, Tarrou lost his peace and began his scrupulous pursuit of secular sanctity, a sanctity without divine forgiveness

---

* Camus, *The Plague*, p. 225. One of the few stories Camus's mother ever told him about his father concerned a public execution he had witnessed and how it had horrified his father. He rushed home, said nothing, lay down, and vomited. See Camus's "Reflections on a Guillotine" in *Resistance, Rebellion, and Death*, p. 132.

or grace. He resolved to rid himself any way he could of the plague and to do nothing to infect others, never joining forces with the myriad murderous agents of pestilence. Like Dr. Rieux, he would walk instead "the path of sympathy"[34] in the hope of attaining peace.

The last two of the narrative's focal plague fighters—Rambert and Father Paneloux—undergo their "conversions" before our eyes, as it were. When the state of plague is declared in Oran and the city is shut off from the world, neither of these men is prepared to take a stand against the death stalking the streets. For very different reasons, they don't see resistance as their fight, and both focus on escape. Neither feels he really "belongs" here, in the struggle. Rambert finds himself trapped in plague-ridden Oran by accident, and he wants out, to return home to his lover and the life he has lost. His happiness lies outside these walls, far away, and regaining it is all he cares about. As a news reporter, he "covers" others' sufferings and losses, harvesting his stories from them and leaving untouched, unscathed. This time, however, he has lost his footing and fallen into his story.

After multiple abortive attempts to find a way out of Oran and back to his life, Rambert came to realize that resisting the plague was everyone's business. He never renounced his pursuit of happiness. He only postponed and shared it. He saw that his desire for a full and happy life was inseparable from the same desire in everyone else. He wasn't the only person in Oran suffering from separation and loss. When he learned of Rieux's separation from his wife and of her death, Rambert felt ashamed of himself and said so, but Rieux assured him that "there was nothing shameful in preferring happiness." Rambert's response to Rieux's graciousness revealed just how far he had come since arriving in Oran: "Certainly . . . but it may be shameful to be happy by oneself."[35] So, in the end, Rambert took a share in others' happiness, joined the plague fighters, and, in doing so, walked in the footsteps of Jan in *The Misunderstanding*, except that he never lied or played games and so found his way back to the life and love he had lost.

Paneloux, on the other hand, is an Augustine scholar and a Jesuit priest. The evil he encounters in his study of Augustine is abstract, sterile, and far from infectious, compared to the street version. Evil in Augustine's theology is the dark fruit of sin. Sin is the problem, not death. Without sin, death has no sting. All that the afflicted people of Oran needed to do, as Paneloux understood their plight, was to repent of their sins and "God would see to the rest."[36] In preaching this message of blind faith and passive acceptance, Paneloux not only distanced himself from the sanitary groups but undermined their efforts. His was precisely the stance taken by many of the Christian clergy and hierarchy in Occupied France. After the French armistice with Germany, Paneloux's first sermon could be heard not just from the fictional pulpit in Oran's cathedral but from myriad pulpits across wartime France.

What shattered Paneloux's confident diagnosis of suffering and death as the wages of sinfulness was the torturous death of a young child, whose sinfulness even Paneloux, armed with Augustine's *nemo bonus*, was unable to maintain. Fiercely confronted and challenged by Rieux, Paneloux joined the plague fighters and labored side by side with the other members of the sanitary groups. This fight was his after all, as evidenced in his second sermon when he came down from his elevated pulpit and stood among the people of Oran, using the pronoun "we" instead of pointing his finger at them with the pronoun "you." He was one of them now. Paneloux never lost his faith, and neither Rieux nor Tarrou ever embraced it; but now—at one in the common human struggle against death and suffering—nothing could separate them.

This war and reconciliation between Rieux and Paneloux—and, by extension, between Camus and Christianity—leave us with many questions to address, which will happen in the next chapters, as we move from resistance to revolution and then turn to *The Rebel*, the philosophical and historical companion volume to *The Plague*. For now, to bring these reflections on *The Plague* to a tentative end and to provide a toothing-stone to what follows, we might ponder a brief entry in Camus's *Notebooks* after the war as he was turning to *The Rebel*:

> According to the Egyptians, the just man must be able to say after his death: "I have not caused suffering to anyone. Otherwise he is punished."[37]

CHAPTER NINE

Revolution

I began the war of 1939 as a pacifist and I finished it as a Résistant. That inconsistency . . . has rendered me more modest."[1] Truth be told, Camus's "inconsistency" was a good deal more complicated than this brief postwar admission reveals. After all, he attempted to enlist in the French forces in 1939 but was rejected as medically unfit for military service. Otherwise, he might have found himself entrenched on the Maginot Line awaiting the German Wehrmacht. In his willingness to take up arms, Camus had not lost or renounced his deep abhorrence of killing or his pacifist inclination. It was just that, as he put it, "a man may go to war without consenting to war."[2] From his admittedly diminutive colonial podium, Camus had advocated and argued for international disarmament and European unity, but there was no stopping the imminent storm in the north whose surge would soon swamp all of Europe. In November 1939 Camus voiced his own distress in what he entitled a "Letter to a Man in Despair":

> You write that you are overwhelmed by the war, that you would agree to die, but that what you cannot bear is the universal stupidity, this bloodthirsty cowardice, and this criminal simple mindedness which still believes that human problems can be solved by the shedding of blood.[3]

Denied a place in the army of the Third Republic and thus spared a front-row seat in the disastrous Battle of France, Camus eventually made his way into the ranks of the Resistance. We are able to follow the nature and path of his active engagement once he relocated to occupied Paris, in the summer of 1943, and began living two lives, one "in the open" as an editor for Gallimard and a celebrated literary and theatrical figure, and the other "underground" as Albert Mathé, editor of *Combat*, a clandestine newspaper whose first subversive issue appeared in December 1941. Camus's war would be, in the years ahead, a war waged with words, grounded in "the belief that in the end words will prove stronger than bullets."[4]

Combat and a host of other Resistance publications were pivotal in the war—armed and unarmed—against the Nazi occupation and its Vichy collaborators. Written, printed, and distributed at great personal risk, these broadsheets and flyers contradicted fascist claims that the war was over and resistance was futile. In the face of Nazi propaganda, the underground press sought to reassure the people of France that the Resistance was alive and active, hiding in plain sight, ever ready to strike from the shadows, and committed to making the occupation a growing nightmare for the Germans. Together, these publications formed a crucial battle line against the Nazi effort to control the minds and break the will of the French. They served to inform, rally, and sustain the will of the people to defeat the fascist forces; and, at the same time, they strove to inspire the French populace to envision and commit themselves to a future, postwar France, more just, fair, and free than the France that had so fundamentally betrayed its people and lost its soul.

From March 1944 to November 1945, Camus penned front-page editorials for *Combat*, and it was in this persona as journalist—not as novelist, philosopher, playwright, or director—that most people knew him, though not by face or his actual name until the liberation. In his role as editorialist, Camus became one of the most influential and revered voices of the Resistance. His voice, unlike that of many others, often transcended politics and strategy to address matters of the spirit. "In other words," as Camus wrote in September 1944, "we are determined to replace politics with morality.

That is what we call a revolution."[5] And it was the morality, or immorality, of killing that most preoccupied and burdened him during the war years and for the remainder of his life.

> The only really serious moral problem is murder. The rest comes after. But to find out whether or not I can kill this person in my presence, or agree to his being killed, to find that I know nothing before finding out whether or not I can cause death, that is what must be learned.[6]

France and all of Europe were drenched in blood; and virtually no one, if they'd been honest with themselves, could have claimed to have had clean hands. Whether perpetrator or bystander, armed or unarmed, vocal or silent, everyone was conscripted into what Hobbes had centuries earlier coined "the war of all against all."

One of Camus's first and foremost concerns in *Combat* was to draw a line or make a distinction between the aggressor and the aggressed, between those who took up arms with fervor and those who did so reluctantly, as a last resort. For Camus and others like him in the Resistance, the road to war was a disastrous detour that led nowhere they wanted to go. The most that could be hoped for was to finish it and then recover what would remain of their country and their lives. Far from entertaining visions of glorious victory and world dominance, they had to witness savage death and great suffering before they were willing to inflict either. "It took us all that time to find out if we had the right to kill men, if we were allowed to add to the frightful misery of this world."[7]

For Camus this meant accepting Machiavelli's perception that in any contest between "armed prophets" and "unarmed prophets," the armed prophets always prevail, while the unarmed prophets invariably come to ruin.[8] Camus was quick to point out, however, that there was more to be seen and said about contests between "prophets."

> . . . contrary to what we sometimes think, the spirit is of no avail against the sword, but . . . the spirit together with the sword will

always win out over the sword alone. . . . I have never believed
in the power of truth in itself. But . . . when expressed forcefully
truth wins out over falsehood.[9]

In *The Plague*, friendship emerged as the morally compelling bond
between all human beings, echoing a humanistic tradition that resonated through ancient literature from Gilgamesh to Homer, Euripides,
and Augustine. Camus had a special gift for forming and honoring friendships, and he found it excruciating when trust between friends broke down.
He spoke to this pain in the first of his "Letters to a German Friend,"
when he lamented,

We had to stifle our passion for friendship. Now we have done
that. We had to make a long detour, and we are far behind.[10]

Camus made it clear in his wartime writings that he never saw or
embraced violence and murder as a way forward. Rather, it was a way of
holding ground, saving lives, and eventually being able to start over. With
all the irresistible force of gravity, Camus was drawn throughout his life
toward international fellowship and pacifism.

As the scales of war tipped toward an Allied victory and Nazi defeat, it
became both possible and imperative to look to the future, to imagine what
France could and should be when no longer flattened under the German
boot. *Combat*'s masthead—*From Resistance to Revolution*—had, from the
start, looked to this transition, to the necessity of postwar transformation.
Pushing rewind to reinstate the *status quo ante bellum* was not only magical
thinking; it was repugnant. The Third Republic had not merely fallen to
a vastly superior enemy force. The rest of Europe had done that—suffered
defeat—but France had cut a deal. Uniquely and shamefully, France had
formed a pact with Germany, embraced its agenda, betrayed its own
people, and turned its back on its allies. The French elite, politicians,
bankers, industrialists, clergy, journalists, and cultural icons—not all,
but in shocking numbers—had conveniently collaborated with the Nazi

occupation to preserve their privileges and status. Then, eschewing the high road, a trail of minions had fallen in behind them, doing what was needed to enforce and advance the new normal.

The diverse consortium of anarchists, communists, academics, aristocrats, poets, émigrés, Catholics, Jews, Muslims, and others who locked arms in the Resistance was far less numerous than the Vichy collaborators and their silent majority. During the occupation, for obvious reasons, Résistants could not be counted. They were phantoms, at once everywhere and nowhere. Before the liberation, no Résistant could afford to be outed, whereas after the liberation nearly everyone in France outed themselves and, truly or falsely, boasted what they had done for the Resistance. The truth, however, seems to be that a solid 90 percent of the French population had either openly supported the collaborationist Vichy regime or else kept their heads down and stayed clear of any active involvement in the Resistance. Speaking from within the Resistance and as someone who had put his life at risk daily, Camus generously commented that no one who survived those years, including himself, had done enough. Only the dead could claim that.

Camus was not inclined to accuse or judge those who had remained silent and done nothing, those who had clung to their lives and the lives of their loved ones, taking no risks and perpetrating no crimes.* There was another cohort, however, neither bystanders nor Résistants, who had innocent blood on their hands. These were the informers, the murderers, the torturers, the French Malitia (*Milice*), the political leaders of the Third Republic, the traitors of Vichy, the collaborators, the myriad infected enablers who had spread the "brown plague" to their own advantage and the death of others. Their crimes could not be overlooked or go unpunished. In his editorials, Camus called for a revisioning, a remaking of France, a revolution, not a return to the good old days, because those days had not been good for the poor and underprivileged, the working class, immigrants, and the colonized

---

* Here we may well recall the kindness of Rieux toward Rambert, assuring him that there is nothing shameful in preferring happiness to heroism, leaving it to Rambert to question and accuse himself. See *The Plague*, p. 188.

in Africa, Indochina, and the Pacific. Résistants had not suffered and died only to reinstate the same self-serving politicians and discredited ruling class that had handed over the country to the Germans.

France, as Camus and countless Resistance comrades saw it, needed cleansing before it could be reborn. Already, across France, there were makeshift trials and summary executions of notorious, or in some cases not-so-notorious, collaborators. Camus proposed swift and evenhanded justice that would honor rather than forget the victims of Vichy and Nazi betrayals and atrocities. He had never supported vigilantism or personal vendetta. Two months after the liberation of Paris, he made his position clear:

> We have never called for blind or precipitous justice. We detest arbitrary judgment and criminal stupidity, and we would prefer that France keep her hands clean. But to that end we want justice to be prompt, and we want all prosecution for crimes of collaboration to end at some fixed date. We want the most obvious crimes to be punished immediately, and then, since nothing can be done without mediocrity, we want the errors that so many Frenchmen have indeed committed consigned to carefully considered oblivion. [11]

In the national purge (*l'épuration legalé*) that followed, the severity of punishment would, in theory, match the gravity of the crime. For the most heinous crimes, there would be execution. While Camus never stopped believing that "every death sentence is an affront to morality,"[12] he argued in 1944 that what France needed was a Saint-Just, not a Talleyrand. In the early months of the purge, the first execution was that of Georges Suarez, a writer and journalist. Among his crimes were endorsing the German occupation, editing a French newspaper (*Aujourd'hui*) under Nazi control, and writing Pétain's biography—crimes that were no match for the villainy of so many others. Nevertheless, Camus acquiesced in his execution with these words:

We have no taste for murder. The human person embodies all
that we respect in the world. Our instinctive response to this
sentence is therefore one of repugnance. It would be easy for
us to say that our business is not to destroy men but simply to
do something for the good of the country. In fact, however, we
have learned since 1939 that we would betray the good of the
country if we acted on this impulse. [13]

Having called for revolution, Camus countenanced revolutionary justice for a limited period so that the nation could move on—justice that
was swift, decisive, and pitiless. His most vocal and vehement opponent
in this policy was François Mauriac, a prolific poet, novelist, critic, and
playwright, who went on to win the Nobel Prize for Literature in 1952,
five years before Camus followed him to Stockholm. More to the point
of their public confrontation in late 1944 was the fact that Mauriac was a
devout Catholic who opposed the death penalty and advocated mercy and
forgiveness, rather than pitiless, revolutionary justice.

The debate between Mauriac and Camus, conducted in the editorial
pages of *Le Figaro* and *Combat*, began with Mauriac's October 19, 1944
article entitled "Justice and War." Camus responded the very next day in
Combat, agreeing with Mauriac that there was more to France than the
Resistance and that there was no need "to gun down our fellow citizens
at street corners," but parting ways where, as Camus put it, "the force of
revolutions joins with the light of justice . . . and . . . we will be obliged to
destroy a living part of this country in order to save its soul." [14] As a devout
Catholic, Mauriac had a very different understanding of salvation, personal
and national. For Camus it was all about justice, and for Mauriac it was
all about mercy. As a Christian, Mauriac insisted that it was not his role
to condemn, to which Camus answered that it was precisely because he
was not a Christian that it was his duty not to forgive. If anyone had that
right, insisted Camus, it was the loved ones of those who had been tortured
and killed because of or by the accused. "A Christian," wrote Camus on
October 25, 1944,

may believe that human justice is always supplemented by divine justice, hence that indulgence is always preferable. But we invited M. Mauriac to consider the dilemma of those to whom the notion of divine judgement is foreign yet who retain a taste for man and hope for his grandeur. They must either hold their peace or become converts to human justice. [15]

In fact, both felt repugnance at the purge's adoption of capital punishment. Mauriac saw it as a sin, while Camus saw it as a dark duty to the dead.

At this point there could be no meeting of minds between Mauriac and Camus. Theirs was a complex clash of generations, beliefs, politics, and personalities. What got lost in their mutual acrimony was all that they actually had in common,* beginning with the fact that they had each served in the Resistance. Regrettably, both writers were highly skilled in weaponizing words and inflicting wounds that made any reconciliation or consensus seem unlikely. All that changed in a matter of months, however, as the purge persisted beyond any "fixed date," spreading like a virus and infecting the nation. In a hollow mockery of the justice Camus had promoted, judgments were often blatantly biased and sentences shockingly inequitable. Trials produced "absurd sentences and preposterous instances of leniency." [16] As Camus admitted in August 1945: "The word 'purge' itself was already rather distressing. The actual thing became odious. . . . The failure is complete." [17] This failure made Camus reject once and for all the death penalty, convincing him that avenging the dead was no way to remember them. The way to honor the fallen was not to commit murder in their name but to disavow murder in all its forms. Now a born-again pacifist, Camus confessed on January 5, 1945, less than three months after his quarrel with his Catholic opponent began, that "M. Mauriac was right. We are going to need charity." [18] An even more convincing indication of

---

* There was much for Camus to admire in Mauriac's life, such as the fact that Mauriac condemned the Catholic church's support for Franco, joined the Resistance in 1941, opposed French rule in Vietnam, condemned the use of torture by the French army in Algeria, and wrote the foreword to Elie Wiesel's Holocaust memoir *Night*.

Camus's re-conversion to pacifism was the fact that he joined François Mauriac in opposing the execution of Robert Brassilach, whose egregious wartime crimes far exceeded any offenses committed by Georges Suarez, whose execution Camus had supported in 1944, at the start of the purge. Many of the most eminent literary figures in France also signed on to Mauriac's petition to Charles de Gaulle to commute Brassilach's death sentence. They were ignored, however, and Brassilach stood before a firing squad on February 6, 1945, shouting "Long live France" moments before he died.

Brasillach's France, however, was what Camus hoped he and his fellow Résistants would leave behind. On August 21, 1944, after four years of German occupation, the battle for liberation raged in the streets of Paris. The end was in sight, and *Combat*, "in a Paris liberated from shame," was able "to appear at last in the light of day."[19] Speaking for himself and his comrades in the Resistance, Camus wrote that having begun with resistance, it was time to move on to revolution:

> We want without delay to institute a true people's and workers'
> democracy. . . . In the present state of affairs, such a program
> goes by the name "Revolution." This can probably be achieved
> in a calm and orderly fashion, but it is the price that must be
> paid if France is to regain the pure countenance that we loved
> and defended above all.[20]

The Third Republic, in Camus's eyes, had failed to represent and protect the people of France. It was a government neither of the people nor for the people. "To live with one's back to a wall is a dog's life. But people of my generation and of the generation just now taking its place in factories and classrooms have lived and are living more and more like dogs."[21] France was infested with rot, and it had to be remade, not merely reformed. To this end, we have already seen how Camus supported a purge to remove the rot, honor the fallen, restore justice, and reclaim the integrity of a sullied nation.

We have also seen how soon and how badly the purge went awry, only adding to the national shame it was meant to address. Rather than uniting a nation in recovery, the purge further divided it. At the same time, as soon as France was free to redefine itself, the life-and-death solidarity of the Resistance began to dissolve. The bond that had held Résistants of every stripe together suddenly snapped when their common enemy wasn't there to focus on and fight. Partisan discord broke out in the ranks, and personal ambitions trampled the public good. Communists, whose contributions to the Resistance had been so pivotal, refused to cooperate in a common effort, while others sought to marginalize or exclude them altogether. Camus—neither Communist nor anti-Communist—spoke instead for the non-Communist Left and regarded himself as a "democrat," which he defined as "a person who admits that his adversary may be right, who therefore allows him to speak, and who agrees to consider his arguments."[22] Camus soon came to the conclusion that "Marxists do not believe in persuasion or in dialogue,"[23] and he was unwilling to sacrifice freedom for their flimsy assurances of future justice. Justice without freedom, as Camus saw it, described a prison cell. "I choose freedom," Camus wrote in his *Notebooks*. "For even if justice is not realized, freedom maintains the power of protest against injustice and keeps communication open."[24] For all its imperfections, Camus saw democracy as the only viable way ahead for a fractured France and fractious world. "There may be no good political regime, but democracy is surely the least bad of the alternatives."[25]

The reality that Camus confronted and had to accept in postwar France was that the Resistance was over and revolution was not on the table. The Resistance had sacrificed and suffered for years, only to bring back the same flawed republic, the same corrupt ruling class, the same self-serving bureaucrats. The *Combat* masthead—*From Resistance to Revolution*—had been wishful thinking. Instead of dialogue, discord prevailed. Camus concluded from this failure that "we had yet to find the words needed to bring us together, words that would have united us without requiring us to renounce our differences."[26] Disillusioned but not despairing, on September 1, 1945, one year after the liberation of France, Camus signed off as a *Combat* editorialist with these words:

> Our idea was not . . . to rival Marx and Christ. It was not our
> intention to make fools of ourselves. Being neither Communists
> nor Christians, we simply wanted to make dialogue possible by
> pointing out differences and highlighting similarities. In this
> respect, our year of work has ended in abject failure. [27]

Camus, who had grown and flourished in the intense fraternity of the
Resistance, suddenly found himself more isolated than he had perhaps ever
been. He was used to being at the center of things, not looking in from
the margins. The world had stumbled from one war into another—from a
world war against fascist aggression into a cold war that threated the planet
with extinction. Instead of disarming and sowing the seeds of a lasting
peace, the world was preparing for a future cataclysmic confrontation with
weapons of unimaginable destruction.

Unable to embrace any political party or ideology, Camus stepped back
from the public arena and "decided to suppress politics in order to replace
it with ethics." [28] He saw his world becoming every day more murderous,
more inclined to silence opponents than to listen to them, a world in which
force had replaced persuasion.

> We have witnessed lying, humiliation, killing, deportation, and
> torture, and in each instance it was impossible to persuade the
> people who were doing these things not to do them, because
> they were sure of themselves and because there is no way of per-
> suading an abstraction, or, to put it another way, the representa-
> tive of an ideology. . . . The long dialogue among human beings
> has now come to an end. . . . Between the very general fear of
> a war for which everyone is preparing and the very specific fear
> of lethal ideologies, it is therefore quite true that we live in
> terror. . . . We gasp for air among people who believe they are
> absolutely right, whether it be in their machines or their ideas.
> And for all who cannot live without dialogue and the friendship
> of other human beings, this silence is the end of the world. [29]

After the purge had failed and the revolution vaporized, Camus's "agenda" focused on ethics rather than politics. Rather than create or promote a political party or movement, his concern was to create community—human community—beyond any walls or borders, aspiring "to do battle within the historical arena in order to save from history that part of man which does not belong to it."[30]

> What I think needs to be done at the present time is simply this: in the midst of a murderous world, we must decide to reflect on murder and choose. If we can do this, then we will divide ourselves into two groups: those who if need be would be willing to commit murder or become accomplices to murder, and those who would refuse to do so with every fiber of their being.[31]

Once again, as he had at various points in his life, Camus was evolving. In the next several years, he turned inward and began to craft two works— *The Rebel* and *The Just*—that would make him an outcast and cost him many friends. At the same time, he discovered a new friend who helped light his way, an unlikely soul mate who confirmed him in the path he was on. Regrettably, she had already died, which did not diminish her effect on him, "for one can feel as close to a dead person as to a living one."[32] She was, in Camus's eyes, "the only great spirit of our times."[33] In her thirty-four years, Simone Weil had been many things: a prodigious scholar of ancient literature and philosophy, a champion of the working class, a veteran of the anarchist Durutti Column in the Spanish Civil War, a factory worker, and a religious mystic. At age ten she announced she was a Bolshevik and at age twenty-eight she experienced her first mystical experience. Like Camus she contracted tuberculosis, rejected Marxism and the oppressive Russian state, and envisioned a nonviolent revolution that would preserve the peace, establish both liberty and social justice, honor the dignity of work, and respect the needs of the soul. Weil, a Jew, and Camus, a "pagan,"[34] acknowledged the sacred and were drawn to it. Each of them lingered on the threshold of the Catholic church but in the end declined baptism.

When in 1948, three years after Weil's death, Camus first read the manuscript of her masterwork, *L'Enracinement* (published in English as *The Need for Roots*), he found in it both inspiration and confirmation at a time when he was in need of both. He saw in Weil's writing both a critique of Marx and a way forward for the revolution he had sought to promote, commenting that it was "impossible to imagine the rebirth of Europe without taking into consideration the suggestions outlined in it by Simone Weil."[35] *L'Enracinement* contained the fullest expression of Weil's political philosophy, even as Camus was laboring to craft his own. It may not be an overstatement to say that she became for him a muse and a companion. In all, Camus edited eight of Weil's books for the Gallimard *Espoir* series that Camus directed. We may sense how deeply Weil's voice resonated in Camus when we read how she described what it would mean to be rooted, and to live in a community where the needs of the soul are met:

> To be rooted is perhaps the most important and least recognized need of the human soul. It is one of the hardest to define. A human being has roots by virtue of his real, active, and natural participation in the life of a community, which preserves in living shape certain particular treasures of the past and certain particular expectations for the future. This participation is a natural one, in the sense that it is automatically brought about by place, conditions of birth, profession, and social surroundings. Each human being needs to have multiple roots. It is necessary for him to draw well-nigh the whole of his moral, intellectual, and spiritual life by way of the environment of which he forms a natural part.[36]

Camus cited Simone Weil only several times in his writings, but her presence and influence are evident throughout *The Rebel*. We know from Weil's mother that Camus, until shortly before his fatal car crash, frequently visited the Paris apartment in which Simone had been raised until her family fled to Britain and to which her mother returned after the war.

As Camus edited one after another of Weil's posthumous manuscripts for publication, he discussed them with her mother and consulted her on various points. Camus's most remarkable and poignant visit to the childhood home of Simone Weil occurred on the day before he flew to Sweden to receive the Nobel Prize. He went there to "collect his thoughts"[37] and to request a photo of Simone Weil to take with him to Stockholm. In further recognition of his close bond with the woman who in 1943, shortly before her death, sent an anonymous letter to de Gaulle and signed it *un résistant intellectual,*

> Camus made mention in Stockholm of his intimate ties to Weil. When asked by a reporter which writers he felt closest to, Camus named the poet René Char and Simone Weil. When the journalist observed that Weil was dead, Camus replied that death never comes between true friends.[38]

In his Nobel acceptance speech, Camus spoke of the responsibilities of the writer and acknowledged his "limits and debts."[39] Surely among those debts was what he owed to Simone Weil, whose words doubtlessly shed light on and sustained the years in which he labored his way through *The Rebel,* to which we turn next.

CHAPTER TEN

Rebellion

I n the years following the liberation, Camus was in retreat on several fronts. The war and its murderous aftermath left him scarred and disheartened. The purge divided and poisoned France, the fellowship he had known in the Resistance disintegrated, and no one showed up for the liberal, nonviolent socialist revolution he had envisioned. More personally, he struggled with his health, his marriage, and his friends. He stopped writing editorials for *Combat* and, in 1947, left the paper altogether. He began his withdrawal from politics and public life and went inward, to study, think, and write. There was nowhere else for him to go. He had seen the war as a monstrous detour, a road to nowhere, and the ideological highways laid down across Europe and the world led nowhere he wanted to go. In theory, communism led to collective social justice, and capitalism led to boundless personal freedom. Both, in Camus's eyes, led to death, of body and of soul. The choice between them amounted to a choice between death by hanging and death by firing squad. In other words, to no choice at all. To a world deadlocked in Cold War and a nuclear countdown threatening the world with extinction, Camus for the moment had nothing to say except no. No to both.

Like Augustine, his ancient mentor, Camus had become a question to himself, a question directed at his nature as a human being. It was his species that troubled him. As he put it, "In the forties I had ... found myself face-to-face with men whose acts I did not understand. To put it briefly, I did not understand that men could torture others without ever ceasing to look at them."[1] Was indifference to the suffering of others, the readiness to inflict pain and death without qualm or remorse, a grotesque aberration or rather a useful skill, more easily learned than unlearned? How could anyone dismiss the atrocities of totalitarian terror and total war as abnormal deviations, given their bewildering scale: more than seventy-five million war dead, with countless others wishing they were? The German death camps from 1940 through 1945, on any given day, provided an experience of incomprehensible hell for a million inmates, while the Soviet camps consistently "housed" somewhere between ten and twenty-five million lost souls. Mass murder and psychopathic brutality—far from mutant anomalies—were mainstream, too close for comfort to the human core.[*] What Camus had come to realize but not accept was that

> crime could be reasoned, could turn its system into power, spread its cohorts over the whole world, conquer and rule. In other words, Camus found it impossible to understand that crime could be not only organized but rationally justified and legalized.[2]

Far from a monstrous exception, murder is the order of the day. "Camus formulates against the modern world the same indictment as Tolstoy. For Camus, as for Tolstoy, modern society does not recognize any other norm than violence and the accomplished fact, hence it can legitimately be said that it is founded on the murder."[3] For Camus, interrogating the murderousness that comes all too easily to our species was inseparable from envisaging an alternative way of living with others that would never justify, much less institutionalize, murder. War, armed revolution, capital

---

[*] "We used to wonder where war lived, what it was that made it so vile. And now we realize that we know where, that it is inside ourselves." Camus, *Notebooks 1935–1942*, p. 141.

punishment, and institutionalized violence were simply off the table for Camus. They were dead ends, however inevitable they appeared and familiar they had become. He was unwilling to embrace either freedom without justice or justice without freedom. Both were unacceptable. While Sartre and a number of Camus's other friends on the liberal left in France had made a devil's bargain with Stalinist Russia, convinced that Communism represented the world's best, if flawed, chance for achieving social justice, Camus had come to see Bolshevist Communism as humanity's worst enemy,* a totalitarian state analogous to Hitler's National Socialism. This view would cost Camus many of his friends and leave him isolated.

> After saying one day that . . . I could no longer accept any truth
> that might place me under an obligation, direct or indirect, to
> condemn a man to death, various people whose intelligence I
> respect told me that I was living in utopia, that there was no
> political truth that might not someday lead to such an extremity,
> and that one was obliged either to run that risk or to accept the
> world as it is.[4]

Camus's critics had a point. Camus was indeed living in a utopia, but not one they understood or appreciated. Camus's utopia, like Plato's republic, was short on brick and mortar, but rich in truth, a community without walls that has long outlived him and his peers. In fact, the analogy with Plato sheds revealing light on Camus's postwar struggles and endeavors, and helps us to better understand his retreat from the political arena, not only to create fiction or drama but most urgently to explain himself, to construct

---

* In his *Notebooks*, Camus had made a list of "what the collaborationist left approves of, passes over in silence or considers inevitable." His "open list" included: "the deportation of tens of thousands of Greek children . . . the physical disposal of the Russian peasant class . . . the millions of people in concentration camps . . . political abductions . . . near daily political executions . . . Anti-Semitism . . ." See *Notebooks 1951–1959*, pp. 87–88. Camus, *Combat*, p. 260.

an argument, and (as Plato's critics put it) to "daydream."* Camus's political vision and expectations had long struck many of his contemporaries as so impractical, so idealistic, that they amounted to wishful thinking. Camus was no politician. Ideas and words were what he brought to the task of revisioning postwar France, Europe, and the world. He eventually came to understand and more or less accept what he could contribute and what he could not.

> My role . . . is not to transform the world nor mankind. I have not enough virtue nor sufficient wisdom for that. But it is perhaps to serve, in my place, those few values without which a world, even transformed, isn't worth living in, without which a man, even new, is not worthy of respect.[5]

Living in a murderously corrupt world and accepting how little he could do to make his world over or better did not come easily to Camus, any more than it did to Plato. The parallels between them in this regard are closer than one might imagine. Plato, like Camus, lived in tumultuous, war-ravaged times, in a city that had been occupied by the enemy and then emerged ferociously divided. Plato was roughly twenty when he met Socrates and his life changed course. His interest and engagement in politics waned as a new flame flickered in him. With Socrates as his teacher, Plato turned to philosophy, to the pursuit of the good, the true, and the beautiful. Then, in Plato's twenty-ninth year, his life and world went dark on the day the city he loved murdered his mentor, the man he most revered, the embodiment of all he believed in and aspired to. Fleeing Athens in fear and despair, Plato took time off, nearly twenty years' worth, wandering widely in the Mediterranean world, sojourning in Egypt, North Africa, Sicily, and southern Italy.

---

* See Plato's *Republic*, 540d. The Greek word here (εὐχή) means a "mere wish," a "prayer," an "aspiration," or, as I suggest, a "daydream."

Plato was convinced that the violence and corruption he had witnessed in Athens would never cease there or anywhere unless wisdom, virtue, and political power were somehow to converge. Only when a philosopher, a lover of wisdom, becomes king or a king becomes a philosopher could there be enduring peace and justice without resort to violence, bloodshed, war, or executions. A daydream if there ever was one. Yet Plato thought he had glimpsed the possibility of such a rare and unlikely convergence in the royal court of Syracuse, where he became the mentor of a virtuous, keen-minded young prince named Dion, in whom the love of truth burned bright. While Plato never fully gave up on that dream, nothing ever came of it in either the short or the long run. In 380 B.C.E., in his late forties, he finally returned to Athens.

Camus, too, in his own version of Platonic despair over the murderous folly all around him, took time out to recover his health, clear his mind, and restore his soul. His widest travels took him to the United States, Canada, and South America; closer to home he returned to Algeria and vacationed in Provence, where he would eventually find a home and his final resting place. Meanwhile he was writing what he saw as his greatest work, the one he felt most closely resembled himself. Here, too, he was following, perhaps unwittingly, in the footsteps of Plato. Neither Camus nor Plato ever founded, ruled, or helped govern a polity of any sort. What each of them did do was found a city, as it were, of the spirit, a city of ideas and words that would likely never take shape in a republic or prevail in politics but might help prevent or forestall the extinction of all that is human in us. If indeed wisdom is a matter of recollection, the *Republic* of Plato and Camus's *The Rebel* remind us of our common humanity and of all that we owe to each other on that account.

When Plato returned to Athens after nearly twenty years adrift, he founded the Academy, a place of dialogue and reflection, not debate and action, a house of truth, not power. Several years later, Plato shed crucial light on his founding of the Academy and its significance when he wrote the *Republic*, a book focused on justice, as is *The Rebel*. In it, Plato made clear the esoteric nature of the only sort of "city" that lovers of justice and wisdom might realistically establish and inhabit—a commonwealth of the mind, a school. In Book Four of the *Republic*,* Socrates turns to his star pupil, Glaucon, and announces that they've done just that. In dialogue with Socrates and each other, the small circle of truth-seeking interlocutors** have founded the city of their dreams, of their highest aspirations and best thoughts. It is there, invisible to the eye, encircling them. It *is* them. In other words, Plato's Academy is the closest embodiment of the just city, representing not the convergence of wisdom and power but rather the shared pursuit of wisdom without power.

The Academy and the *Republic* are both, in truth, constructed in thought and speech, reflection and dialogue. Plato was the architect of both. The Greek title of the *Republic*, *Politeia*, is the word not for a city *(polis)* or polity but for what it means to be a citizen, to live in community with others, concerned with the common good. "To be political, to live in a *polis*," explains Hannah Arendt, "meant that everything was decided through words and persuasion and not through force and violence."[6] *The Rebel*, too, has everything to do with nonviolent persuasion, community, and the common good. It embodied, even constituted, the revolution that Camus had envisioned and hoped to see established. Instead of creating a polity, Camus, like Plato, wrote a book and realized his "daydream" in words, words that continue to provoke dialogue, nourish community, and help keep the human flame lit. Plato's Academy and Camus's revolution are "utopias." As the word suggests, they are "no-place," nowhere in particular, not limited to one time or one place, and thus everywhere.

Camus, in all his writings, drew from ancient sources, neglected, if not disdained, by most of his fellow Parisian "intellectuals." Camus's spiritual kinship with antiquity set him apart from them, while it attracted him, as we have seen, to the work of Simone Weil. Another young writer, a fierce

---

* See Plato, *Republic*, 427c. The Socrates enshrined in Plato's *Republic* and other dialogues is the living embodiment of Plato's martyred mentor.

** Socrates, Glaucon, Polemarchus, Adeimantus, and Cephalus. Thrasymachus had stormed out early in the dialogue.

yet sympathetic spirit barely known to him, was Hannah Arendt. She, too, had found her early footing in ancient Greek philosophy and, like Camus, had written her thesis on Augustine. They are thought to have met personally only twice. First in 1946, when she described him as "a new type of person, who simply and without any 'European Nationalism' is a European."[7] Later, in 1952, as Camus and Sartre dueled in the French press over *The Rebel*, Arendt wrote in a letter to her husband, Heinrich Blücher, "Yesterday I saw Camus: he is, undoubtedly, the best man now in France. He is head and shoulders above the other intellectuals."[8] At that moment, however, Camus was more obviously head to head with Sartre & Co. The fault line that had always been there between them, until now dormant and more or less harmless, had yawned open, never to close. In *The Rebel*, explained Nicola Chiaromonte at the time, "Albert Camus attempted to do something that Jean-Paul Sartre has never found the time to do, namely, to give an account of the reasons which led him to take the position he took with regard to the political ideologies of our time, and more particularly Communism."[9] Camus sought open dialogue and respectful debate, to which Sartre had already shut the door, preferring ridicule to refutation. In retrospect, finding common ground in *The Rebel* was probably a bridge too far for both of them. When still friends, Camus and Sartre had once joked about having nothing whatsoever in common, and *The Rebel* had, in important ways, proved them right.

The Rebel was Camus's political manifesto. In it, he made clear his adamant refusal to embrace the murderous ideologies of his time and explained the ground on which he stood. It was a bold public statement. It could hardly have been otherwise. His was a public voice. In writing *The Rebel*, Camus confronted the most influential voices and political powers of his time, and—like Martin Luther before the imperial court at Worms—he declared, "Here I stand!" and he explained why. He gave a full accounting of himself and of his convictions. In doing so he drank from his deepest roots: the sun and sea of Algeria, the rock of Sisyphus, the wisdom of the ancients, the common decency of the Chambonnaise, and the courageous solidarity of the Resistance. In *The Stranger* and *The Myth of Sisyphus* Camus had affirmed the defiant will to live in the face of death, the insatiable love of life, and the primal ethic of more life over less life. In *The Rebel*, he took the next step, avowing a truth lost on Meursault and Sisyphus but exemplified in *The Plague* by Tarrou, Rambert, and their fellow plague fighters: the truth that we are all in this together. In a world where I am not alone, where there are innumerable others like me, shouldering the same infamous rock, "more life" means more life for *them*, for *us*, not just for me. "From the moment that life is recognized as good, it becomes good for all men."[10] This means I cannot logically or ethically affirm my life and not affirm the life of others. I cannot reject suicide without rejecting murder.

> Murder cannot be made coherent when suicide is not considered coherent. . . . In terms of the encounter between human inquiry and the silence of the universe, murder and suicide are one and the same thing, and must be accepted or rejected together.[11]

The Rebel is not about mortality or about the universal denial of life and meaning by an indifferent universe. It is not about the human condition; it is about human history, where death sentences are passed and executed by people with faces, people sure of themselves and of what they are doing, people convinced they are right. *The Rebel* is about saying no to them, no to the self-righteous murderers, and no to the rest of us, the bystanders who look the other way and step aside to let them do their work in our name or on our behalf. The truth is that no one has clean hands. "We can't stir a finger in this world without the risk of bringing death to somebody."[12] In all this Camus points a finger at himself as well as others. He never exempts himself from the archetypal sin of fratricide. He knows that he, like everyone else, bears the mark of Cain. He knows that all anyone can aspire to is not innocence but "reasonable culpability,"[13] not sainthood but a "mild, benevolent diabolism."[14]

In taking his stand against "legal" murder, murder by the books, murder for the right cause, Camus took his bearings and inspiration from the villagers of Le Chambon, who understood that "the very first thing that cannot be denied is the right of others to live"[15] and from his Resistance comrades, who in his words embodied "the complete, obstinate refusal . . . to accept an order that sought to bring men to their knees."[16] In 1948, Camus wrote and staged an anti-Fascist allegory entitled *State of Siege*, a play focused on freedom . . . "the only living religion in the century of tyrants and slaves . . . liberty."[17] In it, Camus created a fictional reign of terror set in Cadiz,* reminiscent of Paris under Nazi occupation and reflective of totalitarian Spain under Franco. In it, a "nothing" of a man, appropriately named Nada, the loudmouthed town drunkard, all too readily assumes the role of a bureaucratic functionary and spokesman for the regime, whose aim is "to fix things up in such a way that nobody understands a word of what his neighbor says." Accordingly, Nada's advice to his fellow citizens is to get with the program, and to "live on your knees rather than to die standing."[18] Better to bend than to break. The message of the play, however, is resistance, to rise from your knees, stand, and say no.

Camus begins *The Rebel* with this question: "What is a rebel?" His answer is simple: "A man who says no." Camus is quick to add, however, "He is also a man who says yes."[19] Camus's paradigm for the rebel is the slave, who has had all he can take, all he can accept, of submission, of life on his knees. He rises to his feet and, regardless of the consequences, informs his master that the master has gone too far, crossed a line, and that it—the master's mastery and the slave's slavery—is over. There is nothing new about this confrontation, this contest of master and slave. Not incidentally, it plays a pivotal role in the philosophy of Hegel, Camus's focal villain—his Moriarty—in *The Rebel*. What is new is how Camus understands the dialectic of master and slave and what conclusions he draws from it. For Hegel, master and slave are locked in a self-defeating, life-and-death struggle for recognition, a trial by death, in which the aim of each party is the destruction and death of the other. In *The Rebel*, Camus radically transforms this struggle from a contest of wills, a battle of egos,

---

* In response to criticism from the French Catholic philosopher and playwright Gabriel Marcel, Camus defended at length his decision to set *State of Siege* in Spain rather than in Eastern Europe. See Camus, "Why Spain," in *Combat*, pp. 297–301.

to a discovery of solidarity. Camus's "slave" has no interest in turning the tables on his "master" and dominating him. His goal is not mastery but mutual understanding and recognition.

Camus's rebellious slave sees his bondage as an affront both to himself and to his master. In that sense it isn't personal. His refusal to accept any longer the commands of his master is not a matter of defiant self-assertion. It may begin that way, but something happens when he takes his stand. He discovers that the ground he stands on transcends him. It is common ground, the same ground his master stands on.

> With rebellion, awareness is born . . . the sudden, dazzling perception that there is something in man with which he can now identify himself, even if only for a moment. Up to now this identification was never really experienced. [20]

The rebel's defiance springs not just from personal grievance but also from moral outrage. Slavery is more than a personal transgression, a wrong done to the slave. It violates and disfigures master and slave alike. It is objectively evil, not just personally offensive. Camus, in simple but far from simplistic terms, is saying here that there are moral limits, human limits, not just personal or private limits. If he can't claim this, there is no point in his going any further. In that case, he needs simply to concede that "everything is permitted" and go back to writing fiction.

Admittedly, Camus finds himself here at a relative loss for words, as was Bertrand Russell when he tried to articulate his conflicted position on objective morality: "I cannot see how to refute the arguments for the subjectivity of ethical values, but I find myself incapable of believing that all that is wrong with wanton cruelty is that I don't like it." [21] So, too, for the rebellious slave, who, we may assume, finds it hard to convince himself that the only thing wrong with his degrading servitude is that he doesn't like it. But how can Camus or anyone today make the case that good and evil, right and wrong, are more, much more, than a matter of personal likes or dislikes? In a secular, postmodern (or as some would claim a post-human) world, a world in which moral blindness, unlike color blindness, is commonplace, how can anyone make a persuasive appeal to common decency, much less a case for moral consensus? Camus put the dilemma this way: "Is it possible to find a rule of conduct outside the realm of religion and its absolute values? That is the question raised by rebellion."[22] Objective good and evil was a question that Hannah Arendt struggled to make sense of throughout her life. In the end she suggested that evil, even the darkest evil, may find its matrix in banality, the absence of critical thinking. For Socrates, the "unexamined life" was not worth living. Arendt took this further in *Eichmann in Jerusalem* and made the case that an unexamined life can pose a lethal threat to others, millions of others. "If," as Arendt reflected in her last work, "the ability to tell right from wrong should turn out to have anything to do with the ability to think, then we must be able to 'demand' its exercise from every sane person no matter how erudite or ignorant, intelligent or stupid, he may happen to be."[23] Camus is making just that demand of his readers and his times in *The Rebel*.

In denying his master's dominance, the slave voices his own injured humanity, not his injured pride. In doing so, he affirms not just his humanity but his master's humanity. Camus is unequivocally clear on this: "The slave who opposes his master is not concerned . . . with repudiating his master as a human being. He repudiates him as a master."[24] Slavery is unnatural, a violation of their shared nature. "Analysis of rebellion leads at least to the suspicion that, contrary to the postulates of contemporary thought, a human nature does exist, as the Greeks believed."[25] With these words, Camus plants his feet firmly in the traditions of ancient Greek philosophy and literature and, for that matter, religion, severing any tether connecting him with not only existentialism but much of modern thought. He understood that what is at stake is our common human nature—humanity—the one "value" we all share. If we deny it in ourselves or in others, we are lost. "If men cannot refer to a common value, recognized by all as existing in each one, then man is incomprehensible to man."[26] With this assertion of human nature in place, he takes a further, seemingly more audacious, step.

In truth, however, all he does is sum up what he has already argued and point out where it inevitably leads.

> It is for the sake of everyone in the world that the slave asserts himself when he comes to the conclusion that a command has infringed on something in him which does not belong to him alone, but which is common ground where all men—even the man who insults and oppresses him—have a natural community.[27]

Camus's assertion of a "natural human community" represents his revision of the Aristotelian claim that man, human being, is by nature a political animal. By labeling us as "political animals" Aristotle is not saying that we are naturally scheming, partisan, manipulative, ambitious, self-serving, and power hungry. What he means is that the natural habitat of human beings is the *polis*, a city. Every Greek *polis* had to have an acropolis, a theater, and an agora. The acropolis was a sacred space, the place of gods or goddesses and their temples, the place of civic religious ritual. The agora was secular space for commerce, government, and political assembly. The theater was where sacred and secular met, in drama and the arts. These were all public spaces in which citizens lived out their public lives. Their private lives were another matter and took place elsewhere. Aristotle's point was that human nature requires, for its fruition, for its full unfolding, participation in civic life, "*polis*-life" (*politeia*).

The "natural human community" that Camus points out and affirms is something quite different from the civic life Aristotle held up as the optimal human habitat. What Camus claims is that "human solidarity is metaphysical," not political. In Aristotle's Athens there were slaves, foreigners, and women, none of whom held citizenship; and even among citizens there were divisions, inequalities of wealth and privilege. Aristotle's *polis* was, in a word, "physical," not "metaphysical," visible, not invisible, to the naked eye. Camus envisions and proposes a human community far more radical, in which by nature all human beings are equal. Like Plato's republic, Camus's "natural human community" is utopian, "invisible" or, rather, visible only to the mind, which does not mean unreal or untrue. On the contrary, its reality and truth are certain. "It was axiomatic," explains Hannah Arendt, "that the invisible eye of the soul was the organ for beholding invisible truth with the certainty of knowledge."[28] In asserting the metaphysical solidarity of all human beings, Camus was only saying to those who would dismiss him that "there are more things in heaven and earth . . . than are dreamt of in your philosophy."[29]

All this, of course, was sheer nonsense to Sartre and to most philosophers and intellectuals of the modern period. By the 20th century, metaphysics had long since gone the way of alchemy, superstition, and religion. Reason had assassinated faith, and then itself became the victim of physics. So how could Camus speak of human solidarity as a metaphysical reality? Camus was no metaphysician, yet he was by his own admission "the son of Greek philosophy."[30] But it was not, as it happens, from Greek philosophy that Camus inherited his understanding of the essential nature of human solidarity. It was from Augustine, who regarded all forms of dominance, servitude, subordination, coercion, and punishment as unnatural. The natural human community was, in his view, one of equals. No matter when or where we find ourselves, it is not the community we see around us with the naked eye. All human government, as we know it, necessarily relies on coercive power. By that fact, according to Augustine, it is a form of slavery, more or less harsh or benign. Regardless of their character, all physical or historical states or polities are artificial, not natural. They are human constructs necessitated by sin. The inequality, division, and violence they inevitably, to one degree or another, institutionalize are human inventions that deny, undermine, and corrupt our common humanity. This is what life is like, according to Augustine, in the City of Man. If this view strikes us as too dark and strident for Camus to embrace, we would do well to listen to what he had to say about government as he witnessed it in his day with the naked eye:

Men of somber learning reflect daily on the decadence of our society and look for its deeper causes, which no doubt exist. But for simpler souls, the evil of the present age is characterized by its effects, not by its causes. It is called the state, whether police or bureaucratic. Its proliferation everywhere on a variety of ideological pretexts makes it a mortal danger for all that is best in each of us, as does the insulting security it derives from mechanical and psychological methods of repression. In this sense, contemporary political society is contemptible, regardless of its content. [31]

As Camus said so often, he was pessimistic with regard to the human condition but optimistic regarding his fellow human beings. The grounds for this optimism lay in the solid, irrefutable first truth revealed in the act of rebellion: "I rebel—therefore we exist." [32] From here, Camus could go on. "The world I live in disgusts me," Camus confessed in 1948, "but I feel myself in solidarity with the suffering people in it." [33] He would cling to that solidarity as if his life depended on it.

CHAPTER ELEVEN

Limits

I n a murderous world, what meaning does it have for Camus to assert
that "we exist," that "we"—all of humanity—are a community? Camus's
proclamation of a metaphysically grounded "natural human community" in
Part One of *The Rebel* has a familiar ring to it, reminiscent of the Christian
apostle Paul's words in his Letter to the Galatians: "There is no longer
Jew or Greek, there is no longer slave or free, there is no longer male and
female, for you are all one in Christ Jesus."[1] But Camus's world is not only
murderous, it is also godless. Camus eschews religious faith, while at the
same time invoking the transcendent reality of human nature and human
community. The immediately perplexing point here is that he is prepared
neither to believe in God nor to deny the absolute, the transcendent, the
sacred.* Murder, as Camus understands it, is a metaphysical crime, a violation of the sacred. Human life and community are, for Camus, "sacred" in
the sense of "inviolate." Killing is thereby "unnatural" because it violates
our shared nature and common bond as human beings. If Camus's seemingly gratuitous invocation of a common human nature raises questions for
us, we are not alone in this. He, too, is at a loss here. In his *Notebooks* he

---

* For the meaning of *sacred* in a godless world, we do best to look to the origins of the word
  in the Latin *sacer*, which means to "set apart," to "mark out" and "wall off." A sacred area, a
  sanctum or sanctuary, is protected, safe, inviolate.

asks himself the very question we would want to put to him: "If there is a human nature, where does it come from? Obvious that I ought to give up all creative activity so long as I don't know."[2]

Camus had long been discomforted, even tormented, by the disconnect between his tacit appeals to ethical absolutes and his outspoken disavowal of religious beliefs and sanctions. In a letter dated December 11, 1946, Camus shared with his mentor Jean Grenier the dilemma that haunted him as he labored on *The Rebel*:

> If there are no eternal values, Communism is right and nothing is permitted, human society must be built whatever the price. If it is wrong, then the Gospel and Christianity must be followed. Never before has this dilemma been given an image more distressed and insistent than today. And men like myself who dream of an impossible synthesis, who refuse violence and lies without having to justify their opposite, and who, nevertheless, cannot keep from screaming, are going crazy.[3]

Grenier, with no easy answer to his young friend's quandary, offered at least the reassurance that "the mere fact of believing that there are eternal truths, let's say that there must be some, even incarnated, is enough to dismiss the Communist solution."[4] In other words, he concurred with Camus in his renunciation of murder and violence as acceptable means to a better future, and fully recognized the corner in which that renunciation left him. Refusing to justify murder was one thing; defending that refusal was another. Invoking Bertrand Russell and rejecting wanton cruelty on the grounds that he didn't "like it" would hardly prove convincing to the circles in which Camus moved and wrote. For that, Grenier suggested,

> You may find yourself falling back on Christianity. I think it could provide you greater balance; I don't see how you could *believe* in it. Since your birth you have lived in environments in

which Christ is no more real than Buddha, and in which the
Church arouses hostility.[5]

Camus, however, was not prepared to "fall back on Christianity" or
ancient metaphysics. In a murderous world, a world prepared to anni-
hilate itself, Camus found himself more compelled to speak out than
to retreat into silence to ponder Plato or meditate on scripture. Besides,
murderers are not likely to be dissuaded or even delayed by metaphysics
or theology. Camus knew what he knew, even if he didn't know and
couldn't explain how he knew it.[*] His moral outrage at the inhumanity
and his compassion for the suffering he saw all around him provided, at
least in the short run (which was all he and humanity had), solid enough
ground on which to take his stand. In this stand, Camus, who might
fairly be described as a religious man without a religion or, like Tarrou,
an aspiring saint without God, found himself increasingly isolated in
French intellectual circles, predominantly either Marxist or Christian.

Had he known him, Camus would have found a rare and welcome
intellectual comrade in fellow philosopher J. Glenn Gray, who, like
Camus, had emerged from the war convinced that killing represents a
metaphysical crime against our shared human nature, a violation of our
common humanity. Gray was born only months apart from Camus in
1913. On an otherwise unremarkable spring day in 1941, Gray found two
pivotal pieces of mail side by side in his mailbox: notification of his PhD in
philosophy from Columbia University and his draft notice from the Selective Service System. From 1941 to 1945, he went on to serve with an army
counterespionage unit in North Africa, Italy, France, and Germany. Then,
fourteen years after returning from the war, Gray wrote *The Warriors*, his
memoir, described by Hannah Arendt in her introduction as a "singularly

---

* We don't reason our way to everything we know. This is especially true when it comes to
discerning what is the right thing to do in a given moment. The ancient Greeks called this
φρόνησις (*phronesis*), or practical wisdom. Socrates was guided through his life by what he
called his δαίμων (*daimon*), his spiritual muse, as it were, the inner voice that held him back,
in moments of intellectual or moral risk, from embracing falsehood or doing wrong.

earnest and beautiful book" remarkable in its "self-taught concreteness" and "unswerving fidelity to the real."[6] Gray, like Camus, came to his deepest convictions not from books but from experience, from life, not libraries. "A walk across any battlefield shortly after the guns have fallen silent is convincing enough," wrote Gray. "A sensitive person is sure to be oppressed by a spirit of evil there, a radical evil which suddenly makes the medieval images of hell and the thousand devils of that imagination believable."[7] This is because, as Gray explains, "there is a line that a man dare not cross, deeds he dare not commit, regardless of orders and the hopelessness of the situation, for such deeds would destroy something in him that he values more than life itself."[8]

Gray writes on the same page as Camus when he concludes, "Nothing corrupts our soul more surely and more subtly than the consciousness of others who fear and hate us. Such is our human nature that we cannot possess power that others dread without becoming like the image of their fear and hate."[9] Gray and Camus witnessed the same world at war, the same humanity at war with itself. They faced the same perilous future and came to the same conclusions. "A man who cannot be persuaded," wrote Camus in 1946, "is a man who makes others afraid . . . we live in terror because persuasion is no longer possible, because man has been delivered entirely into the hands of history and can no longer turn toward that part of himself which is as true as the historic part, and which he discovers when he confronts the beauty of the world and of people's faces."[10]

Returning now to the central argument of *The Rebel*, when Camus proclaimed that "we exist," that we are metaphysically *one*, he knew he was addressing a murderously divided world, a "community" at each other's throats. Incidentally, Paul also confronted bitter division when he reminded the fractious Galatians (his first Gentile converts, who also happened to be Celts) that they were "all one in Christ Jesus." Camus, by contrast, claimed that we are all one *in truth*. We see this truth when we turn inward in thought and reflection. It is, as it were, self-evident. Just as obvious, however, is the fact that we, humanity, are *not one*. When we open our eyes and look around, we see that we are clearly not *at one* with each other. These two claims or declarations—"We are one" and "We are not one"—are both true, but in different ways. Our common humanity makes us one. It binds us to each other, makes us responsible for each other, answerable to each other. It is we who defy and defile that bond.

When Cain, the fratricide, with feigned innocence and bloody hands, asks, "Am I my brother's keeper?" he already knows the answer, as do we. In theory, yes. He's your brother. In practice, no. Look at your hands! So, when Camus writes, "We are," he has to take it back and admit that "we are, but not yet." Humanity, the natural human community, is a work in progress. It is a work to be undertaken, not watched from afar. Shouldering the rock of Sisyphus is a common, not a solitary, undertaking. Human solidarity requires shared resolve.

In a godless world, silent to humanity's cry for meaning and justice, it is pointless to shake your fist at the sky or rail against an indifferent universe. It is human indifference and, worse, human hostility and cruelty that are the problem.

> When the throne of God is overturned, the rebel realizes that it is now his own responsibility to create the justice, order, and unity that he sought in vain within his own condition, and in this way to justify the fall of God. Then begins the desperate effort to create, at the price of crime and murder if necessary, the Dominion of man. This will not come about without terrible consequences, of which we are so far only aware of a few. [11]

It is at this point that the rebel enters history, shoulders the rock, and takes on the task of fashioning a better world. "From the moment that man believes neither in God nor in immortal life, he becomes 'responsible for everything alive, for everything that, born of suffering, is condemned to suffer from life.'" [12] The rebel knows that in a world without gods, "we are alone." [13] Wars, plagues, injustice, oppression, slavery, predation, poverty, racism, tyranny . . . the list goes on; and all these affronts and atrocities lie at humanity's door, awaiting action. "Now that God is dead, the world must be changed and organized by the forces at man's disposal."[14] Persuasion and goodwill are among those forces, but they are often in short supply and prove futile. The question then becomes whether any realistic change can be accomplished without the exercise of force, which eventually comes down to lethal force. The ending of wars, the overthrow of tyrannies, the liberation of slaves, the righting of injustices . . . these all involve internecine conflict within the human family. The rebel sets out to affirm humanity and foster community but soon finds himself facing off against other members of that same human community who have blood in their eyes. It comes down to this: if history is any witness, nonviolent revolution is an oxymoron in all but a few exceptions.

Camus's focus in *The Rebel*, his defining concern, was murder—not random crimes of passion, not onetime murderous paroxysms, but legal, authorized, institutionalized murder, committed by people confident that they are in the right, doing their duty, making the world a better place, contributing to a better future, convinced, in other words, that they are innocent.

> In more ingenuous times, when the tyrant razed cities for his own greater glory, when the slave chained to the conqueror's chariot was dragged through the rejoicing streets, when enemies were thrown to wild animals in front of the assembled people, before such naked crimes consciousness could be steady and judgment unclouded. But slave camps under the flag of freedom, massacres justified by philanthropy or the taste for the superhuman, cripple judgement. On the day when crime puts on the apparel of innocence, through a curious reversal peculiar to our age, it is innocence that is called on to justify itself.[15]

The answer, as Camus saw it, lay not in silence or cloistered withdrawal. He was no monk or renunciate. Neither was he, in the end, an absolute pacifist. Camus was a realist who simply understood reality quite differently from many of his peers. He was a man earnestly engaged in his times and its struggles, who consistently called for radical change, revolution, but within ethical limits. When he was accused by Roland Barthes of withdrawing from politics and rejecting "the solidarity of our history-in-the-making," he defended himself, arguing,

> It is not legitimate to reproach me or, above all, to accuse me of rejecting history unless it is proclaimed that the only way of taking part in history is to make tyranny legitimate. . . . Far from being installed in a career of solitude, I have, on the contrary, the feeling that I am living by and for a community that nothing in history has so far been able to touch. [16]

In *The Rebel* he chronicled the many ways in which revolts in the past had gone wrong, betrayed their origins, and failed—the ways that Prometheus had devolved into Caesar, the ways that compassionate solidarity had spawned totalitarian tyranny. More specifically, he traced—in philosophy, literature, and politics—the history of nihilism and terror, the European history that had yielded its bloodiest harvest in National Socialism and Stalinist Communism.* Camus understood Stalinism, like Nazism, as a totalitarian regime notorious for its systematic, bureaucratic murderousness. In his eyes, these regimes represented two parallel forms of terror: "rational terror" in the case of Stalinist Russia, and "irrational terror" in the case of the Third Reich.** Like Hannah Arendt, Camus saw terror as "the essence of totalitarian government."[17] Camus and Arendt shared and sought to develop "what might be called

---

* In his account of the origins and history of revolution and nihilism, Camus referenced in *The Rebel* an exhausting plethora of individuals and texts, which the noted scholar and translator Philip Thody actually counted. By his count, Camus cited by name 160 writers, 96 historical figures, and 20 fictional/mythical characters. See Thody, *Albert Camus: 1930–1960*, p. 139.

** Camus, like Hannah Arendt, was widely denounced for the parallels he drew between Stalinism and Nazism. Arendt, in her monumental work, *The Origins of Totalitarianism*, categorized Russia as fully totalitarian only after the Moscow Trials, between 1936 and 1938, and Germany only after 1938 in the first years of the war.

a political ethic of revolt, one that seeks to resuscitate the modern, universalist ideals of human autonomy and democratic self-governance by embodying them in an ethic of limits."[18]

> Camus, like George Orwell, had the feelings of the common man and the mind of the intellectual. He saw revolt as it really is for the ordinary person—a protest against suffering and injustice and not an attempt radically to transform the nature of the world—and pointed out that the right way to protest against the injustice, the cruelty and the disorder of nature is to try to realize the specifically human qualities of order, mercy and justice.[19]

The first question Camus and any would-be rebel must ask, when contemplating protest and revolution, is "whether we have the right to kill our fellow men, or the right to let them be killed. In that every action today leads to murder, direct or indirect, we cannot act until we know whether or why we have the right to kill."[20] The dilemma confronting any would-be rebel, then, is that acting eventually leads to murder, and doing nothing amounts to letting others be killed. It's a question of ethics, not strategy or politics: What is permitted? In *The Rebel*, Camus considers and critiques two categorically opposed responses to this question: everything is permitted versus nothing is permitted, nihilism versus asceticism, absolute freedom versus absolute justice. Both extremes were unacceptable to Camus; "after all, nothing is true that compels me to make it exclusive."[21] Absolute freedom conveys the right to dominate, to deny any truth and take any life. Absolute justice destroys freedom and negates the individual.

> The revolution of the twentieth century has arbitrarily separated, for overambitious ends of conquest, two inseparable ideas. Absolute freedom mocks at justice. Abstract justice denies freedom. To be fruitful, the two ideas must find limits in each other. No man considers that his condition is free if it is not at the same time just, nor just unless it is free.[22]

The rebel who is uneasy either as a murderer or a bystander should abandon the absolute and accept the relative, making due with a measure of freedom and a measure of justice. In arguing for moderation, Camus invoked one of the central tenets of ancient Greek wisdom. In a world and age rent asunder by conflicting ideologies, Camus's appeal to limits represented a radical proposal.

Another polarity running through Camus's analytical critique of 20th-century nihilism and revolution is the divide between victims and executioners. In 1946 Camus wrote eight consecutive essays, serialized in *Combat* under the general title *Neither Victims nor Executioners*. It's clear from this title that Camus argued for the rejection of both options, either killing or being killed. Plato, in the *Republic*, similarly made a case against both absolute power and absolute weakness, arguing that only gods wield absolute power and only dumb beasts are so weak as to be at the disposal of men. In short, for human beings, dominion is ultimately impossible and subjection unnecessary. Nevertheless, the fact that absolute power (except perhaps the power of total nuclear annihilation) is not within human reach has never stopped people from aspiring to it.

> The regicides of the nineteenth century are succeeded by the deicides of the twentieth century, who draw the ultimate conclusions from the logic of rebellion and want to make the earth a kingdom where man is God. The reign of history begins and, identifying himself only with his history, man, unfaithful to his real rebellion, will henceforth devote himself to the nihilistic revolution of the twentieth century, which denies all forms of morality and desperately attempts to achieve the unity of the human race by means of a ruinous series of crimes and wars.[23]

Camus leaves no doubt regarding who he sees as the executioners and their advocates. The victims, on the other hand, are too many to be counted or named, and merit our grief and compassion. It is the ideology of victimhood, the acquiescence in, even celebration of, submissive suffering at which Camus takes aim. Sacrifice lies at the core of Christian doctrine and devotion. The crucified Christ, and those who follow him into martyrdom, are the exemplars of the Christian life. It is the lamb led to slaughter and not the ravenous lion that Christians are called to imitate.

What makes both Christianity and Stalinist Marxism misguided and dangerous, in Camus's eyes, is their presumed knowledge of the future and their blind submission to history. Marxism, like Christianity, grounds itself in an eschatological vision of the end times. For each, the course of history is fixed and its outcome certain. For Christians that means the kingdom of heaven at the end of time, and for Marxists the classless society at the end of history. Neither Christians nor Marxists can effectively resist, much less alter or prevent, the outcome of history. Christians look with confidence to the second coming of Christ and his eternal reign for the perfect justice and just rewards that eluded them in this life, just as they look with fear to the retribution their sins deserve. Marxists, on the other hand, as individuals, can, in the great scheme of things, do no wrong, or right for that matter, because their deeds and misdeeds are in the end inconsequential. Christians and Marxists, victims and executioners alike find in their beliefs sure confirmation in their respective "callings."

Christianity and Marxism each lay claim to a unique revelation. "For Christians," comments Camus in his *Notebooks*, "revelation stands at the beginning of history. For Marxists, it stands at the end. Two religions."[24] For those like Camus, living without privileged revelations, with only their wits to guide them, the journey through time is precarious and uncertain. Camus's understanding of experiential time is consonant with that of ancient Greek literature and philosophy. We humans are temporal beings. We belong to time. At any given moment, part of our lives is already behind us, and the other part lies ahead of us. We know our past, but we don't know our future. We know what's happened but we don't know what's coming. We might think of this not as "the fog of war" but as "the fog of life." In a world in which, as Hannah Arendt reminds us, the past is irreversible and the future is unpredictable,[25] we must act thoughtfully, humbly, scrupulously. We cannot ever know with any certainty the outcomes of our words, decisions, and deeds. How, then, with this understanding of time and of what Hannah Arendt calls "the frailty of human affairs," might anyone hope to justify the taking of human life in the cause of rebellion? What do moderation and ethical limits mean to the rebel who contemplates murder?

Camus's clearest formulation and fullest response to these questions came in *The Just Assassins*, or simply *The Just* (*Les Justes*), a five-act classical French tragedy first performed on December 15, 1949. It is a work dedicated to Jean Grenier. In it Camus focused on the 1905 assassination of the Russian grand duke Sergei Alexandrovich, the czar's uncle, by a small group of Russian Socialist Revolutionaries, whom Camus referred to in *The Rebel* as "The Fastidious Assassins" (*Les Meurtriers Délicats*).[26] Amid Camus's catalogue of failed, misguided, murderous revolutionary theories, organizations, and endeavors, this small band of idealist revolutionaries stands out as the exemplar, to be admired and emulated by rebels willing to lose their lives but not their souls in the pursuit of justice.

> History offers few examples of fanatics who have suffered from scruples, even in action. But the men of 1905 were always prey to doubts. The greatest homage we can pay them is to say that we would not be able, in 1950, to ask them one question that they themselves had not already asked and that, in their life or by their death, they had not partially answered.[27]

Rebellion within ethical limits requires a profound respect for life, every life. Murder must never be taken lightly, and never justified. Murder, while never right, may, however, be judged in certain circumstances to be necessary. But *how* necessary? What measure is to be used to ensure that a life is not taken needlessly? How can anyone know with certainty that murdering a particular dictator or spy or informer or functionary will achieve or crucially contribute to the desired end? Toppling a regime is like bringing down a building. Either you determine where the weight-bearing walls or stanchions are located and remove them, or you simply demolish the entire structure and everything in it with explosives. Even if killing cannot be avoided, overkilling can. Would-be assassins need to try to talk themselves out of murdering their victims with the same desperation they would employ if the roles were reversed. If I take my victim's life as seriously as I take my own, then chances are I am taking their life seriously. To ensure this, the killer must have as much at stake, as much to lose, as the killed.

In *The Just*, the designated assassin, Ivan Kaliayev, aborts his mission at the last moment. Poised to throw his bomb at the grand duke's carriage, he freezes when he sees the grand duke's niece and nephew sitting at his side. They weren't meant to be there. Kaliayev had prepared himself to throw his bomb at the face of tyranny, the grand duke's face. Murdering children was another matter. His mission unaccomplished, Kaliayev returns to his comrades to explain himself and hope for their understanding. All but one of his group embrace Kaliayev's decision, all but Stepan Fedorov, a hard-core revolutionary zealot, embittered by his recent torture and imprisonment. Stepan accuses Kaliayev of playing at revolution and ridicules his scruples over killing children. His point is that sometimes not killing enough amounts to killing for nothing. It becomes a futile gesture. Stepan says he would gladly blow up all of Moscow to hasten the future reign of justice and equality, the certain fruition of their historical struggle. Kaliayev is less certain where their revolution will lead, less confident that murder can ever be a force for life or that conflict can ever foster fellowship. It is clear to Stepan that Kaliayev simply doesn't believe in the revolution. He is genuinely shocked that Kaliayev feels entitled to kill anyone at all if he isn't certain about the future, about the coming dawn of the classless society. Without such ideological certainty, nothing is permitted, whereas with it everything is permitted. Stepan dismisses Kaliayev's and his comrades' "limits" as senseless sentimentality, undermining rather than advancing their cause.

> There are no limits! The truth is that you don't believe in the revolution, any of you. If you did believe in it sincerely, with all your hearts . . . how, I ask you, could the deaths of two children

be weighed in the balance against such a faith? . . . So now, if
you draw the line at killing these two children, well, it simply
means that you are not sure you have the right. So, I repeat, you
do not believe in the revolution.[28]

Stepan has a point, and Camus gives him the floor.* *The Just* is a tragedy
not unlike Sophocles's *Antigone*, in which Antigone is right but Creon
is not wrong.

Eventually, Kaliayev is given a second chance and he murders the
grand duke without taking the lives of children or anyone else. True to
his convictions and his character, Kaliayev makes no effort to escape. He
gives himself up to judgment and punishment. When offered a pardon,
he chooses death.

The rebel has only one way of reconciling himself with his act
of murder if he allows himself to be led into performing it: to
accept his own death and sacrifice. He kills and dies so that
it shall be clear that murder is impossible. He demonstrates
that, in reality, he prefers the "We are" to the "We shall be."[29]

Kaliayev embraces his victim in the fellowship of death. In doing so,
he affirms that he and the grand duke are in truth brothers. He has not
discounted or dismissed the life of his brother. He has not taken the life
and death of the grand duke any less seriously than he has his own. In
dying with his victim, he asserts that "murder is thus a desperate exception or it is nothing. . . . It is the limit that can be reached but once, after
which one must die."[30] Otherwise, he would be not just a man who has
killed. He would be a killer; and the next time would be easier.

---

* Looking back at *The Just*, Camus later reflected, "I tried to achieve dramatic tension
  through classical means—that is, the opposition of characters who were equal in strength
  and reason," which is not to say that he was torn between their arguments. "My admiration
  for my heroes, Kaliayev and Dora," he explained, "is complete." See Camus, *Caligula and
  Three Other Plays*, ix–x.

Murder and suicide are logically and morally one. Camus began *The Rebel* affirming this fundamental principle: "From the moment that life is recognized as good, it becomes good for all men. Murder cannot be made coherent when suicide is not considered coherent. . . . If we deny there are reasons for suicide, we cannot claim that there are grounds for murder."[31] Rebellion is rooted not in a death wish but in a life wish, a love of life that extends to all life. "Claiming the unity of the human condition, it is a force of life, not of death. Its most profound logic is not the logic of destruction; it is the logic of creation."[32] The "insane generosity" of rebellion, far from sacrificing the present to the future, instead gives "all to the present."[33] True rebellion, unlike its nihilistic perversion, never violates in the present what it hopes to affirm in the future, never sacrifices the "We are" to the "We shall be," never pretends that the end justifies the means. "Does the end justify the means?" asks Camus. "That is possible. But what will justify the end? To that question, which historical thought leaves pending, rebellion replies: the means."[34]

On March 7, 1951, Camus put down his pen after making this brief entry in his *Notebooks*: "Finished the first writing of *The Rebel*. With this book the first two cycles come to an end. Thirty-seven years old. And now, can creation be free?"[35] Meursault's life ended under a guillotine's blade; Kaliayev's at the end of a rope. Camus asks of us, his readers, to imagine these avatars of Sisyphus and Prometheus as happy—happy in life, happy in death. Yet neither was free. Both were chained to their fates: Sisyphus to his rock, Prometheus to his pillar. Where, we wonder, will we find Camus's next hero, and will he be happy?

CHAPTER TWELVE

Hell

I n each of the first two cycles of his writings, Camus held up to his readers an iconic hero, a paradigmatic figure recruited from ancient Greek myth. Sisyphus—defined by his hatred of death, scorn for the gods, and love of life—proved to be a solitary, murderous character who stolidly embraced his fate but failed to recognize himself in others. Prometheus—like Sisyphus an enemy of the gods and a lover of life—focused his hatred on the death and suffering we inflict on each other and labored to replace conflict with community. The "hero" of the Nemesis cycle is cut from very different cloth. Camus calls him A Hero of Our Time, an all-too-familiar figure whose face we see reflected every day in the mirror. As for Nemesis, Daughter of Night, she is faceless. Without shrine or cult[*] she is beyond bribes or supplications, deaf to all pleas for mercy, blind to any change of heart. Like gravity, Nemesis is a fact of life, a force of nature, operating on all alike, playing no favorites. "Nemesis—the goddess of measure," explains Camus in his *Notebooks*: "All those who have overstepped the limit will be pitilessly destroyed."[1] It is that simple. Our actions have inescapable consequences. What we do is never overlooked or forgotten. Like the

---

[*] Apart from her one temple and altar at Rhamnous in Attika.

furies of Greek tragedy, Nemesis—goddess of moral outrage and merciless retribution—stalks those who transgress the limits, violate their nature, and imagine they've gotten away with it.

The Nemesis Cycle, like those dedicated to Sisyphus and Prometheus, was meant to extend across three genres: fiction, philosophy, and theater. For a range of reasons, including Camus's untimely death, the projected philosophical volume, tentatively entitled *The Myth of Nemesis*, never made its way onto the page. Instead of creating a new original play to follow on the success of *The Just Assassins*, Camus penned and staged theatrical adaptations of Faulkner's *Requiem for a Nun* and Dostoevsky's *The Possessed*. Camus's other creative endeavors, in the years between the 1951 publication of *The Rebel* and his death in 1960, included directing others' plays, publishing a collection of lyrical essays and short stories, and launching into what he envisioned as his monumental masterwork, a "free creation" and work of love, *The First Man*. That left *The Fall* to represent a fragmentary Nemesis Cycle. Camus began taking notes for *The Fall* during his brief 1954 visit to Amsterdam. Originally conceived as a short story to be included in the volume entitled *Exile and the Kingdom*, *The Fall* grew in Camus's imagination and on the page into a short novel, even shorter than *The Stranger*. Despite its diminutive size, *The Fall* cemented Camus's standing as the most celebrated French writer of his generation and made all the more likely his reception of the Nobel Prize for Literature a year and a half later. Sartre, no longer among Camus's chief admirers, nevertheless heralded *The Fall* as perhaps the "finest" of Camus's works and "certainly the least understood."[2] Being misunderstood, of course, was nothing new for Camus, and in this case it may have only added to the number and appreciation of his readers.

The Fall stands midway between a play and a novel.* "In that work," Camus noted, "I used a theatrical technique (dramatic monologue and implicit dialogue)."[3] The monologue unfolds across five days and takes

---

* For this reason it is not only widely read but on occasion performed. A recent 2020 New York production of *The Fall*, adapted for the stage by Alexis Lloyd, featured the Belgian actor Ronald Guttman as Clamence.

the form of a classical five-act French tragedy. We hear only one voice in *The Fall*, that of Jean-Baptiste Clamence, who acknowledges and responds occasionally to a nameless interlocutor, dutifully attentive, day after day, to Clamence's dramatic confessions.* We might reasonably doubt the actual existence of this silent, unseen interlocutor. Clamence could just be talking to himself. He is that alone, that lost. Regardless, he speaks to the reader. Each reader, one at a time, is his silent companion and disciple along the streets and canals of Amsterdam and across a table in Mexico City, a seedy sailors' bar in the city's red-light district where Clamence practices his profession and awaits his clients, who "come from the four corners of Europe . . . (and) chilled to the bone . . . ask in all languages for gin at Mexico City."[4] But how is it that Clamence has found his way here? The answer is simple and staring at us: the only way to get here is to fall. Clamence will explain to us, across five days, if we follow him to the end, how he (and we) have fallen.

In *The Fall*, we cannot help but notice that we are far from the sun-soaked Mediterranean, the land of light, the world of Greek gods and heroes, and find ourselves, instead, in "a desert of stones, fogs, and stagnant waters."[5] Years earlier, Camus had already noted that his inner, imaginative world was turning dark and cold:

> I have read over all these notebooks—beginning with the first. This was obvious to me: landscapes gradually disappear. The modern cancer is gnawing me too.[6]

Where, then, are we? In the symbolic geography of *The Fall*, where is it that we come upon Clamence? Just how far, how low, has Clamence (and we with him) fallen? Camus could not be more clear on this point. By his own admission, Clamence inhabits the deepest abyss of hell, the lowest circle of Dante's inferno:

---

* *The Fall* is drenched in Catholic themes, images, and ideas. The *Confessions* of Augustine and Dante's *Inferno* are unmistakably among the most pervasive of these influences.

. . . we are at the heart of things here. Have you noticed that Amsterdam's concentric canals resemble the circles of hell? The middle-class hell, of course, peopled with bad dreams. When one comes from the outside, as one gradually goes through those circles, life—and hence its crimes—becomes denser, darker. Here we are in the last circle. The circle of the . . .[7]

When we descend, or perhaps plummet, through the nine circles of Dante's *Inferno*, we come in the end to the very pit of hell and the frigid waters of Cocytus, the river of lamentation. Here we find the last and lowest class of the damned, embedded in ice. The torment of these lost souls in Dante's ninth circle comes not from burning but from freezing. Who are they and what is their consummately heinous crime? As soon as we hear their names, we realize what they've done to merit the same "eternal pain" inflicted on them by Satan, the "King of Hell."

"That soul that suffers most," explained my Guide,
"is Judas Iscariot, he who kicks his legs
on the fiery chin and has his head inside.
Of the other two, who have their heads thrust forward,
the one who dangles down from the black face
is Brutus: note how he writhes without a word.
And there, with the huge and sinewy arms, is the soul
Of Cassius. . ."[8]

The sin of these three—Judas, Brutus, and Cassius—was one of betrayal, the betrayal of a friend. This same betrayal of friendship is the cause of Clamence's fall, the reason why he and we, his readers and coconspirators, find ourselves in hell's last circle. But why, we may wonder and protest, should we see ourselves in Clamence, his crime, and his punishment?

The Fall is obviously confessional, but whose confession is it? Who in "real life" is Clamence? When *The Fall* was first published in France, Camus seemed to many the likely face behind the mask. The Conscience of

Europe, the secular saint of the modern age, was coming clean, admitting
that he, too, was deeply flawed, fully human. It was lost on no one that
The Fall, beginning with its title and the name of its "hero" Jean-Baptiste
Clamence,* was rooted in the Bible, not in Greek myth, and that Camus
was now drinking from a different stream. A number of readers and notable
critics, particularly the Catholics among them, imagined he was every day
closer to religious conversion and baptism or, more accurately, re-baptism.**
They had speculated as much for some time, which had led Camus to comment, in the preface to his theatrical adaptation of *Requiem for a Nun*, "If
I had translated and produced a Greek tragedy, no one would have asked
me if I believed in Zeus."[9] Camus never denied that *The Fall* was, in part,
autobiographical and that he saw aspects of himself and his life reflected in
Clamence; but he insisted at the same time that he was not Clamence. To
see Jean-Baptiste Clamence as a simple pseudonym for Albert Camus was
to miss the point. Others claimed that Camus was holding up Clamence
as a model to be emulated, as if *The Fall* were an edifying text, a master
class in narcissistic nihilism. To set that record straight, Camus inserted
this epigraph from Lermontov in the English translation of *The Fall*:

> *Some were dreadfully insulted, and quite seriously, to have held up*
> *as a model such an immoral character as* A Hero of Our Time;
> *others shrewdly noticed that the author had portrayed himself and*

---

* As we will discuss later in the next chapter, the name "Jean-Baptiste Clamence" alludes
directly to John the Baptist, who in all four Christian gospels is described as "the voice of
one crying in the wilderness" (*vox clamantis in deserto*), a phrase borrowed from the prophet
Isaiah, 40.3.

** In fact, Camus as an infant had been baptized Catholic and had as a boy made his First Communion, after which he quit the church, declaring time and again that he was no atheist, but
neither did he believe in God. He did, however, read the Bible throughout his life, and, if
the published account of Rev. Howard Mumma is to be believed, Camus requested a private
baptism as a Presbyterian but was denied it several months before his death. See Howard
Mumma, *Albert Camus and the Minister*. On the other hand, Germaine Brée, a close friend
of Camus's for decades, told me about a late 1959 conversation with Camus at his home in
Lourmarin, when she asked him outright if he was then close to conversion. His answer was
that he was no closer than he had ever been to believing in God and embracing Christianity.

*his acquaintances. . . . A Hero of Our Time, gentlemen, is in fact
a portrait, but not of an individual; it is the aggregate of the vices of
our whole generation in their fullest expression.* [10]

The aggregate of all vices, the sum and distillation of all evil—this is the
traditional profile of Satan, "the Prince of Darkness," "the King of Hell,"
whose signature sin is pride.

In *The Fall*, Clamence, not Camus, is the Hero of Our Time. Yes,
Camus sees himself, and we can see him, in Clamence. But Clamence is
essentially a mirror. All who stand before that mirror and gaze into it will
see something of themselves reflected there. The "modern cancer" gnaws
us all. The first symptom of this deadly cancer is cynicism. "My most
constant temptation," confessed Camus in his *Notebooks*, "the one against
which I have never ceased fighting to the point of exhaustion: cynicism." [11]
Clamence is, to his core, a cynic. He no longer believes, if he ever did, in
any essential bond between himself and others, in any "natural human
community." Instead of community there is only contention, endless rivalry.
As Thomas Hobbes recognized and wrote in the 17th century, every one
of us aspires to be God, to have the first and the last word, to create and to
judge. The snag, however, is that there are so many of us, with competing
visions, ambitions, desires. We are just so many doomed gods. Instead of
reigning on high, from a summit, we find ourselves, like Clamence, falling
into "a desert of stones, fogs, and stagnant waters," where "Hell is—other
people." [12]

Clamence, to be clear, is not Satan, not even his full-fledged avatar.
Camus has no doubts about the presence of evil, but that doesn't mean he
believes in fallen angels, much less Satan. Clamence holds court not actually in hell but in its foyer, a well-populated makeshift hell, where those
"who don't want to improve ourselves or be bettered . . . merely wish to be
pitied and encouraged in the course we have chosen."

In short, we should like, at the same time, to cease being guilty
and yet not make the effort of cleansing ourselves. Not enough

cynicism and not enough virtue. We lack the energy of evil as well as the energy of good. Do you know Dante? Really? The devil you say! Then you know that Dante accepts the idea of neutral angels in the quarrel between God and Satan. And he puts them in Limbo, a sort of vestibule of his Hell. We are in that vestibule, *cher ami*.[13]

The first sign of Clamence's apostasy, his despair of human solidarity, is the fact that *The Fall* is a monologue. Like *The Stranger*, it is written in the first person. "I, I, I is the refrain of my whole life, which could be heard in everything I said."[14] The "we"—the great achievement of the Prometheus Cycle—is gone, discarded; we are back to the "I" of Meursault and the Sisyphus Cycle. But not precisely. Meursault represented the zero point. His consciousness was morally unevolved; his humanity inchoate, not corrupted. His connection and bond with others had not yet dawned on him. He had not yet been "converted" to full human fellowship. Clamence, at the other end of that line, is devolved in his humanity, well on his way into the post-human world heralded by some of today's futurists. He is quite literally a lapsed human. Meursault was pre-moral; Clamence is post-moral, consciously so. Meursault was strangely innocent but judged guilty; Clamence, who could not be more guilty, glories in passing judgment on all who fall into his lair and under his spell.

The first tenet of Clamence's cynical creed is that altruism is a delusion. It simply doesn't exist, except as the rarest of anomalies: "true love is exceptional—two or three times a century, more or less."[15] For most of us, there's no such thing as selfless love, self-sacrifice, or, for that matter, true friendship. "That's the way man is, *cher monsieur*. He has two faces: he can't love without self-love."[16] Clamence acknowledges our hunger for friendship, but his advice is:

Don't think for a minute that your friends will telephone you every evening, as they ought to, in order to find out if this doesn't happen to be the evening when you are deciding to commit

ALBERT CAMUS AND THE HUMAN CRISIS 171

suicide, or simply whether you don't need company, whether you
are not in a mood to go out. No, don't worry, they'll ring up the
evening you are not alone, when life is beautiful. . . .

You see, I've heard of a man whose friend had been impris-
oned and who slept on the floor of his room every night in
order not to enjoy a comfort of which his friend had been
deprived. Who, *cher monsieur*, will sleep on the floor for us?[17]

Clamence, by his own admission, has given up on friendship. He still
uses the word, but only "as a convention." "I have no more friends, I have
nothing but accomplices."[18]

Clamence sums up his views on friendship, love, altruism, and shared
humanity in his first discourse with the laconic listener he calls his *"cher
ami"*: "A single sentence will suffice for modern man: he fornicated and read
the newspapers."[19] Here, in one sentence, Clamence cynically dismisses both
passion and compassion and, in doing so, distances himself and his generation
from both Meursault and Rieux. What fornication and reading the newspaper have in common is their lack of genuine intimacy and engagement,
their distance from "the human other," despite the illusion of involvement that
they provide. Fornication, as Clamence practices and represents it, is mere
self-gratification, assisted masturbation. It's all about Clamence, his fantasies
and satisfaction. The same is true as he "stays in touch" with the news. The
faces sharing his bed or confronting him on the printed page stimulate his
experience, make him feel less alone, but the moment he exits the room or
puts down the paper, all is forgotten. The connection is instantly severed, the
bond easily broken, because they were never real. The morning newspaper
enhances his breakfast coffee and croissant, and the evening edition puts his
day behind him and makes him feel connected with his world, even though
he isn't and couldn't care less. As for his sexual liaisons, they, too, occupy
only the moment, offer their own form of ephemeral gratification, and then,
in an instant, become yesterday's news.

Cynicism and self-gratification are hardly the worst of Clamence's
human failings, however. As is the case with Satan, Clamence's signature

sin is pride, a pride so preposterously inflated that it nearly defies compre-
hension. His ultimate fantasy and ambition are to define and dominate his
world and everyone in it. Sin, as Augustine understood it, is the imitation
of God. It is not a matter of doing what God would never be caught dead
doing, as it were. It is, instead, a matter of doing, or pretending to do,
what only God can do. In the book of Genesis, it is God alone who speaks
over the void and summons from it a universe, a world, and every being
in it, culminating in the creation of *Adamah*. Then, in due course, every
other living thing is brought before *Adamah* to give it a name. "Naming"
here means much more than giving to each thing a nametag. The text is
clear on this much: whatever name *Adamah* gives to a thing, that is what
it will *be*, not just what it will be called. It is a question of metaphysics
or substance, not linguistics or nomenclature. If what we call a "cow" is
brought before *Adamah* or Adam,* he isn't just saying it should be called a
"cow" as opposed to a *vache* or a *kuh* or a *bó*. He is, rather, determining what
this living beast before him *is for him*: a pet, a companion, a milk source,
a plow-engine, a leather jacket, or a meal. God alone, in Genesis, has the
first word, the radically creative word; Adam has the second word. God
had a void before him when he spoke the world into existence *ex nihilo*.
He looked within himself, conceived a desire, and then projected that
desire into a reality before his eyes. Adam, in contrast, has a complete
world before him when he speaks. Take the cow. He doesn't create it out of
nothing. It's already standing there on all four legs, staring at him. Adam
only construes it, decides what he wants to make of it or how he wants to
use it. Adam's speech act is perilous. The risk in it comes from the fact that
he will have to answer to God, the Maker of all things, including the cow,
for what he calls and does with the creation. A river, for instance, can be
construed as mysterious and sacred, or as nourishing and thirst-quenching
for people, animals, and plants, or as a pool to swim in, or a waterway for
travel and trade, or a sewer for waste disposal. The fact is that whatever he

---

* *Adamah*, in Hebrew, is a feminine noun meaning soil or earth, and is sometimes awkwardly
but accurately rendered as "earthling." Traditionally, when personified, this earthling
becomes, problematically, "Adam," whose companion and helpmate is Eve.

"names" it, that is what it will be, *for him*. But he can "get it wrong," violate the world, cause rivers to burn, seas to rise, life to perish. The "names" he gives to his world are powerful, and if he is thoughtless, he can turn any paradise into a hell. Names are like shop signs. They save us time. They tell us all we need to know, for our purposes, about anything or anyone. Orange jumpsuits are shop signs. Yellow six-pointed stars are shop signs. "Yes, hell must be like that: streets filled with shop signs and no way of explaining oneself. One is classified once and for all."[20]

In Clamence's godless world, accountability to the creator is no concern or constraint. What threatens his dream of standing in the shoes of Adam and having the last word is how many other would-be Adams there are out there. Like ants without a queen. Clamence knows he will have to narrow his focus, limit his ambitions, and live in a fantasy of his own making. He knows he can't control or dominate the planet and all of humankind.[*] The only solution, a humbling one, is to start small and lord it over at least something or someone.[**]

> I am well aware that one can't get along without domineering or being served. Every man needs slaves as he needs fresh air. Commanding is breathing, you agree with me? And even the most destitute manage to breathe. The lowest man in the social scale still has his wife or his child. If he's unmarried, a dog. The essential thing, after all, is being able to get angry with someone who has no right to talk back. . . . Somebody has to have the last word.[21]

---

[*] This explains Clamence's predilection for islands. "In a general way, I like all islands. It is easier to dominate them." *The Fall*, p. 43.

[**] This realization echoes one of Augustine's favorite, or at least frequent, bits of practical advice to the effect that if you can't have what you desire, desire what you can have. This, he comments, is "advice given to the miserable, lest one be more miserable." Augustine, *De Trinitate*, 13.7.10. See Meagher, *Augustine*, p. 196.

The act of dominating a dog provides a simple illustration of Clamence's quest to have the last word always. The goal is to have the dog eventually see and regard itself exactly as you see and regard it, to live for your recognition and approval. When you love it, it feels lovable. When you despise it, it feels worthless. It is in its own eyes no more and no less than what it is in your eyes. Look away and it is nothing. Your gaze and regard confer its existence and self-worth.

For Clamence it is no great leap from dogs to women. It remains all about control. In his affairs, mutuality and love had no place. He never loved his women, and he insisted that they never love him. That said, he insisted, "It is not true, after all, that I never loved. I conceived at least one great love in my life, of which I was always the object."[22] Women were for him merely "objects of pleasure and conquest."[23] He expected anonymity in his liaisons—no names, no identities, no stories, only the passion-driven moment, "knowing that it is always better to go to bed with a mystery."[24] These were the "rules of the game" by which they both were to play. His aim was for his lovers to belong to him without his belonging to them. "Sometimes I even went so far," he confesses, "as to make them swear not to give themselves to any other man."[25]

> A certain type of pretension was in fact so personified in me that it was hard for me to imagine, despite the facts, that a woman who had once been mine could ever belong to another. As soon as I knew they would never belong to anyone, I would make up my mind to break off. . . . Some cry: "Love me!" Others: "Don't love me!" But a certain genus, the worst and most unhappy, cries: "Don't love me and be faithful to me!"[26]

Even one-way love is a bond, a snare. It asserts a claim on the other, even if the one claimed rejects it. Disappointment on one side stirs guilt in the other. It's messy, confusing, and painful, or at least annoying. Clamence prefers to spin his web, entangle his prey, and move on. When or whether he returns at all is all up to him. What matters is knowing that his "catch" is not going anywhere and awaits him expectantly. He holds all the cards.

Clamence's happiness depends on his naming, controlling, domineering everything and everyone in his world, his creation, however confined or expansive that world is.

> On my own admission, I could live happily only on condition that all the individuals on earth or the greatest possible number, were turned toward me, eternally in suspense, devoid of independent life and ready to answer my call at any moment, doomed in short to sterility until the day I should deign to favor them. In short, for me to live happily it was essential for the creatures I chose not to live at all. They must receive their life, sporadically, only at my bidding.[27]

"All the individuals on earth or the greatest possible number" has a hapless ring to it. It comes down to "master the world or your dog, whatever you can manage." The bar Mexico City is not the world, but it's better than the cold bedsitter in which we find Clamence huddled in the final act of this tragi-comedy. Clamence's world, his domain, is spun from magical thinking and must be maintained with compulsive care. It's a matter of balancing ambition and risk avoidance. The more carefully he restricts his unscripted exposure to others, the more viable it is for him to sleepwalk through another day.

Clamence's creation is, needless to say, more precarious than a house of cards. Each additional card, each slight extension, can bring it crashing down. It is, in the end, a dream world, from which Clamence might at any moment be awakened. It is an impromptu stage on which he writes the script as he goes, taking the lead, and hoping everyone will just fall in, go along with it, and not shatter the illusion. When they don't, he "collapses in public."[28] He recalls one such episode when, in the big world beyond his bubble, he lost control of the situation and found himself caught in others' gaze, a sudden object of ridicule, "as a result of a series of circumstances, to be sure, but there are always circumstances."[29] Later, he reflects, "When I recovered the recollection of that episode, I realized what it meant . . . my dream had not stood up to facts."[30]

That tremor in Clamence's paradise was, however, only a presage of the "big one," the quake that later shook his makeshift creation to its core. It was past midnight and drizzling. He had just left a woman's bed and was all but alone on the streets as he made his way toward his home on the Left Bank. Crossing the Pont Royal, he passed behind "a figure leaning over the railing and seeming to stare at the river . . . a slim young woman dressed in black." Fifty yards later, walking along the quays, he "heard the sound—which, despite the distance, seemed dreadfully loud in the midnight silence—of a body striking the water."* Then "a cry, repeated several times" and silence.[31] Clamence, trembling, ignored what he told himself to do. He did nothing and informed no one. He went home to bed, and for many days avoided the newspapers.

That was the night that changed everything for Clamence. The curtains closed and the lights went dark on the Parisian stage set he had constructed and the role he had played there. He left his law practice and Paris behind, moved to Amsterdam, and set up court in Mexico City. His new profession was all about penitence and judgment. His relocation to the city of canals was, for Clamence, not a clean break from the past. He brought his guilt with him, as well as the surreal, mocking laughter that had already begun to haunt him in Paris. He never knew when or where it would break out, and it didn't matter that only he heard it. It reminded him of his perennial bad faith, his pride, his pretense, and of the fact that his dream never did and never would stand up to the facts. His final misery and desolation are like that of King Creon in *Antigone*: he rules over a desert, alone.[32] No friends and "no human beings, above all, no human beings. You and I alone facing the planet at last deserted."[33]

---

* This incident is likely a thinly veiled reference to Mme. Francine Camus's attempted escape or suicide, in 1954, when she leapt from the 2nd-floor window of her room in the clinic where she was being treated for severe anxiety and depression. In the fall, Francine fractured her pelvis. Francine's family blamed Camus for his wife's illness and injury, and in part he accepted that guilt. "I have no gift for love," he wrote in a letter to Mamaine Koestler, "nor for suffering, and I wander around without knowing what I am here for." See Todd, *Albert Camus*, p. 319.

CHAPTER THIRTEEN

Judgment

I n *The Fall*, Jean-Baptiste Clamence tells how he, in middle age* and in crisis, changed careers and relocated to a "desert of stones, fogs, and stagnant waters" in Amsterdam. His New Testament namesake, John the Baptist, also went off into a desert at a radical turning point in his life. The parallels between them don't end there. Far from it. Clamence is the living, if distorted, image—the corrupt avatar—of his biblical counterpart. While John the Baptist, the cousin of Jesus, was a prophet true to his calling, Clamence confesses quite frankly that he is a "false prophet,"[1] "an empty prophet for shabby times."[2] John the Baptist, at the beginning of his ministry, went off into the desert wilderness of Judea to fast, pray, and do penance. Then, after a time, he preached repentance to others. The response was astonishing. The solitary penitent suddenly had countless penitents on their knees before him, confessing their sins, seeking forgiveness.

> John the baptizer appeared in the wilderness, proclaiming a baptism of repentance, for the forgiveness of sins. And people from the whole Judean countryside and all the people of Jerusalem

---

* When he launched into his "Mexico City" monologue, Clamence was forty years old, roughly the same age as Camus when was composing that monologue. Camus was forty-two when *The Fall* was published in May 1956.

were going out to him, and were baptized in the river Jordan,
confessing their sins.[3]

This story provides the inspiration for Clamence's final career move and
his ultimate profession. It is all he needs to envision and establish his new
practice at Mexico City.

"I have already told you," he candidly explains to his latest listener and
to every new reader, "I am a judge-penitent. Only one thing is simple in my
case: I possess nothing."[4] Like his biblical forerunner, John the Baptist, we
find Clamence devoid of any significant possessions. Unlike his "mentor,"
he is not clothed in camel's hair, nor does he graze on locusts and wild
honey. That said, his life in Amsterdam is relatively austere by modern,
urban standards. Regardless, the fact is he's a fake. Unlike a real prophet
and baptist, he screens his potential followers. He has no interest in wasting
his time on anyone who will not stick with him to the end or, worse, might
break out laughing at him in the middle of one of his orations.

> Allow me to ask you two questions and don't answer if you
> consider them indiscreet. Do you have some possessions? Some?
> Good. Have you shared them with the poor? No? Then you
> are what I call a Sadducee.* If you are not familiar with the
> Scriptures, I admit that this will not help you. But it does help
> you? So you know the Scriptures? Decidedly, you interest me.[5]

With these words, Clamence appears to express his preference for men
of means and letters, who spend their days in cafés and soirées, among their
own, bolstering their sense of personal privilege and elevated self-worth.
Men ridden with unacknowledged bad faith and self-doubt. Men like
himself, who with a little prodding will see themselves in him.

---

* The name (or "shop sign") for the Sadducees may have been derived from a word meaning
the "righteous ones." They were a group of wealthy, educated Jews, well-connected with the
Jerusalem powers-that-be, Jewish and Roman, but unpopular with the people, from whom
they stayed aloof. John the Baptist called the Sadducees "a brood of vipers."

After taking in his latest follower, his freshest recruit, Clamence—across five days—bares himself, confessing with unguarded candor his countless sins, the full moral catastrophe that his life has represented: his conceits, his debaucheries, his drinking a dying comrade's last cup of water, his theft of a priceless artwork, his all-encompassing cynicism and pride. In his long fall from grace, Clamence has plummeted through each of the rings of hell, splashing finally into the frigid waters of Cocytus to join Judas, Brutus, and Cassius, his fraternal betrayers. Clamence embodies the three traditional Christian categories of illicit desire* that provide much of the scaffolding of Dante's *Inferno*: *libido sentienti, libido sciendi, libido dominandi* (lust of the flesh, lust of the eyes and mind, lust for power). In the world of sin, Clamence has done it all. He is, indeed, "the aggregate of all the vices of our whole generation in their fullest expression,"[6] which means that he has provided something for everyone, something with which to identify, and for which to feel guilt or shame.

Upon the completion of his "general confession"**—a tour de force by any sacramental measure—Clamence prepares to mount the judge's bench and exercise his exalted office as judge-penitent. In the normal order of things, indicted criminals come before a judge and confess their crimes or hear them recounted by a prosecutor. Then, Clamence explains, everyone in the courtroom, beginning with the judge, inwardly confesses to themselves that they, too, are sinners, not saints. Next time it might well be them in the box of the accused, awaiting judgment. How, then, do judges, knowing all they know about themselves, dare to stand and pronounce judgment on others without first passing judgment on themselves? "Should I climb up to the pulpit," wonders Clamence, "like many of my illustrious contemporaries,

---

* See *I John*, 2.16 for the earliest Christian formulation of these three illicit desires or lusts embraced by those who love the world and themselves, not God: *quoniam omne quod est in mundo concupiscentia carnis et concupiscentia oculorum est et superbia vitae.*

** In Catholic sacramental practice, a "general confession" differs from an ordinary or "routine" confession, in which penitents confess only those sins committed since their last confession. In a general confession, penitents endeavor to confess the cardinal sins they have committed across their lifetime (so far).

and curse humanity? Very dangerous, that is!"[7] Laughter could break out any moment, laughter directed at him and at the absurdity of his robes, his courtroom, his self-righteous pretense in judging others—fellow sinners—so like himself, except that they happen to find themselves on the wrong side of the bench, labeled, named, accused. Condemned to ridicule, the judge finds himself judged. At least the condemned criminal looks down at the floor, acknowledging guilt. Then it occurs to Clamence, a "stroke of genius."[8]

> Inasmuch as one couldn't condemn others without immediately judging oneself, one had to overwhelm oneself to have the right to judge others. Inasmuch as every judge someday ends up as a penitent, one had to travel the road in the opposite direction and practice the profession of penitent to be able to end up as a judge. You follow me? Good.[9]

This was the insight, the ingenious plan, that brought Clamence to Amsterdam in the first place to practice his "useful"[10] (as he puts it) but hardly lucrative profession in Mexico City.

> It consists to begin with, as you know from experience, in indulging in public confession as often as possible. I accuse myself up and down. It's not hard, for I now have acquired a memory. I mingle what concerns me and what concerns others. I choose the features we have in common, the experiences we have endured together, the failings we share. . . . With all that I construct a portrait which is the image of all and of no one.[11]

Next is the moment of betrayal, the Judas kiss on the cheek of the client and the reader. It is easy to miss, to disregard its import; but in that kiss, that embrace, lies Clamence's darkest sin, his betrayal of friendship and, with it, his (and our) common humanity. In confessing himself the lowest of the low, he sets the stage for what comes next.

Then imperceptibly I pass from the "I" to the "we." When I get to "this is what we are," the trick has been played and I can tell them off. . . . The more I accuse myself the more I have a right to judge you. Even better, I provoke you into judging yourself. . . . Ah, *mon cher*, we are odd wretched creatures, and if we merely look back over our lives, there's no lack of occasions to amaze and horrify ourselves. Just try. I shall listen, you may be sure, to your confession with a great feeling of fraternity. [12]

This is when, hearing the confession of his client-penitent, Clamence imagines himself at his highest point, at the height of his power. "I dominate at last, but forever. . . . I have found a height to which I am the only one to climb and from which I can judge everybody."[13] He says he feels like no less than "God the Father" at the Final Judgement. He glories in having the last word. The whole multitude of the human race comes before him to be judged, their sins and shabby lives as visible and undeniable as shop signs. Clamence envisions them approaching his throne:

They rise slowly; I already see the first of them arriving. . . . And as for me, I pity without absolving, I understand without forgiving, and above all, I feel at last that I am being adored. [14]

Caught up in Clamence's proclamation of his power, we might overlook the discrediting fact that he delivers his peroration from his bed. He is feverish. Among other things he is suffering from terminal vertigo. He imagines he has risen to a great height, whereas he has in fact fallen to a great depth. Anyone can see that, anyone but himself. He is in the pit of hell, not in the heaven of heavens. He has bottomed out, not summited. Some part of himself suspects as much, and in his weakest moments he admits it. "I occasionally hear a distant laugh and again I doubt. But quickly I crush everything, people and things, under the weight of my own infirmity, and at once I perk up."[15]

There are throughout *The Fall* other voices besides that of Clamence. It is not a simple monologue. Clamence's client clearly has thoughts unspoken and things to say. And we can often guess what they are. Then there is laughter, and the ever-present threat of laughter. There is humor, too, in the tone of the text, ironic and satirical. We can trace all of these voices, of course, including that of Clamence, back to Camus. He is, on every page, the voice behind the curtain. Clamence, like Camus, is no believer, but that restrains neither of them from expressing their views on religion, particularly Christianity. "Believe me," pronounces Clamence, "religions are on the wrong track the moment they moralize and fulminate commandments. God is not needed to create guilt or to punish. Our fellow men suffice, aided by ourselves."[16] We humans are drowning in judgment and guilt. Hell, we are reminded, is other people. We don't need a god to make us miserable, or to create misery for others. Prisons are a growth industry. That business is booming. We judge each other every time we read the newspaper or watch the news; and, if no one comes forth to judge us, we do it for ourselves. "Don't wait for the Last Judgment. It takes place every day."[17]

When Clamence asserts that "God's sole usefulness would be to guarantee innocence,"[18] we can easily imagine Camus's lips moving as his pen writes. From his early studies under the tutelage of Jean Grenier, Camus displayed a particular interest in Christian philosophy and theology. His engagement with religion was never that of a believer seeking inspiration but that of an agnostic seeking understanding. He never saw atheism or blasphemy as credentials, as badges of distinction and personal achievement. "I don't believe in God, it is true: but this does not make me an atheist. I would even agree . . . that irreligion is something rather vulgar and, yes, something rather worn out."[19] He described his own position as one of polite disbelief. The fact was that across his life—from Jean Grenier, to the villagers of Le Chambon, to comrades in the Resistance—he knew and deeply respected too many exemplary Christians, some of them clergy, to dismiss them as frauds or dupes. Never blind to the corruption, hypocrisy, superstition, and sheer ignorance displayed by many Christians and their robed shepherds, Camus never let the rogues blind him to the real thing.

ALBERT CAMUS AND THE HUMAN CRISIS 183

Granted, the prison priest in *The Stranger* received only fury and scorn from Meursault. They were made for each other. The priest was no more evolved in his Christianity than was Meursault in his humanity. Both marked a zero point from which there was no way but up. The crucifix-waving magistrate was no better, a caricature at best. In *The Plague*, when Paneloux delivered the first of his two plague sermons, he was already strides beyond the prison priest. He was learned and thoughtful, an Augustine scholar. His training had not been from a Dick-and-Jane catechism. He was steeped in the church fathers and the medieval scholastics. What he lacked was life experience, particularly the experience of suffering—senseless, innocent suffering. When a child's torturous death shook him to his core, he grew, and his faith grew with him. Rieux, once his foe, embraced him, as Camus eventually embraced Mauriac. They agreed to disagree and put their shoulders to the rock, their common human fate and task.

The next and final advance in Camus's trajectory of religious understanding comes from—of all people—Clamence, the false prophet. It is curious but somehow fitting that Camus would elect this tormented cynic to be the spokesman of his fully developed humanistic "Christology." Neither Camus nor Clamence, we know, were men of faith; and yet the New Testament provides much of the landscape and language in *The Fall*. If Camus and Clamence had a quarrel with Christianity, it was not with Jesus. "I feel a friendship for the first Christian of all," admits Clamence. [20] Camus later aligned himself explicitly with Clamence, making clear that in this regard Clamence speaks for him:

> Like him (Clamence), I have a great feeling of friendship for the first Christian. I admire the way he lived and the way he died.* My lack of imagination prevents me from going any further than this. And that, I may say, is the only point which I have in

---

* Gandhi, like Camus an outsider to Christianity, is said to have once remarked that "I like your Christ, I do not like your Christians. Your Christians are so unlike your Christ."

common with this Jean-Baptiste Clamence with whom people
want to identify me.[21]

And just what did Clamence and Camus see about the way Christ lived
and died that so endeared him to them?

Clamence is clear on at least this much: Jesus was about forgiveness, not
judgment. This was the truth of his life, but the truth, as Clamence sees
it, has been belied by those latter-day Christians who

> have hoisted him onto a judge's bench . . . and they smite,
> they judge above all, they judge in his name. He spoke softly
> to the adulteress: "Neither do I condemn thee!"[22] but that
> doesn't matter; they condemn without absolving anyone. He
> simply wanted to be loved, nothing more. Of course, there are
> those who love him, even among Christians. But they are not
> numerous.[23]

"I am inclined," explains Clamence, "to see religion as a huge laundering
venture—as it was once but briefly, for exactly three years, and it wasn't
called religion."[24] Clamence is referring here, of course, to the three years
of what is traditionally known as Jesus's "public life," when he walked the
earth healing the sick, consoling the afflicted, teaching the misguided,
and forgiving sins, until he was murdered, like Socrates, for his upright
life and true words. Nothing threatens the corrupt more than decency and
truth. But was that the only reason he eventually found himself nailed to
a cross? Clamence doesn't think so. "Say," Clamence queries his audience,
"do you know why he was crucified. . . . The real reason is that *he* knew he
was not altogether innocent."[25]

What Clamence goes on to propose is that Jesus, on the day he suffered,
carried a great burden of guilt in addition to the weight of the cross. He
was a criminal, "brought face to face with his innocent crime," a crime
"that consists less in making others die than in not dying oneself!" It was
a crime he had lived with for a long time, his entire life, and as time passed

"he found it too hard for him to hold on and continue. It was better to have done with it, not to defend himself, to die, in order not to be the only one to live."[26] But what was this "innocent crime" that Jesus had committed by not dying when all the others did? What did he know about himself that so weighed him down? Clamence explains that "he must have heard of a certain Slaughter of the Innocents."[27]

The episode in Jesus's life story that Clamence has in mind here is recounted in only one of the four Christian gospels, and then only briefly:

> When Herod saw that he had been tricked by the wise men, he was infuriated, and he sent and killed all the children in and around Bethlehem who were two years old or under, according to the time that he had learned from the wise men. Then was fulfilled what had been spoken through the prophet Jeremiah: "A voice was heard in Ramah, wailing and loud lamentation; Rachel weeping for her children; she refused to be consoled, because they are no more."[28]

Learning from the magi that a great king had been born in his Judea, Herod felt only fear and rage. His first and final impulse was to murder the child before he became an actual threat. From the little that the magi told Herod about the timing of the infant king's birth, he took no chances and ordered the massacre of every boy born in the past two years. It was only due to divine intervention that Jesus, who obviously fit the description of the doomed, managed to escape unscathed. An angel appeared to Jesus's father, Joseph, in a dream to warn him of the impending massacre so that Joseph might flee at once with his wife and newborn son and escape across the Sinai to Egypt.

The "Slaughter of the Innocents" is the dark side of Christmas. It receives little notice during the holiday season, upstaged by the babe in the manger, the angels on high, the shepherds tending their flocks, and the conspicuous arrival of Oriental magi bearing regal gifts. Clamence, however, seems to have dwelled on the grim massacre of innocent children and imagined its impact on Jesus when he first learned that he alone, of all the "children of Rachel," had survived the mass infanticide aimed at him. All that death because of him!

> Those blood-spattered soldiers, those infants cut in two filled him with horror. But given the man he was, I am sure he could not forget them. And as for that sadness that can be felt in his every act, wasn't it the incurable melancholy of a man who heard night after night the voice of Rachel weeping for her children and refusing all comfort?[29]

Given the man he was—this focus on the deeply vulnerable humanity of Jesus is the key to Clamence's (and Camus's) humanistic Christology. Since the earliest centuries of Christianity one serious challenge for believers was to accept the full, unedited humanity of Jesus. That, however, was the easy part for Clamence and Camus. What is remarkable, and out of character for Clamence, was his sympathetic focus on Jesus and, even more striking, his fondness for him. He admired his kindness in a cruel, unforgiving world, and also his endurance in carrying such a weight of guilt through his every day, when "carrying on, merely continuing, is superhuman. And he was not superhuman, you can take my word for it. He cried aloud his agony and that's why I love him, my friend who died without knowing."[30]

Without knowing what, we wonder? And when was it that Jesus cried aloud in agony? Clamence has already explained what he has in mind:

> Yes, it was the third evangelist, I believe, who first suppressed his complaint: "Why hast thou forsaken me?"—it was a seditious cry, wasn't it? Well, then, the scissors![31]

What Clamence points out here is that in the first two gospels—Matthew and Mark—Jesus, as he dies, cries out to his God, "Why have you forsaken me?"[32] An agonized cry of reproach and despair. In both Matthew and Mark, these were the last words of Jesus, spoken in the ninth hour, at three o'clock in the afternoon, the traditional hour of his death. Luke and John, on the other hand, omitted this cry altogether in their gospel accounts.* The "scissors" (that is, the censors) had come out, as Clamence suggests. Luke recorded, instead, the following revised last words of Jesus as he died at three in the afternoon: "Father, into your hands I commend my spirit."** No trace here of complaint or desolation. John, the fourth evangelist, in his gospel, has Jesus saying even less as he dies: "It is finished." "Then," John adds, "he bowed his head and gave up his spirit."[33] In Luke and John, there is no death agony, of body or of spirit. Jesus offers his death to God in sublime and confident submission. His work is complete. His father's will is done. The prophecies are fulfilled. There is no hint of doubt or consternation. Jesus knows what comes next, as evidenced in Luke by his earlier words of consolation to the man crucified at his side: "Truly I tell you, today you will be with me in paradise."[34]

However extraneous it is to the matter at hand, at this point we may be remarking to ourselves that Clamence certainly knows his Bible! This level of biblical literacy and of concerned theological reflection may seem altogether out of character for Clamence, but surely not for Camus. In his early studies and through all his ensuing endeavors—literary, political, philosophical, and dramatic—Camus drew inspiration and guidance from a lifelong dialogue and engagement with the Bible, the church fathers, and early Christian philosophy, as we have seen evidenced repeatedly. But back to the matter at hand, why should Camus or Clamence care about Jesus's last words—whether they expressed inconsolable abandonment or sanguine submission? What was, what is, at stake in the alleged silencing and revision of the last moments and words of Jesus on the cross? In *The Rebel*, Camus had already directly addressed these questions:

---

* "With Luke true treason begins, causing the disappearance of Jesus' desperate dying cries." Camus, *Notebooks 1951–1959*, p. 131.

** *Luke*, 23.46. These words echo the Canticle of Simeon, known as the Nunc Dimittis, which begins: "Master, now you are dismissing your servant in peace, according to your word." *Luke*, 2.29 (NRSV).

The night on Golgotha* is so important in the history of man
only because, in its shadow, the divinity abandoned its traditional privileges and drank to the last drop, despair included, the
agony of death. This is the explanation of the *Lama sabactani*[35]
and the heartrending doubt of Christ in agony. The agony would
have been mild if it had been alleviated by hopes of eternity. For
God to be man, he must despair.[36]

Mortality, we know well, is part of being human, and so Jesus must die.
All finite beings cease to exist at some point. Human beings, in addition to
being finite, are temporal to their core. They belong to time. Jesus, in his
humanity, was no exception. At any moment in his life, part of his life was
already behind him, and the other part lay ahead of him. He knew his past
but not his future. We know what that feels like. Ordinarily, as we move
through life we think of our past as what lies behind us, and our future as
what lies ahead of us. But if we think about that from the perspective of
sight, outer sight and inner sight, as did the ancient Greeks, we *see* and *know*
the past, not the future,** what is already behind us, not what lies ahead
for us. This means that as we walk through our lives, eyes ahead, we walk
blind. We know what's happened, but we don't know what's coming. As
we near death, we look back on our life, but we look ahead into darkness.
How could it have been any different for Jesus, if he was human, as Christian doctrine insists? As Matthew and Mark record, Jesus died a wretched
death and stared into a night as dark as nothingness. This, again, is Camus's
point: *For God to be man, he must despair.* This, we remember, is also the
reason Clamence was able to say "He cried aloud his agony and that's why
I love him, my friend who died without knowing."[37] The defining reality

---

* All three of the synoptic gospels (Matthew, Mark, and Luke) record that the sky darkened
at noon and remained dark until three, the span of time that Jesus hung on the cross.

** In ancient Greek, οἶδα (*oida*) means "I know." *Oida*, however, is actually the perfect form of
the verb to see. In other words, to say "I know" is literally to say "I have seen." That is how
we know anything, by having seen it. Seeing isn't believing, contrary to the common saying.
Seeing is knowing.

of friendship is κοινωνία (*koinonia*), "solidarity." "Friends," Plato reminds us, "have all things in common."[38] If we die "without knowing," in the dark, so must Jesus.

"Christ came to solve two major problems," wrote Camus in *The Rebel*, "evil and death, which are precisely the problems that preoccupy the rebel. His solution consisted, first, in experiencing them."[39] With plague ravaging his city and having just watched an innocent child die a torturous death, Father Paneloux concluded that those who would follow Christ must embrace the same "solution." They must experience evil, suffering, and death. In fact, they have no choice but to do so. No longer could Paneloux assure his congregation that

> the child's suffering (or theirs) would be compensated for by an eternity of bliss awaiting him . . . how could he give that assurance when, to tell the truth, he knew nothing about it? . . . No, he, Father Paneloux, would keep faith with that great symbol of all suffering, the tortured body on the Cross; he would stand fast, his back to the wall, and face honestly the terrible problem of a child's suffering.[40]

Camus, writing *The Stranger* in his twenties, had created, in the prison priest, a straw man, a convenient and deserving target for Meursault's rage. Later, as he wrote *The Plague*, there were still strands of that same straw sticking out in the figure of Paneloux when he delivered his first plague sermon. Paneloux grew, however, when he witnessed suffering and experienced doubt. He didn't lose his faith; he embraced his humanity. But Paneloux didn't grow all by himself. It was Camus who rewrote him, and so it was Camus who grew before Paneloux did. Throughout his life, Camus never settled for unexamined opinions or half-truths. He never made it easy for himself. He had known and revered too many devout Christians for him to dismiss them and their beliefs as misguided. They were admirable in their humanity. If they were more, he wasn't going to begrudge them that. They had their humanity in common, and that was enough for friends.

What can we conclude, or at least conjecture, from Clamence's reflections on the humanity of Jesus? At the very least, that Clamence is still searching, contrary to first impressions. He is still open to something new. He is, after all, in a figurative hell, or at least its vestibule, shivering with chills, friendless, loveless, in what he has called his "little ease" [41] with nowhere to look but up.* So he does look up, and that's when he sees the snow, descending like doves in huge flakes, and excitedly declares, "Oh. I must go out!" [42]

> What an invasion! Let's hope they are bringing good news. Everyone will be saved, eh?—and not only the elect. Possessions and hardships will be shared and you, for example, from today on you will sleep every night on the ground for me. The whole shooting match, eh! Come now, admit that you would be flabbergasted if a chariot came down from heaven to carry me off, or if the snow suddenly caught fire. You don't believe it? Nor do I. But still I must go out. [43]

The Fall ends on an odd double note. On the one hand, Clamence looks back to the Pont Royal and cries out to the drowned woman to throw herself again from the bridge to give him another chance to save her, admitting in the same breath that it's too late for that. The water's too cold, and he'd probably walk away a second time. On the other hand, there's the snow, transforming the sky, the canals, and all of Amsterdam. So unforeseen, so simply miraculous. Grace may be like that—unbidden, undeserved, free. Clamence couldn't help himself, he had to go out and greet it. Then, who knows . . . ?

---

* The same image appears in *The Stranger* to describe Meursault's cramped prison cell with only one overhead window.

CHAPTER FOURTEEN

Friendship

C lamence's final declaration in *The Fall*—"I must go out"—signals a new beginning. But how can this be? Clamence is in hell, along with his entire generation; a hell of his own making, a hell from which there appears to be no exit. His betrayal of friendship has hurled him there, and his own cynicism has shut the door behind him. Yet wait, he is not quite in hell, but only in its vestibule—purgatory—a way station of remorse, penance, and second chances. All who enter there need not abandon all hope. Like snow—unbidden, undeserved, free—grace is possible if Clamence, the terminal cynic, is only willing to go out into the night and greet it. A fresh beginning, a friend who would sleep on the floor for him, a woman who, already lost, would give him a second chance to save her—he doesn't believe in any of this. It's all too late for him. He's lost. All the same, he can't stop himself.

Mythical Sisyphus, we recall, talked his way out of Hades into a brief reprieve, long enough to make a new start. After that he lived on borrowed time, but who doesn't? In 1957, Clamence was not alone in purgatory. His maker stood beside him. Camus was as beset as he had ever been, and his "faith in life was faltering."[1] In his *Notebooks* he wrote of severe claustrophobia, acute respiratory attacks in which he nearly suffocated, dark depression, anxiety and panic, inability to work. In sum, "a feeling of total madness."[2] He was seized with grief and guilt over his disintegrating marriage and distressed over its likely ongoing effect on his children. The Nobel Prize, instead of bringing delight and affirmation, brought Camus more abandonment and abuse than ever. Even his longtime stalwart patron and friend, Pascal Pia, dismissed Camus, calling him "a secular saint in the service of an anachronistic humanism."[3] Instead of lifting him to new heights, the Nobel Prize disheartened Camus. He feared it spoke more to his past than to his future, a weighty monument to a great writer who no longer had anything of import to say. A mausoleum. In his Nobel acceptance speech, Camus described himself as "a man almost young, rich only in his doubts and with his work still in progress, accustomed to living in the solitude of work or in the retreats of friendship," asking, "how would he not feel a kind of panic at hearing the decree that transports him all of a sudden, alone and reduced to himself, to the center of a glaring light?"[4] Like Clamence, he was a man in crisis, a man seemingly at his highest point, but in reality cold and alone, far from the sea and the sun, in the vestibule of hell.

Regarding war-ravaged Algeria, where "he hurt at this moment, as others feel pain in their lungs,"[5] Camus had fallen silent. He had been vocal when others were silent;[*] now he was silent when those others, on the Right and on the Left, gorged the streets and the press with their cries for blood. Camus had been "the only French journalist forced to leave Algeria for defending the Muslim population"[6] and for exposing in the press the gross injustices of French colonial rule and their disastrous consequences for the poor and oppressed. Now he had nothing to say that others would hear or heed, nothing that would do anything but make things worse, spill more blood, cost more lives. He would work instead behind the scenes, quietly but with purpose, to lessen the suffering and death, intervening in

---

[*] "For the past twenty years, first in Algiers itself, quite alone, and later in France, at a time when the public, including that segment of the public which is most vociferous today, systematically ignored Algerian realities, I defended the right of the Arab people to be treated justly. Because of my actions, I was forced to leave Algeria, where I had been deprived of the means of earning a livelihood." Camus, *Algerian Chronicles*, p. 205.

ALBERT CAMUS AND THE HUMAN CRISIS

more than 150 cases to plead for the lives of Algerian militants sentenced to execution.

Before leaving for Stockholm, Camus had reached a resolve. He would commit himself anew to his calling as an artist, whose "role is not free from difficult duties. By definition he cannot put himself today in the service of those who make history; he is at the service of those who suffer it."[7] He would focus on "the two tasks that constitute the greatness of his craft: the service of truth and the service of liberty."[8] He would "go out" of himself and confront anew, as a writer, the human crisis, the abandonment of friendship, the severing of the human bond, the betrayal of our common humanity.

Camus's last completed work, published in 1957, comprised six diverse short stories published under the title *Exile and the Kingdom*. In them, Clamence and his inner demons made no reappearance. Camus returned to himself and "in the very hour of exile" rediscovered "those two or three great and simple ideas in whose presence his heart first opened."[9] At forty-four, however, that heart, while still beating, was admittedly weary. Camus, body and soul, was tired and disillusioned, but far from defeated. From the pursuit of happiness he turned his gaze and energies to the pursuit of justice and the reduction of suffering. He was driven now less by passion than by compassion. He grew accustomed, but not resigned, to exile. We might well imagine him, in his darkest, most silent moments, crying out, in the words of the poet Gerard Manley Hopkins, "Send my roots rain."[10] Or, perhaps, snow.

Two of the focal characters in *Exile and the Kingdom** embody that cry: Daru in "The Guest" and d'Arrast in "The Growing Stone." In these stories Camus focused on friendship, a grace each time it offers itself in life, a

---

* We can readily imagine what "exile" means in this title. We see its meaning in Camus's life and hear it in his words. The meaning of "the kingdom" is more elusive and enigmatic. In it, Camus appears to have stepped out of Greek myth and into the Bible. "The kingdom" begs the question: what kingdom? The kingdom of heaven, the kingdom of God, the kingdom of man, the kingdom of this world . . . ? They all have a biblical ring to them, an air of mystery and the unknown. Did Camus know what he meant here or was he searching for it?

respite from alienation and loneliness, a return from exile, a homecoming. In turning now to these two stories, we return to where we began in this book, to our common humanity and to the mutual goodwill without which we find ourselves with Clamence, in a cynically frigid, man-made hell.

The key that opens "The Guest" and reveals its riches lies in the story's French title: "L'Hôte." In French, *l'hôte* has two meanings: "the host" and "the guest." What may at first appear confusing is, we shall see, actually clarifying. A similar conflation of *host* and *guest* exists in many languages: *hospes* in Latin, *ospite* in Italian, ξένος (*xenos*) in Greek, to cite a few. What *host* and *guest* have in common is their initial estrangement. They are both strangers to each other. They meet and come together in their mutual estrangement. This is not true, of course, when we host friends or relatives, colleagues or new acquaintances. In the normal order of things we don't invite perfect strangers into our home, to eat and stay with us, without a prior connection, without knowing them or at least knowing who they are, unless, of course, we operate a hotel, a guest house, or a B&B—in other words, unless we are in the hospitality business, in which case we open our doors to anyone and everyone for a fee. But that fee makes the host and guest quite different, even opposite, from each other. Without the fee, the door is closed.

The roots of Camus's story lie not in a business transaction but in the ancient ritual of hospitality, sacred to the civilizations of the ancient Mediterranean and beyond. Among Bedouins in North Africa and the Middle East it is still widely observed. The traditional rites of hospitality provide the stranger, any stranger at the door, with a bath, a fresh cloak, a meal, and a roof, usually for three days (the day of arrival, a day of rest, and the day of departure). These are the basic needs of any wayfarer. As understood and practiced in antiquity, this ritual is offered to strangers by strangers. They do not at first introduce or identify themselves to each other. The one is in need (of nourishment, rest, safety) and the other is in possession of the resources (bed, board, and roof) to address that need. That is all that needs to be clear at first. It is, in fact, essential that guest and host conceal their identities behind the mask of silence. Who the stranger is, where they come from, the purpose of their journey, etc. will be revealed only after the offer of hospitality has been made and accepted, usually at the first meal they share. By masking *who* they are, they unmask *what* they are: fellow human beings. That is enough. That is the point. They may be distantly related or have friends in common; they may share the same religious beliefs and political views, or they may not. If they knew more about one another, they might want no part of each other, or they might embrace each other for the wrong reasons, namely for personal reasons. Hospitality is about their common humanity, not kinship or congeniality.

A traditional Bedouin greeting to strangers says it all: "You are among your family." [11] The human family. Hospitality is about the essential friendship between all human beings, affirmed and sustained in opening our doors to each other and sharing what we have, which comes down to sharing life. Hospitality is about what Camus called "the natural human community." An old Welsh rhyme puts it this way:

> Hail guest, we ask not what thou art;
> If friend, we greet thee, hand and heart;
> If stranger, such no longer be;
> If foe, our love shall conquer thee. [12]

In hospitality, strangers share each other's condition. The presence of a stranger under his roof estranges the host in his own house. "Let a stranger live with you, and he'll estrange your way of life," writes Ben Sira. [13] When a stranger is taken in and made to feel at home, his host feels a little less at home. Hospitality is about the goodwill we owe to every member of our shared human family. The fortunes that divide us are all too readily reversed. We have no claim on them. Our only claim is to the goodwill of others. "Where," asks Aeschylus, "is good will greater than in the host towards the guest?" [14] "One who bids me to eat wishes me to live." [15] The rituals of hospitality come down to the host assuring the guest that he wishes him to live. He wishes him well. He recognizes their human bond, their essential friendship. It is human sympathy, compassion, in its purest, most primal expression.

Camus's "The Guest" is a simple, translucent parable in which a young French schoolteacher named Daru and his nameless, mostly silent, Arab guest reenact the timeless ritual of hospitality. The story is set in the desperately poor desert region of Kabylia,* a region of "horrifying sights in the midst of an incomparable natural environment,"[16] where Daru was born and from which he had gone to war and seen men murder each other. This was "a cruel place to live, even without the men, who didn't help matters. But Daru had been born here. Anywhere else, he felt exiled."[17] He had come home from the war and returned to his birthplace to teach local Arab children in an isolated one-room school, with an extra room that housed him. Besides teaching, Daru distributed government rations of wheat to his students' families to get them through the drought that had left them starving and their animals dead. Beyond the burden of dire poverty and all the assaults on life that come with it, now there was war. Following the FLN's** proclamation of Algerian independence on November 1, 1954, armed revolts and killings broke out and became more numerous and widespread throughout Algeria. Daru wanted no more part of war and killing. He had laid down his arms. He was a teacher now, committed to nourishing the children he taught, their bellies and their minds.

After eight months of drought, there was a blizzard, and his students were not coming to school. He had the day to himself, until he looked out his window and saw Balducci, the local gendarme, on horseback, pulling behind him, on a rope, his bound Arab prisoner. Daru invited them in and made them tea, requesting that the man's hands be set free. Balducci explained that the Arab had killed his cousin in a family dispute over grain, and Daru's "orders" were to deliver the prisoner the next day to Tinguit, a

---

* Kabylia and its desperation were the focus of a series of feature articles under the title "The Misery of Kabylia," that Camus wrote for *Alger républicain* in 1939. Like Daru, Camus was returning in this story to a place he knew well and cared about deeply.

** The *Front de Libération Nationale*, the principal Algerian nationalist movement/party during the Algerian War.

town twenty kilometers away, to be tried for murder and, no doubt, hanged. Daru said he had no intention of following such "orders." His job was to teach children, not to deliver a man, whatever his crime, to execution. It was a standoff, and Balducci had no time for it. Rebellion was in the air. He had been mobilized, and he had more on his plate than a family dispute that had turned deadly. After a cup of tea, Balducci rode off and left the Arab with Daru.

Now they were alone, the two of them, host and guest; but which was which? The Arab was in Daru's home; but Daru, a *Pied-Noir*, a European settler, was in the Arab's land. In one sense Daru was the Arab's host, and in another sense he was the Arab's guest. In either case they were strangers to each other, observing the rites of hospitality; and in doing so they became friends, what the ancient Greeks called guest-friends. Daru welcomed the Arab, invited him to wash up, while Daru prepared a warm bed for him to spend the night and a hot meal for them to share.

Daru set two places at the table and laid it with an omelet, dates, bread, and hot condensed milk. Although they could have conversed—Daru, like his guest, spoke Arabic—they exchanged only a few words. The Arab asked, "Why are you eating with me?" and Daru gave the simplest of answers: "I'm hungry."[18] They were both men, sharing the same hungers, the same needs, the same love of life and fear of death. Now they were sharing the same bread. The Arab asked if he was the judge, but Daru was neither jailer, judge, nor executioner. Tonight they were host and guest, friends. The Arab was free to go any time, and Daru hoped he would.

Later, ready for sleep, they asked each other questions. Why had the Arab killed? Would the gendarme return? What will they do to me tomorrow? The Arab's last words that night were a simple, enigmatically open request: "Come with us."[19] In the small room that was all that Daru had for a home, they lay only feet apart, Daru in his bed and the Arab in a camp cot. Daru always slept naked, and on that night he made no exception. He felt vulnerable, and he was. They both were. The exhausted Arab dropped off to sleep in minutes, while Daru lay sleepless, listening to his guest-stranger's breathing.

In the room where he had slept alone for a year, this presence
disturbed him. But it disturbed him also by imposing on him
a sort of brotherhood, which he rejected in the present circumstances, familiar as it was. Men who share the same sleeping
quarters, soldiers and prisoners, develop a strange bond, as if
shedding their weapons with their clothes, they were joined
together each evening, beyond their differences, in the ancient
community of dreams and fatigue. [20]

The next morning, Daru shook the Arab to wake him; when Daru
saw the sudden terror in his eyes, he tried to calm him: "Don't be afraid.
It's me. Time to eat." [21] After their breakfast, Daru put together a modest
packet of provisions for the Arab, enough for whichever journey the Arab
chose to take. Daru hoped he would choose to live, not to die at the end
of a rope. But that was a choice his guest-friend would have to make for
himself. They walked together in silence for two hours until they reached
a rocky perch from which two roads branched out: the one led to Tinguit, a
token trial, and a rapid execution; the other led south to fertile pastures
and hospitable nomads who would take the Arab in and make him safe.
In addition to the packet of food he had prepared, Daru gave the Arab a
thousand francs, enough to keep him alive for a couple of days. Then Daru
left him. He felt the Arab's eyes fixed on his back. When Daru finally
turned to catch sight of the Arab from afar, his heart ached to see in the
distance that the Arab had decided to walk to his death.

Arriving back at his school in full daylight, Daru walked into the empty
classroom and found that "on the blackboard, among the meanderings of
the French rivers, a clumsy hand had traced in chalk the inscription '*You
turned in our brother. You will pay.*'" [22] The fact that he had done precisely the
opposite was irretrievably lost, as was any possibility of dialogue with his
Arab neighbors. The fact that he taught their children and helped feed their
families was equally irrelevant. Then there was the fact that, in refusing to
deliver up the Arab to the French authorities, he had effectively wiped away
his national service in the war, as easily as chalk is erased on a blackboard.

It was Algeria, 1957. Lines were drawn. There were only two sides, and Daru found himself on both, which meant neither. "In this vast country he had loved so much, he was alone."[23]

"The Growing Stone," the longest and most complex story in *Exile and the Kingdom*, continues and expands the theme of hospitality. It is the last completed story that Camus would write and publish before his death. As if he knew that, he created a work infused and resonant with the rich legacy he would leave us, while at the same time gesturing beyond anything he had yet expressed or written. Put simply, "The Growing Stone" is both a précis and preview. It is set in a remote, riverside Brazilian town,* whose poorest inhabitants were periodically terrorized by the surging, muddy floodwaters that wiped away their humble, low-lying huts variously constructed from mud, branches, tin, and reeds. D'Arrast was both a guest and a deliverer of these people. He was a French engineer, commissioned to construct a jetty that would bring an end to their woes, at least those inflicted by their unruly tidal river. He was in their eyes a Promethean figure, who might as well have come down from Olympus (or heaven) to lessen their suffering.

> To command the waters, to conquer rivers; ah!—a great profession, and surely the poor people of Iguape would remember the engineer's name and for many years to come would utter it in their prayers.[24]

D'Arrast soon learns, however, that he is not the only source of wonders in Iguape on that day. Besides being the day of his arrival, it is the festival of the good Jesus, "when everyone comes to the grotto with a hammer."[25] Socrates, d'Arrast's driver and guide, provides the needed explanation. Long ago, village fishermen discovered a statue of Jesus carried in from the sea and floating down the river. They washed it and set it in the grotto, where a stone began to grow. Each year since, on this day, the villagers come

---

* In the summer of 1949, Camus traveled to South America on an invited lecture tour. His experiences in Brazil and his visit to Iguape, which form the basis of "The Growing Stone," are recounted in his *American Journals* (New York: Paragon House, 1987).

with hammers to chip away a piece of that stone "for a blessing" and as a holy relic. "And then what happens? It keeps growing, you keep breaking. That's the miracle."[26]

At the grotto, d'Arrast witnesses a throng of pilgrims, waiting expectantly with their hammers. "He too was waiting . . . and he did not know for what."

> The truth is, he had not stopped waiting since he had arrived in
> this country a month before. He was waiting . . . as if the work
> he had come to do here were merely a pretext, the occasion for
> a surprise or an encounter he could not even imagine, but that
> had been waiting for him, patiently, at the end of the world.[27]

It is then that Socrates has him meet a man he calls "the champion," a sturdy ship's cook with shaven head, yellow skin, and a black beard neatly trimmed into a square. This man, too, has a miraculous tale. Far out at sea, in open waters, his tanker caught fire. Then his lifeboat capsized, his strength gave out, and he was drowning. He prayed to the good Jesus and made a bargain. If he survived, he vowed that each year from then on he would carry a fifty-kilo stone on his head in the annual procession to the domed church of the good Jesus in Iguape. That's why he is here, for the concurrent festival of St. George, when tomorrow he will once again keep his vow. Before d'Arrast and the cook part, "the champion" asks him if he ever called out in distress and made a promise, to which d'Arrast replies that yes, he thinks he did do that once. "Someone was about to die because of me. I think I called out."*

When the day ended and darkness descended over Iguape, the festival, like a flood, burst its banks and swept the village into a night of feasting, drinking, and wild, pounding music that evoked inarticulate shrieks and

---

* Is this a veiled reference to an occurrence in Camus's life? During the Resistance? When his wife struggled with suicide? Camus clearly did not wish to reveal this; so it is not for us to pry.

howls, as circles of women danced themselves into a trance.* D'Arrast stood off by imself and watched. Then the cook confronted him. "Uncross your arms, Captain . . . you're preventing the saint's spirit from descending."[28] At that d'Arrast let his arms fall to his side. The increasingly god-crazed liturgies that blazed through the night were nothing that d'Arrast had ever imagined, much less witnessed. Motionless, he was nevertheless captivated, and then eventually exhausted, as never before. He "felt faint" and "managed to slide along the walls and crouched over, feeling nauseous."[29] As he called it a night, the cook announced that he was staying on. It was clear already, from the cook's condition, that he would be in no shape in the morning to honor his vow to walk in the saint's procession with a fifty-kilo stone on his head. "Over in Europe," d'Arrast thought to himself, "there was shame and fury. Here, (there was) exile or solitude among these listless and throbbing madmen who were dancing to death."[30]

The next morning d'Arrast walked to the center of the town and found the main square deserted. There he encountered Socrates, who inquired, "So, Monsieur d'Arrast, you like the ceremony? . . . where you come from, it's only the mass. No one dances. . . . Impossible, they're impossible." Then, when d'Arrast explained that he doesn't go to Mass, Socrates wondered, "So, where do you go?" "Nowhere," answered d'Arrast, and Socrates only laughed. Socrates laughed again, this time at the thought of "a lord without a church, without anything!" Finally, when d'Arrast said he just hadn't found his place yet, Socrates offered with open heart: "Stay with us, Monsieur d'Arrast. I love you."[31]

The plan that day was for d'Arrast, the guest of honor, to watch the festive parade from the balcony of the judge's house overlooking the church square. Among the assembled marchers were penitents in black surplices, white penitents carrying red and blue banners, boys dressed as angels, and religious sodalities holding aloft their identifying banners, all followed

---

* The ceremony described in "The Growing Stone" reflects the syncretic Afro-Brazilian ritual dance known as *Candomblé* ("dance to the gods") widely practiced in Brazil by the *povo de santo*, "the people of the saint." *Candomblé* represents a blend of West African, indigenous American, and Roman Catholic elements.

by the reliquary and the effigy of the good Jesus. As d'Arrast watched, the cook, stripped to the waist, joined the procession. He carried atop his head a massive stone block, resting on a cork mat. He had made a promise, and he was resolved to keep it. When the musicians appeared in bright jackets and their ribboned horns blared, the procession moved on and the crowds followed along its designated route, winding through the town. In a matter of hours, they would return to the church square.

Later, as the festive ritual was reaching its climactic conclusion amidst a frenzy of firecrackers, a glorious peal of church bells, and shouts of joy, d'Arrast saw that the cook was missing and ran in search of him. He found "the champion" staggering under the weight of the stone. When the cook saw d'Arrast, "he tried to smile. But motionless under his burden, his whole body was trembling except for his shoulder, where the muscles were visibly knotted in a sort of cramp."[32] He had already fallen along the way. He forced himself to go on, and d'Arrast walked beside him, his hand on the cook's back for support, uttering words of encouragement. "Go on, cook, a little more."[33] The festive procession had become the *via dolorosa*. Suddenly the stone slipped, gashing the cook's side, and he collapsed. D'Arrast lifted him to his feet and steadied him in his arms while others raised the stone to its place on the cook's head and shared its weight. Another agonized step or two and it was over. The cook stared vacantly and shook his head. All he could do was turn toward d'Arrast, his eyes streaming with tears, and mouth the words, "I promised."

Saying nothing, d'Arrast grabbed the cork mat, placed it on his head, and gestured to those nearby to lift the stone in place. The allusion to Simon of Cyrene, who took up the cross of Jesus after he had fallen repeatedly and was no longer able to carry it, is unmistakable here.* Determined to fulfill the cook's vow, d'Arrast labored forth under the stone's crushing weight. Soon he approached the square, where the reliquary and the figure of the good Jesus awaited the stone's arrival. The crowd parted to provide a path

---

* This episode is recorded in all the synoptic Gospels: *Matthew*, 27.32; *Mark*, 15.21; *Luke*, 14.27.

for him, but he walked past them and the church. He changed course and walked toward the riverbank huts, the homes of the *povo de santo*, the scene of last night's festivities. Arms trembling and struggling to breathe,

> he walked faster, finally reached the little square where the cook's hut stood, ran to it, kicked open the door, and in one movement heaved the stone into the center of the room, on to the still-glowing fire. And there, straightening up to his full height, suddenly enormous, inhaling with desperate gulps the familiar smell of poverty and ashes, he listened to the wave of joy surging inside him, dark and panting, which he could not name.*

Soon the hut's inhabitants arrived, stood in the doorway, and gazed. Next, the exhausted cook was led to the stone by his brother. The cook, his brother, and the others, except for d'Arrast, sat in the dirt around the stone as they had around the hearth. D'Arrast stood off by himself, "listening without seeing anything, and the sound of the waters filled him with a tumultuous happiness."[34] These were the waters he had come to master, and they had tamed him instead. The cook's brother moved to make space for d'Arrast beside his brother, and gestured to d'Arrast to sit, and said, "Sit down with us."[35]

Tumultuous happiness and the silent, loving welcome of friends: these may be the most that Camus had ever longed for and arguably never quite found. D'Arrast found it not in a church but in a poor dwelling not unlike his own childhood home. In the final moments of this simple morality tale, we see the rock of Sisyphus, carried by a would-be Prometheus, in whom we glimpse the suffering Jesus, whom Clamence and Camus called friend. Finally, there is the attainment of happiness, tumultuous happiness. It was, we recall, the desire for happiness that lay at the center of Camus's earliest works and infused everything he later wrote. In

---

* Camus, *Exile and the Kingdom*, p. 162. In writing these words, we can imagine that Camus in this place of poverty, silence, and love had experienced a homecoming.

"The Growing Stone" we glimpse, if only in our imagination, what its fulfillment might look like. For Camus, unlike Augustine, happiness lay not in the vision of the divine but in the vision of the human. And yet even Augustine, in the *City of God*, conceded that the happiness of the blessed in eternal paradise lay not only in the enjoyment of God but also in the enjoyment of each other, not only in communion with God but also in human community, the natural human community, finally fulfilled.

In late December 1959, only weeks before he was killed, Camus wrote this to his friend Urbain Polge: "What pleases me is that I have finally found the cemetery where I will be buried. I will be fine there."[36] The modest country cemetery he had found was only a short walk from his home in the Provençal village of Lourmarin, where his only marker today is a rough fieldstone inscribed with his name and sadly shortened life span. If we permit ourselves, we might imagine that d'Arrast had carried it there or that the stone had sprung up from the ground by itself, miraculously. To our immeasurable loss, in real life neither the stone nor Camus is able to grow again when chipped away.

Camus's practical thoughts of death and burial suggest no death wish, but only the ever-presence of death he had lived with since his youth. It's a matter of mortal wisdom—what Euripides called "thinking mortal thoughts." Camus had also given thought to his funeral. In the last year of his life he explained to a friend* that at the funeral of anyone in the village of Lourmarin, the church bell tolls. He added to this that at his funeral he wanted the bell in the town hall, not the church, to toll. In this instruction we may see a reflection of d'Arrast, who decided to carry the stone to the cook's hearth rather than deliver it to the church, as was the tradition, the hearth where he had been welcomed and found happiness.

Camus had a special gift and craving and appreciation for friendship. The human embrace was what brought him joy and consolation. He gave

---

* The friend was Germaine Brée, who shared this conversation with me.

it freely and honored it when offered to him. He also gave it to his readers, his silent, unseen friends from afar, distant not only in space but also in time. He had known not only intimate friendship but its loss and, at times, its betrayal. The car crash that killed him also killed his most dear friend Michel Gallimard. Friends, we recall Plato writing, have all things in common. I can testify to the sustaining friendship he still extends to his readers and can think of no more appropriate words with which to end these reflections on his life and work than words that Euripides left two and a half millennia ago to his readers whom he would never meet:

> The good and decent man,
> even if he lives in some distant place,
> and even though I never set eyes on him,
> I count as friend. [37]

Conclusion

W hat sense is there in writing a "conclusion" when Camus's life and work were never "concluded"? I've asked myself this many times as I neared the end of this book. Any life cut suddenly short in an unforeseen instant leaves us speechless at first, as it should. But then life does go on—not only the lives of the bereaved but also the life of the deceased, who has inevitably left behind memories and a footprint of some sort, large or small. Summoning those memories and considering that footprint, the survivors, still with breath, find words again.

When the world first learned of the car crash that took Camus's life, there was a silent gasp of disbelief and loss. For some that lasted only hours or days, for others far longer. Eventually the gasps turned to words and the silence to a flood of tributes to Camus, his life and his work, all trying to compose a "conclusion" for a life without one. One of the simplest and most profound of these, in my view, was uttered by William Faulkner, whose work Camus had revered and brought to stage.

> When the door shut for him, he had already written on this side
> of it that which every artist who also carries through life with
> him that same foreknowledge and hatred of death, is hoping to
> do: *I was here.*[1]

When the door shut for Camus, he was immersed in writing a new book, for which the working title was *The First Man*. "This was to be his *War and Peace*," his devoted daughter Catherine explained in a 2018 interview.[2]

> What we have is the childhood section. After that he wanted
> to look at the Second World War. . . . He started to think about
> the book early on and said that if he failed to write it, it would
> be as if he hadn't written anything. For him it's a liberation, the
> style is different, less austere, more lyrical.

From these words we begin to grasp just how unfinished Camus's life and work as an artist were. In his eyes, they had hardly begun. Camus expressed as much in a letter to an old friend in the summer of 1959, saying that with *The First Man* he felt he was writing on a whole new level and that the greater part of his writing career lay ahead of him.[3]

The fact is that we will never have Camus's finished work, much less his final words. He cannot sum up his life for us. It is, instead, left to each of us to convey our concluding words about him. All I can do here is try to bring to conclusion this short book.

It has always struck and impressed me that Camus never claimed to have the final answer or to want the last word. He lived with more doubts and questions than he did with certainties or solutions. He craved dialogue and trusted it more than pronouncements, whether by him or by others. It has always seemed fitting to me that Camus, in his last completed work, chose a man named Socrates as the guide for d'Arrast, one of Camus's most transparently autobiographical characters. The ancient Socrates, we know, spent his life in dialogue with others, seeking truth rather than proclaiming it. He was a lover of truth without ever having consummated that love. His search began when someone just back from Delphi reported that the sacred oracle had said that Socrates was the wisest man on earth. Socrates's wisdom, however, consisted in the knowledge of ignorance—being able to spot untruths before embracing, much less spouting, them. He had, we might say, a nose for fallacies, lies, and half-truths. Similarly, his uncompromised decency lay not in resplendent acts of virtue but in simply doing no wrong, as if he had taken the Hip-pocratic oath and never broken it. He claimed he was gifted with an inner *daimon*, a guardian spirit, that warned and kept him from falling into error or evil. Socrates, then, never claimed to be wise, to possess the truth, or to be virtuous. But how much wiser or more virtuous can anyone really aspire to be than to never be in error or do harm? I believe Camus shared that aspiration. He made clear his self-doubts and his ill-suitedness for politics, due to the fact that he could never wish for the death of his rivals or opponents.

> And speaking for myself, I must say that the only actions that interest me are those that can prevent, here and now, the point-less shedding of blood, and the only solutions that interest me are those that preserve the future of a world whose woes weigh on me too heavily to allow me to grandstand for the sake of an audience. . . . I have still other reasons for avoiding these public jousts. In the first place, I lack the assurance necessary to think that I have all the answers.[4]

Surely there would have been appreciably less bloodshed and death then, and since, if more people held such convictions.

In eulogizing Camus, I am wary of saying too much. Silence might be best; but short of that I will appeal to and repeat the eloquently understated tribute Edward Kennedy paid to his murdered brother Bobby, whose life like Camus's was cut short, with work left undone:

> My brother need not be idealized, or enlarged in death beyond what he was in life; to be remembered simply as a good and decent man, who saw wrong and tried to right it, saw suffering and tried to heal it, saw war and tried to stop it.[5]

In the case of Camus, I would simply add that he saw beauty and cel-ebrated it.

Albert Camus and Robert Kennedy lived in dark times. We, too, live in dark times. People who live in dark times search for light, wherever they may hope to find it. That light may not promise a way out, but it makes the moment we are in more bearable. Writing in dark times, Hannah Arendt had this to say of men like Camus, to people like us:

> That even in the darkest of times we have the right to expect some illumination, and that such illumination may well come less from theories and concepts than from the uncertain, flickering, and often weak light that some men and women, in their lives and their works, will kindle under almost all circumstances and shed over the time span that was given them on earth. . . . Eyes so used to darkness as ours will hardly be able to tell whether their light was the light of a candle or that of a blazing sun. But such evaluation seems to me a matter of secondary importance which can be safely left to posterity.[6]

This book is written in gratitude to Albert Camus for the light his brief life cast on those who knew him, either in life or in death, in person or in the words he bequeathed us.

Sources Cited

Arendt, Hannah. "Home to Roost," *New York Review of Books* (June 26, 1975).
———. *Essays in Understanding: 1930–1954*, ed. Jerome Kohn (New York: Harcourt Brace, 1994).
———. *Men in Dark Times* (New York: Harcourt, Brace, 1968).
———. *The Human Condition* (University of Chicago, 1958).
Aristophanes. *The Birds*, tr. William Arrowsmith (University of Michigan, 1961).
Aristotle. *Eudemian Ethics*, tr. Anthony Kenny (New York: Oxford, 2011).
———. *Nichomachean Ethics*, tr. W. D. Ross. The Internet Classics Archive. Online: http://classics.mit.edu//Aristotle/nicomachaen.html.
———. *Physics*, tr. R. P. Hardie and R. K. Gaye. The Internet Classics Archive. Online: http://classics.mit.edu/Aristotle/physics.html.
———. *Physics*, tr. Philip H. Wickstead and Francis M. Cornford. Loeb Classical Library, Harvard University, 1929.
Aronson, Ronald. *Camus & Sartre: The Story of a Friendship and the Quarrel that Ended It* (Chicago: University of Chicago Press, 2004).
Augustine. *Confessions*, tr. Henry Chadwick (Oxford University Press, 1991).
———. *The Happy Life*, tr. Ludwig Schopp (Boston: St Paul Editions, 1939).
———. *The Soliloquies*, in *Augustine: Earlier Writings*, ed. & tr. John H. S. Burleigh (Philadelphia: The Westminster Press, 1953).
Barrett, William. *The Truants: Adventures Among the Intellectuals* (New York: Anchor, 1982).
Brée, Germaine. *Camus* (New Brunswick, NJ: Rutgers University Press, 1972).
Brown, Peter. *Augustine of Hippo* (Berkeley: University of California, 1967).
Camus, Albert. *A Happy Death*, tr. Richard Howard (New York: Knopf, 1972).
———. *American Journals* (New York: Paragon House, 1987).
———. *Caligula and Three Other Plays*, tr. Stuart Gilbert and Justin O'Brien (New York: Knopf, 1963).
———. *Camus at "Combat": Writing 1944–1947*, tr. David Carroll, ed. Jacqueline Lévi Valensi (Princeton University Press, 2006).

———. *Christian Metaphysics and Neoplatonism*, tr. Ronald D. Srigley (University of Missouri, 2007).

———. *Lyrical and Critical Essays*, tr. Ellen Conroy Kennedy, ed. Philip Thody (New York: Knopf, 1968).

———. *Neither Victims Nor Executioners*, tr. Dwight Macdonald (Berkeley: WWWC, 1968).

———. *Notebooks 1935–1942*, tr. Justin O'Brien (New York: Knopf, 1963).

———. *Notebooks 1942–1951*, tr. Justin O'Brien (New York: Knopf, 1965).

———. *Notebooks 1951–1959*, tr. Ryan Bloom (Chicago: Ivan R. Dee, 2008).

———. *The Myth of Sisyphus*, tr. Justin O'Brien. (New York: Knopf, 1955).

———. *Resistance, Rebellion, and Death*, tr. Justin O'Brien (New York: Modern Library, 1960).

———. "The Artist as Witness of Freedom: The Independent Mind in an Age of Ideologies." *Commentary* 8 (December 1949), 534–538. Online: https://www.commentary magazine.com/articles/albert-camus/the-artist-as-witness-of freedomthe-independent -mind-in-an-age-of-ideologies/.

———. "The Human Crisis," Online: https://qdoc.tips/queue/the-human-crisis-albert -camus-lecture-pdf-free.html. A new, definitive translation of Camus's New York lecture, "The Human Crisis," is to be included in a forthcoming volume: *Albert Camus, Speaking Out: Lectures and Speeches, 1937–1958* (New York: Vintage, 2021).

———. *The Plague*, tr. Stuart Gilbert (New York: Modern Library, 1948).

———. *The Rebel*, tr. Anthony Bower (New York: Knopf, 1956).

———. *The Stranger*, tr. Matthew Ward (New York: Knopf, 1988).

———. *The Fall*, tr. Justin O'Brien (New York: Knopf, 1956).

Camus, Albert, and Jean Grenier. *Correspondence, 1932–1960*, tr. Jan F. Rigaud (Lincoln: University of Nebraska, 2003).

Camus, Catherine, ed. *Albert Camus: Solitude and Solidarity* (Zürich: Edition Olms, 2012).

Chiaromonte, Nicola. "Albert Camus," tr. Miriam Chiaromonte. *Dissent* (Summer 1969). Online: https://www.dissentmagazine.org/article/albert-camus.

———. "Sartre versus Camus: A Political Quarrel," *Partisan Review* 19, no. 6 (November– December 1952), 680–687.

Dobie, Madeleine. "We are in a 'Camus Moment.'" *National Book Review* (May 5, 2016). Online: https://www.thenationalbookreview.com/features/2016/5/5/essay-we-are -in-a-camus-moment-but-what-can-the-great-french-algerian-author-teach-us -about-the-world-today?rq=dobie.

Frenz, Horst, ed. *Nobel Lectures, Literature 1901–1967* (Amsterdam: Elsevier, 1969).

Gray, J. Glenn. *The Warriors: Reflections on Men in Battle* (Lincoln, NE: Bison Books, 1998).

Hallie, Philip. *Lest Innocent Blood Be Shed: The Story of the Village of Le Chambon and How Goodness Happened There* (New York: HarperCollins, 1979).

Henry, Patrick. "Albert Camus, Panelier, and *La Peste*." *Literary Imagination* 5, no. 3 (October 2003), 383–404.

Isaac, Jeffrey C. *Arendt, Camus, and Modern Rebellion* (New Haven: Yale, 1992).

Jones, Tom. *The Fantasticks*, book and lyrics (New York: Applause, 1990).

Kaplan, Alice. *Looking for "The Stranger": Albert Camus and the Life of a Literary Classic* (University of Chicago, 2016).

Kierkegaard, Søren. *Concluding Unscientific Postscript*, tr. David F. Swenson and Walter Lowrie (Princeton University Press, 1941).

———. *Fear and Trembling* and *The Sickness unto Death*, tr. Walter Lowrie (New York: Doubleday Anchor, 1954).

———. *The Essential Kierkegaard*, ed. Howard V. Wong and Edna H. Hong (Princeton University Press, 2000).

Lottman, Herbert R. *Albert Camus* (New York: George Braziller, 1980).

McBride, Joseph. *Albert Camus: Philosopher and Littérateur* (New York: St. Martin's, 1992).

Machiavelli, Niccolò. *The Prince*, tr. Harvey C. Mansfield (University of Chicago, 1985).

Meagher, Robert E. *Albert Camus: The Essential Writings* (New York: Harper & Row, 1979).

———. *Augustine on the Inner Life of the Mind* (Indianapolis: Hackett, 1998).

———. *Herakles Gone Mad: Rethinking Heroism in an Age of Endless War* (Northampton, MA: Olive Branch, 2006).

———. "The Human Crisis," Online: https://qdoc.tips/queue/the-human-crisis-albert.

———. *Mortal Vision: The Wisdom of Euripides* (New York: St. Martin's, 1989).

Moorehead, Caroline. *Village of Secrets: Defying the Nazis in Vichy France* (New York: HarperCollins, 2014).

Mumma, Howard E. *Albert Camus and the Minister* (Orleans, MA: Paraclete Press, 2000).

O'Connell, Robert J. *St. Augustine's Early Theory of Man, A.D. 386–391* (Cambridge, MA: Belknap Press, Harvard University, 1968).

Oliver, Mary. *Dream Work* (New York: Grove, 1986).

———. *New and Selected Poems, Volume Two.* (Boston: Beacon, 2005).

———. *Swan: Poems and Prose Poems* (Boston: Beacon, 2010).

Parker, Emmet. *Albert Camus: The Artist in the Arena* (Madison: University of Wisconsin, 1965).

Peyre, Henri. "Albert Camus, An Anti-Christian Moralist." *Proceedings of the American Philosophical Society* 102, no. 5 (October 20, 1958), 477–482.

———. "Camus the Pagan," *Yale French Studies* no. 25 (1960), 20–25.

Pierce, Roy. *Contemporary French Political Thought* (London: Oxford, 1966).

Plato. *The Collected Dialogues*, ed. Edith Hamilton and Huntington Cairns (New York: Pantheon, 1961).

Plotinus. *The Enneads*, tr. Stephen MacKenna (New York: Penguin, 1991).

Rosen, Fred. "Marxism, Mysticism, and Liberty: The Influence of Simone Weil on AlberCamus." *Political Theory* 7, no. 3 (August 1979), 301–319.

Russell, Bertrand. *Russell on Ethics*, ed. Charles Pigden (London: Routledge, 1999).

Sacks, Oliver. *The Man Who Mistook His Wife for a Hat* (New York: Harper & Row, 1970).

Sharpe, Matthew. *Camus, Philosophe: To Return to our Beginnings* (Leiden: Brill, 2016).

Sontag, Susan. "The Ideal Husband," *New York Review of Books* 1, no. 3 (September 26, 1963), 35.

Sophocles. *Philoctetes*, tr. David Grene. In *Sophocles II*, edited by David Grene and Richmond Lattimore (Chicago: University of Chicago Press, 1957), 194–254.

Herodotus. *The History*, tr. David Grene (University of Chicago, 1987).

Terence (P. Terentius Apfer). *Heautontimorumenos* (Boston: Perseus Digital Library, 2007). Online: http://www.perseus.tufts.edu/hopper/text?doc=Perseus%3atex t%3a1999.02.0089.

Thody, Philip. *Albert Camus: 1913–1960* (New York: Macmillan, 1961).

Todd, Olivier. *Albert Camus: A Life*, tr. Benjamin Ivry (New York: Knopf, 1997).

Weil, Simone. *Simone Weil: An Anthology*. Edited with Introduction by Sian Miles (New York: Penguin Classic, 2005).

———. *The Need for Roots* (New York: Harper Colophon, 1971).

Zaretsky, Robert. "The Logic of the Rebel: On Simone Weil and Albert Camus." *Los Angeles Review of Books* (March 7, 2020). Online: https://lareviewofbooks.org/article /logic-rebel-simone-weil-albert-camus/.

Endnotes

PROLOGUE

1   Meagher, *Albert Camus: The Essential Writings*.
2   Euripides, *Herakles*, 273–274. My translation. See Meagher, *Herakles Gone Mad*, p. 81.
3   Camus, "The Artist as Witness," Online.
4   Camus, *Neither Victims Nor Executioners*, p. 1.

One : The Human Crisis

1   Camus, "The Human Crisis," p. 1.
2   Camus, "The Human Crisis," p. 3.
3   Camus, "The Human Crisis," pp. 3–4.
4   Camus, *Neither Victims Nor Executioners*, p. 1.
5   Camus, "The Human Crisis," p. 4.
6   Camus, "The Human Crisis," p. 4.
7   Camus, "The Human Crisis," p. 4.
8   Camus, "The Human Crisis," p. 8.
9   *Camus at "Combat,"* p. 236.
10 *Camus at "Combat,"* p. 236.
11 *Camus at "Combat,"* p. 236.
12 Sontag, "The Ideal Husband," *New York Review of Books*.
13 Dobie, "Camus Moment."
14 Dobie, "Camus Moment."
15 Dobie, "Camus Moment."
16 Lottman, *Albert Camus*, p. 371.
17 Todd, *Albert Camus: A Life*, p. 220.
18 Chiaromonte, Albert Camus, p. 270.
19 Chiaromonte, Albert Camus, p. 266.
20 Camus, "The Human Crisis," p. 3.
21 Arendt, "Home to Roost," *New York Review of Books*.
22 Camus, "The Human Crisis," p. 12.
23 Camus, "The Human Crisis," p. 5.
24 Camus, "The Human Crisis," p. 10.
25 Camus, "The Human Crisis," p. 14.

26   Camus, "The Human Crisis," p. 11.
27   Barrett, *The Truants*, p. 119.
28   Barrett, *The Truants*, p. 119.

Two: Mortality
1   Camus, *Lyrical and Critical Essays*, pp. 6–7.
2   Camus, *Lyrical and Critical Essays*, p. 60.
3   Camus, *Lyrical and Critical Essays*, p. 6.
4   Brée, *Camus*, p. 24.
5   Brée, *Camus*, p. 24.
6   Brée, *Camus*, pp. 24–25.
7   Peyre, "Camus the Pagan," p. 22.
8   Brée, *Camus*, pp. 24.
9   Camus, *Notebooks 1942–1951*, p. 267.
10   Camus, *Notebooks 1951–1959*, p. 203.
11   Camus, *Christian Metaphysics and Neoplatonism*, p. 133.
12   Camus, *Christian Metaphysics and Neoplatonism*, p. 117.
13   Camus, *Les Nouvelles Litteraires*, Paris: May 10, 1951. In *Lyrical and Critical Essays*, p. 357.
14   Lottman, *Albert Camus in New York*, p. 15.
15   Camus, *Christian Metaphysics and Neoplatonism*, p. 118.
16   Augustine, *Soliloquies*, I.i, 1.
17   Augustine, *Soliloquies*, I.ii,7.
18   Augustine, *Confessions*, 10.6 in Meagher, *Augustine*, p. 56.
19   Augustine, *Confessions*, I0.17 in Meagher, *Augustine*, p. 56.
20   Plato, *Phaedrus*, tr. R. Hackforth, 230a.
21   Camus, *Notebooks 1942–1951*, p. 136.
22   Camus, *Notebooks 1942–1951*, p. 144.
23   Aristophanes, *Birds*, tr. William Arrowsmith, p.50.
24   Plotinus, *The Enneads*, III.2.8. In the writings of Plato and Aristotle we find the same hierarchical triad.
25   Camus, *Myth of Sisyphus*, p. 14.
26   Euripides, *Alcestis*, 779ff. My translation.
27   Lottman, *Albert Camus*, p. 45.
28   Barrett, *The Truants*, p. 119.
29   Camus, *Notebooks 1935–1942*, p. 10.
30   Camus, *The Myth of Sisyphus*, p. 89.
31   Camus, *Notebooks 1935–1942*, p. 9.
32   Camus, *Lyrical and Critical Essays*, p. 69.
33   Camus, *Lyrical and Critical Essays*, p. 7.
34   Lottman, *Albert Camus*, p. 51.
35   Camus, *Caligula and Three Other Plays*, p. 132.
36   Lottman, *Albert Camus*, p. 43.
37   Camus, *Caligula and Three Other Plays*, p. 8.

Three: Happiness

1 Peter Brown, *Augustine of Hippo*, p. 119.
2 Robert J. O'Connell, *Augustine's Early Theory of Man*, p. 32.
3 Camus, *Lyrical and Critical Essays*, p. 351.
4 Camus, *Notebooks 1942–1951*, pp. 66–67.
5 "Albert Camus à Athènes," in Matthew Sharpe, *Camus, Philosophe*, p. 268.
6 Camus, *A Happy Death*, 128.
7 Camus, *Caligula and Three Other Plays*, p. 8.
8 Augustine, *The Happy Life*, 4, 33.
9 Augustine, *The Happy Life*, 2, 12.
10 Camus, *The Myth of Sisyphus*, p. 38.
11 Mary Oliver, *Swan*, p. 50.
12 Aristotle, *Physics*, II.1.
13 Tom Jones, "Plant a Radish," *The Fantasticks*, pp. 49–50.
14 Aristotle, *Nichomachean Ethics*, I.4.
15 Aristotle, *Eudemian Ethics*, I.4.
16 Aristotle, *Eudemian Ethics*, I.5.
17 Sophocles, *Philoctetes*, 902–903.
18 Søren Kierkegaard, *Concluding Unscientific Postscript*, p. 363.
19 Camus, *A Happy Death*, pp. 81, 84.
20 Camus, *The Myth of Sisyphus*, p. 13.
21 Camus, *The Myth of Sisyphus*, p. 38.
22 Mary Oliver, *New and Selected Poems*, Vol. 2, p. 34.
23 Camus, *The Myth of Sisyphus*, p. 11.
24 Hong and Hong, *The Essential Kierkegaard*, p. 112.
25 Joseph McBride, *Albert Camus*, p. 185, n.8.
26 Augustine, *Confessions*, I.i.1.
27 Camus, *Notebooks 1942–1951*, p. 158.
28 Camus, *Notebooks 1942–1951*, p. 257.
29 Augustine, *Confessions*, III.iv.7–8.

Four: The Zero Point

1 Kaplan, *Looking for "The Stranger,"* p. 91.
2 Camus, *Notebooks 1935–1942*, p. 181.
3 Camus, *The Stranger*, p. 3.
4 Camus, *Notebooks 1935–1942*, p. 105.
5 Camus, *Notebooks 1935–1942*, p. 103.
6 Camus, *The Stranger*, p. 3.
7 Camus, *Lyrical and Critical Essays*, p. 337.
8 Camus, *The Stranger*, p. 65.
9 Camus, *A Happy Death*, p. 151.
10 Camus, *Lyrical and Critical Essays*, p. 101.
11 Camus, *Notebooks 1942–1951*, p. 20.
12 Camus, *Lyrical and Critical Essays*, p. 336.

13   Camus, *Notebooks 1942–1951*, p. 21.
14   Camus, *Notebooks 1942–1951*, p. 20.
15   Camus, *Notebooks 1942–1951*, p. 141.
16   Camus, *The Stranger*, p. 59.
17   Camus, *Lyrical and Critical Essays*, p. 90.
18   Camus, *The Stranger*, p. 59.
19   Camus, *The Stranger*, p. 59.
20   Camus, *The Stranger*, p. 66.
21   Camus, *The Stranger*, p. 67.
22   Camus, *The Stranger*, pp. 70–71.
23   Camus, *The Stranger*, p. 72.
24   Camus, *The Stranger*, p. 72.
25   Camus, *The Myth of Sisyphus*, p. 10.
26   Camus, *The Myth of Sisyphus*, p. 10.
27   Camus, *Lyrical and Critical Essays*, p. 348.
28   Kierkegaard, *The Sickness Unto Death*, p. 176.
29   Kierkegaard, *The Sickness Unto Death*, p. 176.

Five: Prison
1   Kierkegaard, *The Sickness Unto Death*, in *The Essential Kierkegaard*, p. 351.
2   Camus, *The Stranger*, p. 78.
3   Camus, *The Stranger*, p. 78.
4   Camus, *The Stranger*, p. 79.
5   Peyre, "An Anti-Christian Moralist," p. 477.
6   Camus, *The Stranger*, p. 80.
7   Augustine, *Confessions*, 10.6 in Meagher, *Augustine*, p. 56.
8   Herodotus, *The History*, I.32.
9   Camus, *The Stranger*, p. 81.
10   Augustine, *Confessions*, 11.29 in Meagher, *Augustine*, p. 57.
11   Augustine, *Confessions*, 8.12.
12   Sachs, "A Matter of Identity," in *The Man Who Mistook his Wife*, pp. 110–111.
13   Camus, *The Stranger*, pp. 89–90.
14   Camus, *The Stranger*, p. 92.
15   Camus, *The Stranger*, pp. 92–93.
16   Camus, *The Stranger*, p. 108.
17   Camus, *The Stranger*, pp. 112–113.
18   Camus, *The Stranger*, pp. 116–117.
19   *Gospel of Matthew* 13.45–46.
20   Camus, *The Stranger*, p. 120.
21   Augustine, *Confessions*, 3.2 in Meagher, *Augustine*, p. 58.
22   Augustine, *Confessions*, 10.17 in Meagher, *Augustine*, p. 136.
23   Kierkegaard, *The Sickness Unto Death*, in *The Essential Kierkegaard*, p. 352.
24   Camus, *The Stranger*, pp. 120–123.

Six: Toothing-stones

1   The source here uses the British title, *The Outsider*.
2   Excerpt from a letter to writer-director Rolf Hädrich, September 8, 1954. See *Albert Camus: Solitude and Solidarity*, p. 67.
3   Camus, *The Myth of Sisyphus*, p. 89.
4   Camus, *The Myth of Sisyphus*, p. 89.
5   Camus, *The Stranger*, p. 121.
6   Camus, *The Stranger*, p. 121.
7   Camus, *The Myth of Sisyphus*, p. 91.
8   Camus, *The Myth of Sisyphus*, p. 91.
9   Camus, *A Happy Death*, p. 36.
10 Camus, *The Myth of Sisyphus*, p. 47.
11 Camus, *The Myth of Sisyphus*, p. 54.
12 Camus, *The Myth of Sisyphus*, p. 59.
13 Camus, *The Stranger*, p. 122–123.
14 Camus, *The Stranger*, p. 90.
15 Oliver, *Dream Work*, p. 73.
16 Camus, *The Stranger*, p. 50.
17 Camus, *Caligula and Three Other Plays*, pp. 6–7.
18 Camus, *Caligula and Three Other Plays*, p. 8.
19 Camus, *Caligula and Three Other Plays*, pp. v–vi.
20 Camus, *Caligula and Three Other Plays*, pp. 70–71.
21 Camus, *Caligula and Three Other Plays*, p. 73.
22 Camus, *Caligula and Three Other Plays*, p. 10.
23 Camus, *Caligula and Three Other Plays*, p. 52.
24 Camus, *The Stranger*, pp. 79–80.
25 Also translated and published as *Cross Purpose*.
26 Camus, *Caligula and Three Other Plays*, p. 87.
27 Camus, *Caligula and Three Other Plays*, pp. 83–4.
28 Camus, *The Stranger*, p. 80.
29 Camus, *Caligula and Three Other Plays*, p. vii.
30 Camus, *Caligula and Three Other Plays*, p. 84.

Seven: Plague

1   Camus, *Notebooks 1935–1942*, p. 189.
2   Camus, *Notebooks 1935–1942*, p. 198.
3   Camus, *Notebooks 1942–1951*, p. 20.
4   Camus, *Notebooks 1942–1951*, p. 20.
5   Kaplan, *Looking for the Stranger*, p. 166.
6   Quoted by Geneviève de Gaulle in the 2000 documentary *Sisters in Resistance*.
7   Camus dedicated *The Myth of Sisyphus* to Pascal Pia.
8   Camus, *The Plague*, p. 115.
9   Camus, *Notebooks 1942–1951*, p. 82.

10   Henry, "Albert Camus," p. 395.
11   Camus, *The Plague*, p. 205.
12   Hallie, *Lest Innocent Blood*, p. 243.
13   *Metzger* in German means "butcher."
14   Camus, *The Plague*, p. 197.
15   Camus, *The Plague*, p. 120.
16   Terence, *Heautontimorumenos, The Self-Tormentor*, Act 1, Scene 1. My translation.
17   Thucydides, *The History of the Peloponnesian War*, III.82.
18   Thucydides, *The History of the Peloponnesian War*, II.48.
19   Thucydides, *The History of the Peloponnesian War*, I.22.
20   Camus, *The Plague*, p. 278.
21   Camus, *Lyrical and Critical Essays*, p. 199.
22   These are the opening lines of Camus's review of Sartre's *La Nausée* (*Nausea*), published in 1938.
23   Camus, *The Plague*, frontmatter.
24   Camus, *The Plague*, p. 67.
25   Camus, *Notebooks 1942–1951*, p. 36.
26   Camus, *The Plague*, p. 278.
27   Camus, *The Plague*, p. 115.

Eight: Rats
1   Camus, *The Plague*, p. 7.
2   Camus, *The Plague*, p. 7.
3   Camus, *The Plague*, p. 59.
4   Camus, *The Plague*, p. 278.
5   Thucydides, *The History of the Peloponnesian War*, I.22.
6   Camus, *The Plague*, p. 148.
7   Camus, *The Fall*, p. 11.
8   United States Holocaust Memorial Museum. https://encyclopedia.ushmm.org/content/en/article/martin-niemoeller-first-they-came-for-the-socialists
9   Camus, *The Plague*, p. 150.
10   Camus, *The Plague*, p. 41.
11   Camus, *The Plague*, p. 19.
12   Camus, *The Plague*, p. 31.
13   Camus, *The Plague*, p. 113.
14   Moorehead, *Village of Secrets*, frontmatter.
15   Camus, *Notebooks 1935–1942*, p. 140.
16   Camus was mistaken here and elsewhere in stating that Augustine and the Catholic church teach that unbaptized infants are doomed to eternal damnation.
17   Camus, *Resistance, Rebellion, and Death*, p. 54.
18   Augustine, *Confessions*, 5.14. In Meagher, *Augustine*, p. 64.
19   Augustine, Letters, 2.1.6. In Meagher, *Augustine*, p. 50.
20   Camus, *The Plague*, p. 120.
21   Camus, *Notebooks 1942–1951*, p. 60.

22 Camus, *Notebooks 1942–1951*, p. 254.
23 Camus, *The Plague*, p. 231.
24 Camus, *The Plague*, p. 233.
25 Camus, *The Plague*, p. 230.
26 Camus, *The Plague*, p. 116.
27 Camus, *The Plague*, p. 117.
28 Camus, *Caligula and Three Other Plays*, p. 8.
29 Camus, *The Plague*, p. 118.
30 Camus, *The Plague*, p. 120–121.
31 Camus, *The Plague*, p. 222.
32 Camus, *The Plague*, p. 224.
33 Camus, *The Plague*, p. 227.
34 Camus, *The Plague*, p. 230.
35 Camus, *The Plague*, p. 188.
36 Camus, *The Plague*, p. 91.
37 Camus, *Notebooks 1942–1951*, p. 188.

Nine: Revolution

1   From a letter Camus wrote in 1950, published after his death. See Parker, *The Artist in the Arena*, p. 68.
2   From "The War"—an editorial Camus wrote for the *Soir-Républicain* on September 17, 1939. See Parker, *The Artist in the Arena*, p. 49.
3   Camus, *Notebooks 1942–1951*, pp. 148–149.
4   *Camus at "Combat,"* p. 276.
5   *Camus at "Combat,"* p. 28.
6   Camus, *Notebooks 1942–1951*, p. 134.
7   Camus, *Resistance, Rebellion, and Death*, p. 6.
8   Machiavelli, *The Prince*, VI, 24.
9   Camus, *Resistance, Rebellion, and Death*, p. 7.
10 Camus, *Resistance, Rebellion, and Death*, p. 6.
11 *Camus at "Combat,"* p. 90.
12 *Camus at "Combat,"* p. 233.
13 *Camus at "Combat,"* p. 89.
14 *Camus at "Combat,"* p. 81.
15 *Camus at "Combat,"* p. 89.
16 *Camus at "Combat,"* p. xv.
17 *Camus at "Combat,"* pp. 249–250.
18 *Camus at "Combat,"* p. 165.
19 *Camus at "Combat,"* p. 12.
20 *Camus at "Combat,"* p. 13.
21 *Camus at "Combat,"* p. 257.
22 *Camus at "Combat,"* p. 287.
23 Camus, *Notebooks 1942–1951*, p. 124.
24 Camus, *Notebooks 1942–1951*, p. 104.

25 *Camus at "Combat,"* p. 287.

26 *Camus at "Combat,"* p. 253.

27 *Camus at "Combat,"* p. 251.

28 Parker, *The Artist in the Arena*, p. 78.

29 *Camus at "Combat,"* p. 258–259.

30 *Camus at "Combat,"* p. 275.

31 *Camus at "Combat,"* p. 275.

32 Lottman, *Albert Camus*, p. 615.

33 In *L'Express*, February 11, 1961, cited in Roy Pierce, *Contemporary French Political Thought*, p. 121.

34 See Peyre, "Camus the Pagan."

35 Weil, *Simone Weil: An Anthology*, p. 57.

36 Weil, *The Need for Roots*, p. 43.

37 Rosen, "Marxism, Mysticism, and Liberty," p. 317.

38 Zaretsky, "The Logic of the Rebel." Online.

39 Camus, Nobel acceptance speech, in *Nobel Lectures*.

Ten: Rebellion

1   Camus, unpublished manuscript, 1952. See Brée, *Camus*, p. 22.

2   Brée, *Camus*, p. 220.

3   Nicola Chiaromonte, "Sartre versus Camus," p. 682.

4   Camus, *Combat*, p. 260.

5   Camus, *Actuelles I*, p. 264, in Brée, p. 9.

6   Hannah Arendt, *The Human Condition*, p. 26.

7   Isaac, *Arendt, Camus, and Modern Rebellion*, p. 17.

8   Isaac, *Arendt, Camus, and Modern Rebellion*, p. 17.

9   Nicola Chiaromonte, "Sartre versus Camus," p. 680.

10 Camus, *The Rebel*, p. 6.

11 Camus, *The Rebel*, p. 6.

12 Camus, *The Plague*, p. 228.

13 Camus, *The Rebel*, p. 9.

14 Camus, *The Plague*, p. 248.

15 Camus, *The Rebel*, p. 8.

16 Parker, *The Artist in the Arena*, p. 76.

17 Camus, *Caligula and Three Other Plays*, p. ix.

18 Camus, *Caligula and Three Other Plays*, p. 186.

19 Camus, *The Rebel*, p. 13.

20 Camus, *The Rebel*, pp. 15 and 14.

21 Russell, *Russell on Ethics*, 165/Papers, 11:310–311.

22 Camus, *The Rebel*, p. 21.

23 Arendt, *The Life of the Mind*, p. 13.

24 Camus, *The Rebel*, p. 23.

25 Camus, *The Rebel*, p. 16.

26 Camus, *The Rebel*, p. 23.

27 Camus, *The Rebel*, p. 16.

28 Arendt, *The Life of the Mind*, p. 6.

29 Shakespeare, *Hamlet*, Act 1, scene 5.

30 "Albert Camus à Athènes," in Matthew Sharpe, *Camus, Philosophe*, p. 268.

31 *Camus at "Combat,"* p. 298.

32 Camus, *The Rebel*, p. 22.

33 *Camus at "Combat,"* November 28, 1948.

Eleven: Limits

1   *Galatians*, 3.29 (NRSV).

2   Camus, *Notebooks 1942–1951*, p. 144.

3   Camus and Grenier, *Correspondence*, Letter 108, p. 93.

4   Camus and Grenier, *Correspondence*, Letter 111, p. 98.

5   Camus and Grenier, *Correspondence*, Letter 111, p. 98.

6   Gray, *The Warriors*, p. ix.

7   Gray, *The Warriors*, p. 51.

8   Gray, *The Warriors*, p. 186.

9   Gray, *The Warriors*, p. 229.

10 Camus, *Camus at "Combat,"* pp. 258–259.

11 Camus, *The Rebel*, p. 25.

12 Camus, *The Rebel*, p. 70.

13 Camus, *The Rebel*, p. 104.

14 Camus, *The Rebel*, p. 108.

15 Camus, *The Rebel*, pp. 3–4.

16 Camus, *Lyrical and Critical Essays*, pp. 340–341.

17 Arendt, *Essays in Understanding*, p. 341.

18 Isaac, *Arendt, Camus, and Modern Rebellion*, p. 104.

19 Thody, *Albert Camus: 1930–1960*, pp. 138–139.

20 Camus, *The Rebel*, p. 4.

21 Camus, *Lyrical and Critical Essays*, p. 165.

22 Camus, *The Rebel*, p. 291.

23 Camus, *The Rebel*, p. 132.

24 Camus, *Notebooks 1942–1951*, p. 188.

25 Arendt, *The Human Condition*, pp. 188–247.

26 Camus, *The Rebel*, pp. 164–173.

27 Camus, *The Rebel*, p. 167.

28 Camus, *Caligula and Three Other Plays*, pp. 258–259.

29 Camus, *The Rebel*, p. 282.

30 Camus, *The Rebel*, p. 282.

31 Camus, *The Rebel*, pp. 6–7.

32 Camus, *The Rebel*, p. 285.

33 Camus, *The Rebel*, p. 304.

34 Camus, *The Rebel*, p. 292.

35 Camus, *Notebooks 1942–1951*, p. 270.

Twelve: Hell

1   Camus, *Notebooks 1942–1951*, p. 156.
2   Thody, *Albert Camus: 1930–1960*, p. 176.
3   From Camus's last interview, in December 1959. See Hughes, *Albert Camus*, p. 131.
4   Camus, *The Fall*, p. 15.
5   Camus, *The Fall*, p. 17.
6   Camus, *Notebooks 1942–1951*, p. 162.
7   Camus, *The Fall*, p. 14.
8   Dante, *Inferno*, Canto xxxiv, 61–68.
9   Thody, *Albert Camus*, p. 175.
10   Camus, *The Fall*, frontmatter.
11   Camus, *Notebooks 1942–1951*, p. 249.
12   Sartre, *No Exit*, p. 45.
13   Camus, *The Fall*, pp. 83–84.
14   Camus, *The Fall*, p. 48.
15   Camus, *The Fall*, p. 57.
16   Camus, *The Fall*, pp. 33–34.
17   Camus, *The Fall*, pp. 31–32.
18   Camus, *The Fall*, p. 73.
19   Camus, *The Fall*, pp. 6–7.
20   Camus, *The Fall*, p. 47.
21   Camus, *The Fall*, pp. 44–45.
22   Camus, *The Fall*, p. 58.
23   Camus, *The Fall*, p. 58.
24   Camus, *The Fall*, p. 61.
25   Camus, *The Fall*, p. 62.
26   Camus, *The Fall*, p. 63.
27   Camus, *The Fall*, p. 68.
28   Camus, *The Fall*, p. 53.
29   Camus, *The Fall*, pp. 53–54.
30   Camus, *The Fall*, p. 54.
31   Camus, *The Fall*, pp. 69–70.
32   Sophocles, *Antigone*, line 639.
33   Camus, *The Fall*, pp. 72–73.

Thirteen: Judgment

1   Camus, *The Fall*, p. 147.
2   Camus, *The Fall*, p. 117.
3   *Mark*, 1.4–5 (NRSV).
4   Camus, *The Fall*, p. 10.
5   Camus, *The Fall*, p. 9.
6   Camus, *The Fall*, frontmatter.
7   Camus, *The Fall*, p. 117.
8   Camus, *The Fall*, p. 117.

9   Camus, *The Fall*, p. 138.
10 Camus, *The Fall*, p. 139.
11 Camus, *The Fall*, p. 139.
12 Camus, *The Fall*, p. 140.
13 Camus, *The Fall*, p. 142.
14 Camus, *The Fall*, p. 143.
15 Camus, *The Fall*, p. 142.
16 Camus, *The Fall*, p. 110.
17 Camus, *The Fall*, p. 111.
18 Camus, *The Fall*, p. 111.
19 From a *Le Monde* interview in August, 1956. See Thody, *Albert Camus*, p. 175.
20 Camus, *The Fall*, pp. 135–136.
21 Thody, *Albert Camus*, p. 175.
22 A reference to *John*, 8.1–11.
23 Camus, *The Fall*, p. 115.
24 Camus, *The Fall*, p. 111.
25 Camus, *The Fall*, pp. 111–112.
26 Camus, *The Fall*, p. 113.
27 Camus, *The Fall*, p. 112.
28 *Matthew*, 2.16–18 (NRSV).
29 Camus, *The Fall*, pp. 112–113.
30 Camus, *The Fall*, p. 114.
31 Camus, *The Fall*, p. 113.
32 *Matthew*, 27.46 and *Mark*, 15.34.
33 *John*, 19.30 (NRSV).
34 *Luke*, 23.43 (NRSV).
35 The last death-cry of Jesus, "why have you forsaken me?" *Matthew*, 27.46 and *Mark*, 15.34.
36 Camus, *The Rebel*, p. 32.
37 Camus, *The Fall*, p. 114.
38 Plato, *Phaedrus*, 279c.
39 Camus, *The Rebel*, p. 32.
40 Camus, *The Plague*, p. 202.
41 Camus, *The Fall*, p. 109.
42 Camus, *The Fall*, p. 145.
43 Camus, *The Fall*, pp. 145–146.

Fourteen: Friendship
1   Camus, *Notebooks 1951–1959*, p. 31.
2   Camus, *Notebooks 1951–1959*, p. 198. See pp. 221, 229–230.
3   Bronner, *Camus*, p. 135.
4   From the opening of Camus's Nobel Banquet Speech. Online: www.nobelprize.org.
5   From "Letter to an Algerian Militant," Camus, *Algerian Chronicles*, p. 113.
6   Camus, *Algerian Chronicles*, p. 214.

7   From Camus's Nobel Banquet Speech. Online: www.nobelprize.org.
8   From Camus's Nobel Banquet Speech. Online: www.nobelprize.org.
9   Camus, *Lyrical and Critical Essays*, p. 17.
10   Gerard Manley Hopkins, "Thou art indeed Just, Lord, if I Contend." Online:
     https://www.poetryfoundation.org/poems/44404/
11   Meagher, "Strangers at the Gate," p. 11.
12   Meagher, "Strangers at the Gate," p. 12.
13   Meagher, "Strangers at the Gate," p. 13.
14   Meagher, "Strangers at the Gate," p. 15.
15   A Scottish proverb. See Meagher, "Strangers at the Gate," p. 15.
16   Camus, *Algerian Chronicles*, p. 83.
17   Camus, *Algerian Chronicles*, pp. 37–83.
18   Camus, *Exile and the Kingdom*, p. 78.
19   Camus, *Exile and the Kingdom*, p. 79.
20   Camus, *Exile and the Kingdom*, pp. 80–81.
21   Camus, *Exile and the Kingdom*, p. 82.
22   Camus, *Exile and the Kingdom*, p. 86.
23   Camus, *Exile and the Kingdom*, p. 86.
24   Camus, *Exile and the Kingdom*, p. 132.
25   Camus, *Exile and the Kingdom*, p. 140.
26   Camus, *Exile and the Kingdom*, p. 141.
27   Camus, *Exile and the Kingdom*, p. 141.
28   Camus, *Exile and the Kingdom*, p. 150.
29   Camus, *Exile and the Kingdom*, p. 153.
30   Camus, *Exile and the Kingdom*, p. 155.
31   Camus, *Exile and the Kingdom*, p. 156.
32   Camus, *Exile and the Kingdom*, p. 162.
33   Camus, *Exile and the Kingdom*, p. 162.
34   Camus, *Exile and the Kingdom*, p. 166.
35   Camus, *Exile and the Kingdom*, p. 166.
36   "Afterword" in Camus, *Notebooks 1951–1959*, p. 261.
37   Euripides, fragment 902, tr. R.E. Meagher, in Meagher, *Mortal Vision*, p. 151.

Conclusion
1   William Faulkner, *Homage Albert Camus 1913–1960, Nouvelle Revue française*.
     March 1960, 538. In Joseph Blotner, *Faulkner: A Biography*. p. 678.
2   From interview with Dominic Cavendish, November 14, 2018. "Albert Camus'
     daughter on the impact of his death." *Gulf News*, November 14, 2018. Online.
3   See the INA (*Institut National de l'Audiovisuel*) 1974 interview with Mouloud
     Mammeri. Online.
4   Camus, *Algerian Chronicles*, p. 24.
5   From Edward Kennedy's funeral Mass eulogy for his brother, St. Patrick's
     Cathedral, New York, June 8, 1968. Online: www.jfklibrary.org
6   Arendt, *Men in Dark Times*, pp. ix-x.

Index

151, 156; death of, 15, 205, 207,
211; desire to know by, 46; as editor
of *Combat*, 123–126, 130–132,
136; education of, 26–29, 34;
engagement with the past by, 27–28;
on existentialism, 47; family life of,
192; on free will, 42; on government,
148–149; on happiness, 38–41, 49,
203–204; on human nature, 136–137,
150–151; illness of, 26, 33–34, 93–94;
influence of Augustine on, 27–30,
47, 50, 67, 68–69; as intellectual, 22;
legacy of, 15–16; on Marxism, 159;
misunderstanding of, 17–18; in New
York, 9–15; as pacifist, 122, 125, 129–
130; in Paris, 51, 123; as philosopher,
39, 50, 53–54; philosophy of, 28–29,
46; politics of, 131–133, 138–139,
142–143; postwar years for, 136, 138–
139; relevance of, 16–17; Resistance
movement and, 123–132; Sartre and,
142, 148; on totalitarianism, 156–157;
travels of, 140; writings of, 1–3, 5,
17–18, 34–35, 47–48; youth of, 24–25.
See also specific works
Camus, Catherine, 7, 55, 208
Camus, Francine, 94, 176
Camus, Lucien, 36
capitalism, 136
capital punishment. *See* death penalty
Cassiciacum, 37–38, 40, 54
Catholic Church, 97, 98, 168
Le Chambon-sur-Lignon, 95–98, 106,
110, 111, 143–144
Chiaromonte, Nicola, 19–20, 142
Chouraqui, André, 96
Christ, Jesus, 183–190
Christianity, 27, 28, 31, 47, 112–114, 121,
151–152, 159, 182–185
"Christian Metaphysics and
Neoplatonism" (Camus), 34
Christmas, 185
Christology, 183, 186
Cicero, 49–50

The City of God (Augustine), 75, 204
City of Man, 148
Cold War, 23, 132, 136
Combat, 96, 123–126, 130–132, 136,
158
common decency, 110, 112–115, 146
common good, 5, 43n, 141
common humanity, 5, 6, 21, 22, 24, 146,
152–154
communication, 19, 21
communism, 19, 131, 136, 138, 142, 151,
156
community, 6, 22, 133, 141, 147–148,
150, 153–155, 195, 204
compassion, 5, 21, 152, 171, 193
Coney Island, 9
confession, 76, 77, 179–181
Confessions (Augustine), 30, 49, 67–72,
115
consciousness, 32, 40, 49, 62–63, 81,
117–118
consequences, 164–165
conversions, 114–115, 120
cooperation, 5
crime, 137
crisis, moment of, 11
critical commentary, 3–4
cynicism, 169, 170, 171

D
Dante, 166–167, 170, 179
Darwin, Charles, 4
death: of Camus, 205, 207; certainty
of, 74–75, 78, 86, 204; of Christ,
186–189; consciousness of, 32–34,
36; denial of, 32; experience of, 29;
indifference toward, 13, 14. *See also*
murder
death penalty, 22, 119, 127–130, 137–138,
143
decency, 110, 112–115, 146
Defoe, Daniel, 94, 105
de Gaulle, Charles, 130, 135
democracy, 131

Robert Emmet Meagher's books include:

Personalities and Powers, Herder & Herder, 1968

Beckonings, Fortress, 1971

Toothing-Stones: Re-thinking the Political (editor), Swallow, 1972

Cave Notes: First Reflections on Sense and Spirit, Fortress, 1974

An Introduction to Augustine, New York University, 1978 and Harper & Row, 1979

Camus: The Essential Writings, Harper & Row, 1979

Mortal Vision: The Wisdom of Euripides, St. Martin's, 1989

Helen: Myth, Legend, and the Culture of Misogyny, Continuum, 1995

Euripides' *Hekabe*, Bolchazy-Carducci, 1996

Aeschylus' *Seven Against Thebes*, Bolchazy-Carducci, 1996

Euripides' *Helen*, University of Massachusetts, 1987

Euripides' *Iphigenia at Aulis & Iphigenia in Tauris*,
University of Tennessee / Bolchazy-Carducci, 1993

Euripides' *Bakkhai*, Bolchazy-Carducci, 1995

Augustine on the Inner Life of the Mind, Hackett, 1998
[Reprint of *An Introduction to Augustine*]

The Essential Euripides: Dancing in Dark Times, Bolchazy-Carducci, 2001

The Meaning of Helen: In Search of an Ancient Icon, Bolchazy-Carducci, 2001
[Reprint of *Helen: Myth, Legend, and the Culture of Misogyny*]

The Epic Voice (co-editor with Alan D. Hodder), Praeger, 2002

Ancient Ireland: An Explorer's Guide (co-author with Elizabeth P. Neave), Interlink, 2003

Herakles Gone Mad: Redefining Heroism in an Age of Endless War, Interlink, 2006

Killing from the Inside Out: Moral Injury and Just War, Cascade, 2014

War and Moral Injury: A Reader, co-edited with Army Lieutenant Colonel (ret)
Douglas Pryer, Cascade, 2018